HERE'S HOW WE'LL DO IT

Here's How
We'll Do It

An Informal History of the Construction of the Shoals

Marine Laboratory, Appledore Island, Maine

by

John M. Kingsbury

BULLBRIER PRESS
Ithaca, New York
1991

Information on the programs of the Shoals Marine Laboratory can be obtained from: Shoals Marine Laboratory, Stimson Hall, Cornell University, Ithaca NY 14853.

Other books by John M. Kingsbury:

Deadly Harvest
Oil and Water, The New Hampshire Story
Poisonous Plants of the United States and Canada
200 Tropical Plants
Seaweeds of Cape Cod and the Islands
The Rocky Shore

Here's How We'll Do It is available singly or in quantity from:

Bullbrier Press
Ten Snyder Heights
Ithaca, NY 14850

Copyright 1991 © John M. Kingsbury

ISBN 0-9612610-3-X

Library of Congress Cataloging-in-Publication Data:

Kingsbury, John Merriam, 1928-
    Here's how we'll do it : an informal history of the
  construction of the Shoals Marine Laboratory, Appledore Island,
  Maine / John M./ Kingsbury.
        p.   cm.
    Includes index.
    ISBN 0-9612610-3-X
    1. Shoals Marine Laboratory--History. 2. Marine
  laboratories--Maine--Appledore Island--Design and construction--
  History.
    I. Title.
  QH91.65.U62S465   1991
  574.92'0720741'95--dc20

> *Dedicated to Louise Kingsbury and Joanna Kingsbury Smith, ex officio partners in this venture from the beginning.*

ACKNOWLEDGMENTS AND CAVEATS

Special thanks go to John M. Anderson, Arthur Borror, Jan Robert Factor, Jay Freer, Ronald Harelstad, Frederick T. McGill, Jr., and Philip Sze, all of whom reviewed the manuscript for accuracy. Remaining errors may be laid to the vagaries of the author's aging memory.

Major events are organized in strict chronological order as shown in the chapter heads; the chronology of some minor or extended events has been treated more loosely.

Quotations, except where stated otherwise, were composed by the author as reasonable facsimilies of what was actually said, the exact words of which are now lost.

Photographs have been selected for content from several sources and are of varying quality. Often the name of the photographer is no longer known. Warm thanks to those named; equal thanks plus apologies to those unidentified.

Production of the manuscript was encouraged, sight unseen, by a grant from the James B. and Martha Kinne Palmer family through David Palmer. The prescient poem, *Appledore*, is reproduced with kind permission of its author, Frederick T. McGill, Jr.

The most important acknowledgments have been saved for last. Without the can-do people on Star Island, the Appledore project could not have been started. Without strong-minded achievers on Appledore Island, all thinking strongly and individually but cooperating nevertheless, it would not have moved forward. Dominic and Rachel Gratta are unique. Without them, nothing would have been the same.

Even so, top acknowledgment goes to the students generically, specifically, and individually who furthered this venture as prime motivators, volunteer laborers, construction workers, contributors, paying customers, and occasional sufferers, and who are now making the Shoals Marine Laboratory proud in their personal and professional achievements. Equal appreciation goes to Shoals Lab faculty and staff members (also students once) who gave (in consequence, perhaps) more of themselves on Star and Appledore Islands than they were ever paid for. Special thanks is owed John Anderson and Arthur Borror, each of whom served as acting director on Appledore from time to time when I had to leave the island.

Without each of you, the Appledore Project would not have worked out quite the same, and without all of you together, it could not have succeeded. No one appreciates this better than the author of this record.

6

The central campus of the Shoals Marine Laboratory as it appeared in 1981 after the close of the initial construction phase described in this book. Clockwise from left bottom the buildings are: Laighton House, Brown House (now owned by the University of New Hampshire and fully reconstructed), Kiggins Commons, Dormatory 1, Coast Guard Building, Dormatory 2, Dormatory 3, Palmer-Kinne Laboratory, and the radar tower. Not pictured: Grass Foundation Laboratory, Celia Thaxter's Garden, Werly Fuel Tank, docks, moorings, vessels, and roads. The road from Laighton to the Coast Guard Building, pictured here, was constructed in 1971.

CONTENTS

Appledore

Appledore is deep in death;
  One by one the fence-rails fall;
The wind lays on its sultry breath,
  Where vines of poison ivy crawl.

Year on year foundations crumble;
  Slowly fade the human signs;
Comes the day when gate-posts tumble,
  Sink into the poison vines.

A dozen guards protect the dead,
  And watch for death on every breeze,
While Science in a creaking shed
  Performs its daily autopsies.

Soundlessly the ivies strangle
  Lesser life within the brush,
While cries of gulls above the tangle
  Serve to punctuate the hush.

The island is a little Earth;
  Like Earth it has its hopeful dreams;
It labors for a second birth,
  Which may be nearer than it seems.

Who will tear the vines away?
  Who will prop the sagging rafter?
Who will go again to play?
  Who will try a little laughter?

The island bears a golden name;
  With golden hours its past is rife;
Like gold its waters sparkle still;
  Who'll bring the island back to life?

Frederick T. McGill, Jr.

This poem was composed in 1940, which was about 30 BC (Before Construction).

Chapter One

INTRODUCTION

The Shoals Marine Laboratory exists to provide instruction and field experience in marine subjects for undergraduate collegiate students. Research is important, too, but secondary. In these characteristics the Shoals Lab, now 25 years old, is the largest of its kind in America, perhaps in the western hemisphere, whether measured in numbers of students, range of courses, or credit hours taught. Students come not only from the parent institutions but also from colleges throughout the United States, Canada, and beyond.

The role of the Shoals Marine Laboratory was conceived in the instructional programs at the Marine Biological Laboratory of Woods Hole in the early 1960s. The institutions that made it physically possible are Cornell University, the University of New Hampshire, the Star Island Corporation, and, briefly, the State University of New York. Of these, Cornell is the principal parent.

This is not intended as a detailed history of the creation of the Shoals Marine Laboratory, though if you winnow it right most of the important dates, facts, and figures will shake out. Nor is it primarily a record of significant doings over a period in the history of the Isles of Shoals, or of Kittery, or of Portsmouth, or of the University of New Hampshire, or of Cornell University, though historians of these places and institutions may some day relish this bit of the record.

Derelict buildings in 1966. Left to right (current or recent names), Laighton House, Hewitt Hall, Winkley House (mostly hidden behind; now entirely collapsed), University of New Hampshire House, and Rice House (torn down in 1970).

It is, rather, a glimpse of the spirit behind an unlikely enterprise, one that on the face of it could not succeed—but did anyway. The character of the work, here set forth, and the work of some of the real characters involved, reveals a bit of the soul of an institution that has now won an international reputation for the innovative excellence of its teaching program and, more important, for its profound and lasting effect on the lives of students.

Here, too, are gathered some good Down East stories, because the story of the Shoals Lab is really the story of how certain New England towns, townspeople, and institutions accommodated an invading academic community and other foreigners.

Could something like this happen again? Probably, but not in exactly the same way. Coastal communities are now more populous, more administered, less personal. The towns, the State of Maine, the Coast Guard, the Army Engineers watch more closely. Universities are much more concerned for protecting themselves against litigation. All ways of corporate life are more complex and convoluted. Inevitably, good old common sense has less scope of operation. Perhaps individuals are not now willing to risk as much of themselves or their resources as 25 years ago. Perhaps a simple handshake understanding, like so much else, is a thing of the past. The Shoals Lab came into being at a golden moment when much was needed—and much was possible. Here's how we did it.

═══════════════════════════

THE DELICATE MATTER OF BUILDING PERMITS

Permits are the political currency of advance or stagnation. Nearly always, permits are mainland inventions. Small offshore islands live by a different order of priority. This was especially true at the start of Appledore Island's rebirth as an academic venue.

Consider the daunting realities of an uninhabited, unimproved, rugged granite 95-acre island ten miles offshore (town dock to rock-bound island shore) in the often stormy, often foggy Gulf of Maine and the immediate problems of no dock, no trails, no habitable buildings, no fresh water, no communication facilities, no vehicles, no sanitary facilities, no food services, and essentially no money with which to attack these needs. In these circumstances, mainland realities such as building permits may understandably not even come to mind.

How the newcomers faced these initial challenges will become clear as this tale proceeds. This narrative starts instead with a story out-of-chronology to demonstrate right at the beginning some of the underlying flavor of the enterprise as it developed.

Disposing of human waste properly, especially from a predicted eventual population of one hundred persons or so on an almost soilless granite island, is not easy. Getting the required permit from the State of Maine to do so legally would be, it turned out, even more difficult. How that was accomplished is not the story I wish to tell here; rather, what happened in consequence of possessing such a license.

Returning from Augusta one midsummer day in 1973 with that hard-won but vital piece of paper, I climbed the stairs to the Offices of the Town of Kittery, Maine. Without the official endorsement of the local town, the state sewage permit had no effect. Appledore Island is within the political boundaries of the Town of Kittery, though true Shoalers pay as little attention to that fact as possible, and most Kittery townspeople don't even realize it.

At that time the town offices were located upstairs in small red brick building on the main street. I presented my document at the office barrier and stated my purpose.

Class on the rocks.

"You need to see the Building Inspector. He's not in."

"Can I wait?"

"He's not likely to be in for a while."

"But I'm from the Shoals. We don't have a telephone out there, so I can't call ahead for an appointment. And I don't know when I can get back to town again."

"Oh. Well, perhaps the Assessor can help you."

For two summers we had been building new buildings and renovating old ones on Appledore Island. Since 1972, truckloads of gravel, cement, concrete blocks, lumber, building materials, and supplies had been moving steadily across the town dock in Pepperrell Cove behind Frisbee's Store, "The Oldest Family-owned Grocery Store in America."

In any coastal town in Maine, one of the more important local activities in the daily routine is to pass by the town dock to see what is going on. Thus it was the rare inhabitant of Kittery who didn't know something major was happening on Appledore Island, even if he didn't know Appledore was within the bounds of Kittery.

In the Assessor's office I explained about the state sewage permit and the need for the town to sign on. Charlie Tetrault, the Assessor, like others in town, surely knew that serious work had been in progress on the island for some time. But he asked, "You're going to do some building out there?"

Taking the hint, I told him generally what Cornell University contemplated, assuming that he knew full well something was already happening.

"You'll need a building permit for each new building, and the buildings will have to meet all of the town's zoning requirements. Now then, just what are you going to need permits for?"

The idea of zoning or needing building permits at the Isles of Shoals simply had not previously crossed my mind or anyone else's. What did cross my mind on that instant was that I had better tread very carefully in the next few minutes.

The conversation continued in a Down East combination of future and subjunctive verbs in a way that kept both parties technically honest yet led forward productively.

"If we were to build, here's what we'd start on."

"Well, if you did that, here's what you'd need."

Cornell, after all, was known even in Kittery as a reputable institution, although located somewhere out west beyond the Hudson River, and what we were planning involved investing a substantial amount of capital in an unlikely part of town for an educational venture which, as it turned out, is one of the highest uses of land under Kittery's existing zoning. How could the town do better? Mr. Tetrault also appreciated full well that we were undertaking this effort under the incredibly adverse physical circumstances of an abandoned, heavily vandalized, small, offshore island, which at that time was distinctly more a liability to the town than an asset. Why should the town give us a hard time with paperwork? It didn't.

After an hour or so, I left the Assessor's office with a full set of the necessary building permits and the town's official blessing on our state-approved sewage disposal system. But the building permits were not signed. While the Assessor could fill them out, only the Building Inspector could sign them.

It turned out that the Building Inspector at that time was a senior widowed gentleman (perhaps octogenarian) who came into the town office only occasionally. The Assessor told me how to find his home.

"The house has a large front porch. When you go to the door, tromp on the porch floor and hit the knocker hard. He's pretty deaf, but he's probably there."

I did those things, and the Building Inspector appeared at the door. I hollered a bit and he followed my explanations readily.

"The Assessor filled these out?"

"Right."

"They look OK to me. Three dollar fee for each."

"OK." I handed him the cash. He signed.

Earlier, in the Assessor's office, a question on the building permit application form had required some fast thinking. The town wanted to know what the new buildings would be worth. Should one state a high valuation figure, or a low one, or what? What were the likely consequences in taxes, fees, and further requirements? It hadn't occurred to me to be concerned about such things until that fateful moment.

In the end, I used the Cornell 'guesstimate' for each building. No one—neither Cornell nor the contractor nor I—had any close idea of what the real cost of building on a remote island would be. Only time and circumstances would tell. But Cornell had insisted on a guess for its own records and I had those figures well in mind because it was my obligation to raise those amounts. Those numbers went on the applications. After all, as a nonprofit educational organization we should be able to qualify for a real-property tax exemption anyway.

Now, in the Building Inspector's living room, some more fast thinking seemed necessary. How would the Inspector want to follow progress on the buildings? Would he want to see the wiring before it was closed in? The plumbing? Would he want to assess how much we were actually spending in some direct way? As he signed the permits, I said tentatively, "I suppose you'll want to come out and check on things from time to time."

"Well now, . . . those buildings are out on Appledore, ain't they?"

"Yup."

He looked me long in the eye and responded, *"You'll never get me in a boat!"* And that was that for the next several years.

Chapter Two

PRELUDE
1964, 1965

A very great deal had already taken place before we reached the building permit stage on Appledore Island in 1973. A lease, negotiated with the owners, had to be obtained to use the land. Cornell University required some intense convincing that the project was not only worthwhile but also feasible. Funding had to be obtained. And, somehow, serious work had to begin on a remote offshore island which, except for the isolated summer homes of two working fishermen, was totally abandoned, vacant, and vandalized.

At the real beginning in 1964 there were no docks, no open paths through the tangled vegetation, no roads to move materials on (no vehicles, either), no drinking water or water for mixing concrete—you can't use sea water for that—no public transportation from the mainland to Appledore Island, and not one of the old buildings still standing on the island had a tight roof or a single remaining window or door, outside or inside. None of the common municipal services one takes for granted these days—police, fire protection, rubbish disposal, doctors, hospitals or the like—was available in any practical sense, nor telephone, nor electric utilities, nor gas, nor fuel oil, nor mail, nor delivery services of any kind.

Initially only small boats could reach the rugged granite shores. People, all materials, and all equipment had to be landed over the steep, slippery, seaweed-covered rocks by human hand and muscle alone.

16

Derelict buildings (above); poison ivy (below).

What crumbling buildings there were, were reached by scrambling through the wind-whipped wild cherry scrub, the gull-fertilized blackberry brambles, and especially the poison ivy forests. Yes, forests! Poison ivy on Appledore often grows to a height of ten feet on its own free-standing four-inch trunks.

And the gulls! Several thousand wheeling gulls defend their pervasive nesting territories on Appledore Island in two ways: by aimed bombing or by direct attack. The sudden shrieking swoop of a black-backed gull (always from behind) is a fearsome thing. Gulls can crease the scalp with beak or claws, drawing copious blood and requiring a suture or two to close. (What the gull may have been carrying on bill or feet must be well cleaned out of the wound first.)

What sane, let alone competent, contractor would accept these conditions, especially on a severely limited budget?

WHY BOTHER!

Why bother? You may well ask! In fact, many people, especially college administrators and potential donors, asked exactly that.

Before the second World War, the white laboratory coat of the microbiologist or of the cellular physiologist attracted the imagination of many college-bound high schoolers. It exemplified glamor and the cutting edge of biological science. Following the war, the luster of the lab coat dimmed a bit. Suddenly, diving tanks became an emblem of biological research and the oceans were touted as the last unexplored earthly frontier of science.

Robert Abel of the Federal Interagency Committee on Oceanography (then soon to become the initiating director of the Sea Grant program under the National Science Foundation) gained attention with his catchy observation that, with the advent of the national space program, we knew more about the moon's behind than the ocean's bottom. Jacques Cousteau and *Skin Diver Magazine* hit the high-school population with an immense motivating impact. Many high-school graduates went off to college with a simmering idea of majoring in some branch of marine science.

They found colleges generally unprepared to provide firsthand experience in the marine sciences. Those few existing marine stations on the East, West, and Gulf Coasts, had relatively small, underfunded, and mostly inelastic facilities.

Instead of "go West, young man," for such a student it had always been "go to Woods Hole." Woods Hole is a magical phrase among

Above: Watch out!
Below: "Welcome to Appledore."

biologists. The Marine Biological Laboratory (MBL), one of several marine-oriented scientific institutions at Woods Hole on Cape Cod, is an institution of illustrious ancestry and distinguished scientific attainment. It is also one of the world's oldest and best-known seaside biological institutions. "Go to Woods Hole for a summer." That's what aspiring marine-oriented freshmen and sophomores heard from all sides.

Hundreds, perhaps thousands, of aspiring students wrote to the Marine Biological Laboratory for application materials in those years right after Captain Cousteau grabbed the adolescent interest. My colleague Professor John M. Anderson, the invertebrate zoologist at Cornell, and I (my specialty was marine algae) were both on the faculty of the summer courses at the MBL when this wave of interest hit. One reaction of the MBL to the sudden onslaught of student interest was to elevate the level of its teaching program. In fact it had to in order to keep class size reasonable without turning down some 90 percent or so of the applicants. Courses that had earlier been taught primarily for undergraduates began to show a strong graduate and even postgraduate focus. Typical sophomores and juniors with excellent records at good colleges had smaller and smaller chances for admission. Even Professor Anderson and I were no longer able to count on getting our own best undergraduates admitted to the MBL.

Similar events were taking place at other marine field stations. If not elevated in content, courses were soon stretched to the limit and presented in overloaded facilities by overworked faculty. Despite repeated applications, many undergraduates failed to gain admission for marine field study anywhere before graduating. Thus, in their senior year many good students had to make that most fateful decision of their young lives —whether to go on to graduate school—without ever having had a chance to get their feet wet, or to find out what the life of the marine biologist or oceanographer was really like. What were the results?

Consider the prospective graduate student who has decided on a specific marine subject in which to major, found a faculty member to serve as adviser, gained admission to that specialist's institution, gone there, and settled in. Eventually comes the necessity to work aboard ship or at the shore in the winter, taking a field course or gathering research data.

Most research vessels are not particularly sea-kindly. They roll, pitch, yaw, and generally convey well the sensations of an unstable environment. Seasickness hits with a vengeance . . .and lasts. It's damn cold. The wind and roar of the diesel exhaust drown out easy communication on deck. Exhaust odors assault the already queasy stomach. The sampling gear hangs up on the bottom. An expensive Nansen bottle is lost off the sounding line and no replacement is at hand. Electronic instruments become

Appledore Island in winter.

temperamental and unreliable. The nearest technician who can fix such things properly is several hundred lumpy aqueous miles away. Fog closes in. The Coast Guard issues storm warnings. The vessel heads for a safe harbor before data collection has been finished. Similar problems arise in coastal marine studies from land, located as they often are in remote sites with primitive living conditions and uncertain logistical support.

When real marine science has been thoroughly de-Cousteaued and shown by actual experience for the difficult, sometimes dangerous, often tedious, impersonal, mostly underpaid and demanding work that it really is, the glamor wears off fast and the fledgling student may begin to wonder whether this is the life he really wanted. The only sound basis for a successful career in marine science is an unyielding, hot-burning itch to know more about things marine and a gut feeling that the itch will last a lifetime.

How does an undergraduate assess his marine itch before making that fateful graduate school decision in the latter part of the junior or early senior year? A quiet inland classroom far from the sea is not the best place. Book learning alone is certainly not the best launching.

Each student who changes his mind after beginning graduate work wastes time, tuition, and scarce scholarship resources; ties up expensive faculty time unproductively; occupies high-overhead space; and uses costly equipment or ship services to no useful end.

To those of us on the student firing line in those years, the need was crystal clear for increased field resources dedicated to the educational and experiential requirements of undergraduates interested in marine sciences or oceanography. This was true not only at Cornell, as later detail will show.

WHY THE SHOALS?

Put yourself in mind of a professor or instructor—or more realistically, a university administrator—whom we might need to convince that this remote and inaccessible spot in the Atlantic Ocean was the right place to bring students. How did we do it?

For the record, I had known of the Isles of Shoals since high school, having spent a week or two on Star Island in the summer of 1946 when the conference center had just reopened after the war years. Even though the trained professional eye of the marine biologist was not yet among my abilities, the isolation and character of those remote specks of land made a lasting impression on a young mind. So did the independent soul and iconoclastic ruggedness of the people inhabiting them.

Professional field work and teaching assignments took me to many locations along New England's shores and also to various coasts of the world during the '50s and '60s. All that time I had an intuitive feeling that I should stay away from the Isles of Shoals. Somehow I knew their special magnetism would ensnare me if I ever returned.

A colleague at Cornell finally changed all that. Byron Saunders, a professor of engineering and later Dean of the University Faculty, and his wife, Miriam, had been involved in one of the week-long family programs at the Star Island Conference Center for a number of years. They felt that the conferees should be presented the opportunity to explore the natural history of the island, particularly the marine biology so abundantly displayed between tides. They wanted my wife, Louise (a zoologist), and me to do it. Byron was both persuasive and persistent. After several years of resistance from us they won, and in 1964 we went.

That did it. The need for a new marine field facility and the rightness of the Isles of Shoals for such an undertaking came together like two powerful opposed magnets.

The Isles of Shoals comprise nine islands that are the high points of a submerged mountain ridge. Their geology is interesting of itself and as related to that of the mainland. More important, they rise rather steeply from water of moderate depth in the Gulf of Maine.

The Isles of Shoals, looking toward the northeast; clockwise from left: Lunging, Appledore, Duck (above Appledore), Smuttynose, Cedar, and Star Islands; White Island is beneath the airplane. Below: Seal on Duck Island.

The Gulf of Maine is roughly bounded by Canada and Maine to the north and northeast, the rest of New England to the west, Cape Cod to the south, and major shoal-water fishing banks, especially the Grand Banks, to the east. Within these boundaries water slowly circulates counterclockwise. Thus it washes past the Shoals, coming from the open gulf to the east and not directly from any heavily populated coastal location. Sewage outfalls, accidental discharges at commercial docks, and thermal effluents such as at the infamous nuclear powered generator finally ignited on the distant Shoals horizon at Seabrook, New Hampshire, after great overruns in cost and time, are not the constant immediate threats to the richness of the community of marine organisms at the Shoals as they are along so much of the coast. As waters go, this Gulf of Maine marine water is relatively rich in nutrients and organisms, yet cleaner of coastal pollution than is common at a typical coastal marine field station, most of which, particularly in the Northeast, are not far removed from the consequences of massed human populations.

The water six miles offshore at the Shoals varies less in temperature and salinity from moment to moment and season to season than does marine water along shallower coasts. The tidal range is large (ten feet average) exposing at low tide a broad expanse of intertidal shoreline well populated by a stable and rich assemblage of diverse marine organisms made possible by the cleanliness and constancy of the surrounding waters.

The area of the Isles of Shoals has been known as a rich fishing ground since 1600 or earlier. Whales of several kinds can usually be seen near the islands each summer; sometimes they come close by. Seals raise young on the ledges of Duck Island. The islands are breeding grounds for several species of gulls, herons, and other marine birds, and they serve as a stopping point on the migratory routes of hundreds of other avian species. During the early construction of the Laboratory, the Shoals simultaneously held the northernmost nesting record for the little blue heron and the southernmost for the black guillemot on the east coast. The ubiquitous herring gull has been a classical subject for study of animal behavior in Europe. This bird was nesting in greater and more accessible profusion at the Isles of Shoals than anywhere else in the United States. These indices of biological richness at the Shoals were known to the local people and thus the information soon came to us, though not all was scientifically documented when the Shoals Lab was first conceived.

Today the Shoals record has been published, principally by the Shoals Lab, and there is no doubt. The extraordinary richness of organisms there can now be fully appreciated. The State of Maine has recognized this richness by designating two parts of tiny Appledore Island as registered natural areas. The interior of the north end of the island was designated a

Above: A few local fish.
Below: Snowy egret and glossy ibis on Appledore Island.

Above: Cormorants nesting on Duck Island.
Below: Humpback whale.

The seaweeds and invertebrates are interesting, too.

state natural area as a heron rookery soon after the state program got started, and most of the coast of Appledore has since been registered for its richness of intertidal and subtidal organisms and populations.

Incidentally, the human species is not the only one to ignore governmental actions. Soon after the first classes came to the Shoals, the ornithologists on our faculty (primarily Dr. Arthur Borror of the University of New Hampshire, known colloquially as UNH, and Dr. Oliver Hewitt of Cornell University) discovered and described the nesting of significant numbers of the black-crowned night heron, snowy egret, and glossy ibis on Appledore Island, and probably the little blue heron as well. At that time these species were inhabiting the dense, scraggly, woody growth in the center of the northern bulge of the island. Someone from the state office came to see for himself and was convinced of the rarity of this ornithological assemblage of nesting herons. He started moving the paperwork for registering the northern end of the island as a state natural area. More than a year later, when governmental paper had multiplied and dispersed sufficiently, the northern interior of Appledore was proclaimed an official State of Maine natural area as a heron rookery. In the meantime, the birds, for reasons known only to themselves and in total disregard of Maine state government, transferred their nesting grounds to the unregistered southern end of the island.

Without exception, all the owners and inhabitants of the several Isles of Shoals are interested in and concerned for the protection of the biological richness of the islands. This concern does not extend to each individual herring gull by every one of the local fishermen, perhaps, but otherwise the generalization holds. The voice of the Laboratory in making recommendations concerning how to protect the environment at the Shoals is not only heard, but is generally well supported.

From the faculty's point of view, neither forms nor requisitions, buses nor bus drivers, accounts nor accountants, front office nor back office stand between a faculty member, his students, and access to the shores of these rich islands. Most faculty members who come out once keep coming back for years.

The Isles of Shoals also have certain practical characteristics, not always immediately obvious, that suit them well as a home for a marine station. Although they are isolated from the detrimental effects of massed human populations, the trip ashore takes only about an hour. In calm seas the Boston Whaler can make it in less than half of that. Ordinary supply needs are met readily in Portsmouth or Kittery. More difficult needs can usually be solved by a trip to Portland or Boston, each about one hour distant from the mainland dock. Academic needs, including a major library, are

28

No buses, forms, or requisitions stand between an instructor, his class, and the Shoals environment (above), and community involvement begins with the unloading line at the Appledore Island dock (below).

satisfied in Durham, New Hampshire, home of the University of New Hampshire, and less than a half hour distant from the dock. It is possible to be parked and in the terminal at Logan International Airport (Boston) with the entire world at your doorstep just two and a half hours after leaving Appledore. Where else is there such a rare combination of an isolated natural marine environment so close to the medical, financial, business, and travel resources of large cities? The Shoals Lab is, in fact, less isolated in some of these ways than is its parent in Ithaca, New York.

The characteristic of the Shoals islands that is most difficult to demonstrate to a skeptical academic community functioning at inland desks is, nevertheless, perhaps the most important of all. It has to do with the efficiency and effectiveness of the teaching program on a distant, isolated island.

Each new class arrives at the Shoals aboard a small Laboratory boat, coming across Gosport Harbor (about a mile) from the dock on Star Island where the ferry lands. The students are accompanied by their heterogeneous luggage. Invariably the first activity a class encounters on Appledore Island is the exercise of getting the luggage to the rooms. Here's how they do it.

The bare granite shore above the Appledore dock rises steeply and ruggedly to the elevation of the island "road." Even today, all luggage must be transferred from boat to dock and up that rocky hill to road and truck solely by hand. This is accomplished by assembling and organizing the entire island population of the moment into a single human chain strung from dock to truck. Then for 10 or 15 minutes suitcases, sacks, duffel bags, cardboard boxes, guitars, knapsacks, and the occasional trunk pass from hand to hand up the hill. This exercise is repeated with cartons and boxes every time the lab vessel makes its weekly supply run to Portsmouth for provisions. A sense of community begins at the dock.

At the moment the newcomer first steps foot on Appledore Island it is abundantly obvious, even without formal announcement, that no public fire department will respond to a fire, no police department to a safety emergency, no ambulance to a medical emergency, and no utility truck to a power outage. Everyone on the island is immediately and inescapably responsible for a share in the public welfare. One person shirking a duty, or one irresponsible act, places visibly more load on the community and each person in it. The feeling of a self-dependent, self-sufficient, and self-regulating community develops and grows rapidly from these roots.

The sense of community and the educational function expand in the absence of diversions. The work at hand is learning. Community resources are directed solely to that end. The kitchen serves (excellent) meals

Performed by students in pairs, transect studies involve using a yardstick, string, line level, and quadrat frame to examine the kind and number of marine organisms at successive levels from above high tide to as far down as students can get.

to meet the academic schedule, not the other way around, as on the mainland. Faculty do not retire from campus at day's end. Instead, discussions continue through meals and into evening hours uninterrupted by television or the lure of the neighborhood bar. The absence of distractions and the presence of real community spirit foster the educational process in a way not possible on any college campus, or even at most field stations. Ask any student who has taken a credit course at the Shoals Lab.

These, then, were the main reasons for choosing the Shoals as the site for a new marine field station. Granted, some of them were intuitive or but dimly seen at the beginning, but taken together they proved over time to be persuasive in overcoming the objections of those who at first said, "Why bother?"

Of paramount importance in developing the Lab, once the choice was made, was the academic philosophy on which the basic program rests. We tried a new idea at the Shoals and here's how we did it.

Instead of offering a collection of courses in individual specialties from which the beginning student is forced to choose, usually taking only one or two at a time, as is done at most other institutions, the six original faculty members and initial guest lecturers at the Shoals cooperated in presenting a single overview course. Instead of learning a lot about the invertebrates and nothing about the algae, birds, fish, geology, or ocean waters, our students were introduced to some of each. Instead of limiting study solely to academic learning, we included practical aspects as well, easily done at the Shoals because the islands live close to practical reality at all times. The faculty, having little else to do, generally listened attentively to each other's lectures. Subsequent discussions and presentations thus entrained a kind of subject integration not encountered in typical team-taught serial courses on the home campus, and they mortared the gaps between presentations of visiting specialists.

The idea of a strong, integrated introductory course with both academic and practical content that originated with the very first class in 1966 has persisted now at the Shoals for more than 25 years. Class study of the intertidal shores by transect was also introduced that first summer. The value of this transect study in fostering first-hand awareness of marine organisms and their habitats has also stood the test of time. That both ideas have survived close attention from several thousand students and successive scores of faculty members is profound testimony to their rightness and is immensely gratifying to me. Most of all, return trips to Appledore Island show unequivocally that the magic manifest at the Shoals during the first few hardship years for motivating and directing undergraduate lives still continues unabated, and perhaps has even increased with the increasing

The Star Island conference center complex seen from the dock (1968).

diversity of subjects that the second director, J. B. Heiser, and his colleagues have brought about. Of course the fact that the second director and many of his current faculty colleagues at the Shoals Lab are themselves Shoals graduates speaks for itself.

This gets ahead of the story. At the beginning there was no assurance that things would work out this way, but the basics were right and intuition urged us all onward. Here's how the big gamble actually began.

IT STARTED ON STAR

The first step was to test the waters, both figuratively and literally. Despite arguments, intuition, and rationalizations such as those above, how would actual students take to intensive study on a small, remote, rugged offshore island? How would faculty cope? In fact, could any of the right people be coerced into making that first trial?

In the late spring of 1965 I arranged to take the students in my spring semester course in marine algae on a brief one-day field trip to the Isles of Shoals. By arrangement we were welcomed at the conference center on Star Island, not yet open for the season, and had a wonderfully productive and stimulating, though all-too-brief time. The students were overwhelmingly enthusiastic. No surprise.

The seasonal conference center on Star Island, which consisted then as now of a large 19th century hotel building, a cluster of venerable cottages, a stone chapel, and several other buildings, began gathering a staff in mid-spring to prepare for opening for its summer season. Getting ready for some 250 guests in the historic but antique buildings on Star Island required considerable effort and the presence of several really resourceful islanders to staff the kitchen, fire up the generators, get the water and sewer systems functioning, repair winter damage to roofs and windows, and the like. This was especially true just after the war when, by forced abandonment for several years, the buildings were in particularly poor repair.

By late May or early June, when most colleges discharge students from the spring semester, the conference center was already functioning at this open-up level and could easily handle a class of 20 or 30 for a week or two, providing the guests didn't expect too much in the way of special attention and did their own housekeeping. The Star Island Corporation welcomed us. Even more important, so did Island Manager Harry Lent, Chef Lenny Reed, Dick Case, Tom Mansfield, Rozzie Holt, and the other early-season islanders who would have to put up with our presence on Star while they got the place ready for the summer season.

The new one-week natural history program Louise Kingsbury and I presented for Star Island conferees in 1964 proved so popular that the conference center management immediately laid plans to develop a full-season naturalist program for all their conferences and asked help in finding a suitable resident naturalist for the 1965 season. I suggested Kenneth J. Dormer, then a third-year undergraduate advisee of Professor John Barlow at Cornell. He accepted the Star Island offer, and the corporation provided him a large room in one of the older buildings to use as a public teaching laboratory. Together Ken and the maintenance staff installed lights, tables, and aquaria there and the Star Island naturalist program was off to a strong start. It has been eminently successful right from that start and is today housed in its own specially designed building.

Demonstrably enthusiastic students, a teaching laboratory, a suitable lecture room, and housing and dining services—here were some starter pieces that could be put together usefully, and here's how we did it.

Above: John M. Anderson; John P. Barlow.
Below: Perry W. Gilbert; Oliver Hewitt.

Chapter Three

FIRST STEPS
1966

ACADEMIC VERITIES

Because Cornell has historically been strong in biological sciences, it has been unexpectedly strong in marine sciences despite its inland location. Why? Biology professor William T. Keeton and I once made an informal analysis of the full spectrum of plants and animals ranging from viruses to the human species as presented in the classificational outline at the back of Bill's best-selling college textbook, *Biological Sciences*. We found that more than one-half of the 69 classes of animals (36 of 69 as Bill listed them) are composed of species that are *exclusively* marine. Nearly three-quarters of all the classes of animals (50 of 69) contain species that are found *mainly* in the marine environment. Finally, more than three-quarters of *all* classes of organisms, both plant and animal (all but 22 classes of 94), contain a significant number of marine species. The old saw "Life arose in the oceans and the majority of biological diversity remains there" is supported well by our figures. To study that diversity, especially to know a good range of animals as they actually live, one must go to the coasts and onto the oceans. Cornell faculty members have done so.

In May 1965, Robert Morison, MD, newly appointed as the first director of the Division of Biological Sciences at Cornell, responded to my request for permission to offer a course at the Shoals by approving "consideration of the Isles of Shoals as a place where Cornell might develop some aspects of a program in marine biology." Two months later a group of nine marine-oriented faculty members at Cornell met in Ithaca with Director Morison, reviewed the situation, and decided to start planning a summer course at the Shoals with the director's blessing. Shortly afterwards, responding to my queries, the Star Island Corporation voted formally to offer to house a two-week course for Cornell in June of 1966 and also to entertain the possibility of renting its holdings on Appledore Island to Cornell for the creation of a full-season marine facility there.

Given a suitable location, could a good faculty representing the necessary subject areas be found, and would these professors be willing to forsake their families and come to this remote spot for up to two weeks in June? Six of the Cornell faculty agreed to give it a shot. They were Professors John M. Anderson (invertebrate zoology), Oliver Hewitt (ornithology and wildlife biology), Perry W. Gilbert (ichthyology, especially elasmobranchs), John P. Barlow (marine ecology and oceanography), Edward Raney (ichthyology), and me (marine algae).

We now had the people and the place, but could we six find an administrative home at Cornell for our proposed course? We needed a formal, legal mechanism through which to bill and receive tuitions, pay course expenses and honoraria, register students, and transmit grades to the university Registrar. These functions are normally performed by departmental or college offices. The six organizing faculty members were members of five different academic departments in three separate administrative units. Even so, and despite careful search and some arm-twisting, *no* academic department at Cornell seemed in the least interested in doing our accounting and paper-work for us.

To appreciate what is involved in paper pushing at Cornell, especially financial paper, the reader must understand the basics of Cornell's Byzantine organization, one that is unusual even for the academic world. A university is composed of colleges. Cornell University is composed of a confederation of four state-financed or "contract" colleges and six fully private or "endowed" colleges that is unlike almost any other in the world. Separate accounting offices and systems are required within the one university to serve its two-headed nature. One, administering the state-supported colleges, must follow all the rules and regulations for the spending of public monies as promulgated continuously by the State of New York. The other, serving the private colleges, uses an accounting system more typical of a large, nonprofit institution. Ownership of equipment vests in the State of New York or in Cornell University, depending on the source of funds, the accounting route followed, and certain other budgetary complexities beyond this discussion.

Cornell's complexity can sometimes be used to advantage. When one part of the university turns something down, an enterprising supplicant can usually find another office that thinks the matter may lie within its official purview. When I had been turned down by several academic departments, it occurred to me to check out Cornell's Summer School (now called the Division of Summer Session, Extramural Study, and Related Programs). Fortunately, William Smith, director of the Cornell Summer School, decided that because our proposed course would be offered outside of the regular academic year he could consider it within his jurisdiction, even though summer courses are normally repeats of material offered during the regular school year and ours was not. In an act of considerable faith, he said he would take us on if we could meet two requirements: get our course approved for credit by the appropriate Cornell college faculty, and show him a realistic balanced budget—where the money would come from (student tuition) and how it would be spent. His approval of our budget would mean, following normal Summer School practice, that the Summer School would stand behind any unexpected deficit if we followed the approved budget to our best ability.

What about course credit? By university legislation, credit for a new course can be authorized only by the faculty of the college in whose area of expertise it falls. The initial Summer Program as proposed at the Shoals would consist mostly of biology. Biology at Cornell is housed primarily in two colleges, the College of Arts and Sciences (endowed accounting), and the New York State College of Agriculture (later renamed the New York State College of Agriculture and Life Sciences) with state contract accounting. Some basic biology is also found in the New York State College of Veterinary Medicine, also with state contract accounting. These colleges are colloquially known on the Cornell campus as the Arts College, the Ag College, and the Vet College.

To complicate this picture further, the Cornell administration had just created a new academic structure to bridge among these colleges and provide better coordination of teaching and research in biology. This new academic straddle was named the Division of Biological Sciences, and it was later to loom large in Shoals Lab politics. Robert S. Morison, the first director of the Division of Biological Sciences, had been only recently appointed as the Shoals Lab came on the scene. He was to have the academic powers of a college dean, but was to receive his funding primarily from the budgets of the deans of the two colleges mostly involved, Arts and Ag. In announcing this arrangement, impossible on the face of it given the normal

Faculty lunch break, mainland field trip. Left to right: Louise Bush, John Kingsbury, John Anderson, Arthur Borror.

resource competition among deans, Cornell's President James Perkins said he expected these three gentlemen to resolve this anomalous funding situation amicably. If they didn't, he added, "it will be resolved in my office."

Approving courses and awarding course credits is about the only really significant collective power remaining to faculty members in universities like Cornell. Deans, provosts, and even presidents cannot authorize academic credit on their own. It is done only by decision of peers. This means it is done by exactly the same people with whom the person proposing the course is competing for students and academic funding. Territoriality enters the picture, something understood well by biologists in relation to all species except sometimes their own.

In some ways, peer review is just another name for the old-boy (gender neutral) network. The ivied tower can occasionally make the halls of Congress look tame in comparison. New undergraduate courses, especially innovative ones outside mainstream thinking, must make their way in these shoal waters whenever credit is sought.

The curriculum committee of the newly formed Division of Biological Sciences refused to approve the course description we initially submitted to it in the autumn of 1965. Credit for the proposed course at the Shoals was not forthcoming. Our peers, who certainly knew the high academic standing of the six petitioners, employed the usual method of academic negation. We were asked for more information, more detail, and greater justification. Some months later, after I had made further detailed submissions and appeared before the separate faculty curriculum committees of the Division of Biological Sciences, the Arts College, and the Ag College, approval did come from each: two credits for a two-week course. In consequence of this delay, copy for the flyer announcing the new course reached the the the printer barely in time for effective dissemination.

This lengthy review process had one beneficial outcome: credit was eventually approved by all college faculties that might have any possible interest in the Shoals program, not just by the faculty of the Division of Biological Sciences. The prestigious Arts College even voted a rare exception in its general policy of refusing to recognize credit earned in Cornell Summer School courses. Its faculty would give credit for ours because it was not otherwise available on campus. We were beginning to earn a reputation for excellence, albeit the hard way.

What about students? Predictably, we were flooded with applications the moment the course, *Field Marine Biology* (later changed to *Introduction to Marine Science*), was announced. That first spring and until we moved to the larger facilities on Appledore Island, we were able to accept only about one in three of the applicants. Our intention had been to admit a class of 20 students. Faced with this huge demand, the admissions committee of the Shoals faculty selected 30 the very first year.

BUILD A FIELD STATION? LET'S NOT BE HASTY

Everything was shaping up very well for the first credit course at the Shoals in the early months of 1966, but organizing and presenting it was a lot of work. The six cooperating faculty members knew that, no matter how excellent the educational results, the work of organizing, setting up, and presenting a course at the Shoals only to have to take it all down again after just two weeks was beyond common sense unless it was understood as a step toward a full-season (three-month) offering. Simultaneously with organizing that first course on Star Island we began pushing for the creation of an entirely new marine field station as soon as possible.

Director Morison was educated as a physician. He had spent most of his professional life, however, as an administrator at a large philanthropic foundation. While he had readily agreed to the two-week course in the conference center on Star Island, it soon became apparent that separate field stations, or perhaps marine stations specifically, held a low place in his esteem. We got the impression, perhaps wrongly, that he had been "burned" at some time in the past by a bad experience with one. Whatever his reason, he was not about to repeat that experience.

What does a college administrator do when faced with an undesired but apparently reasonable request supported enthusiastically by several of his faculty members? Appoint a committee to study the question.

This Director Morison did in November of 1965, naming as chairman a distinguished professor of agronomy, Nyle Brady, who, so far as we could tell, was then only vaguely aware that the great and fertile soils of this country were surrounded by oceans. In 1965 Dr. Brady was serving as Director of Research in the College of Agriculture. We wondered about the academic logic of placing a director of experimentation in charge of a committee to recommend in the area of undergraduate instruction. But that's the kind of logic common on distinguished American campuses as local politics comes into play. So be it. Dr. Morison also appointed several of the initial six Shoals faculty members to the committee, and Dr. Brady had an open mind.

The Brady committee required convincing on these points: that the demonstrated demand would continue, that the proposed station was economically feasible without making inordinate requirements on Cornell for funds, and that the Isles of Shoals represented the best place anywhere (in relation to Cornell's Ithaca locus) for such a venture. To the committee chairman particularly, an offshore island, with attendant supply and communications problems, was definitely not the most obvious place for a field station. Here's how we convinced him.

Anticipating that this need would arise in some form, and rather sooner than later, I had already spent several months in 1965 visiting marine stations from Woods Hole to Halifax, meeting with their directors, and in September had written a large number of letters to colleagues in marine subjects at colleges across this country and Canada asking them to comment on demand for field work among their students and need for increased facilities. The response was gratifying in numbers, promptness, and thoughtful comment. All respondents were enthusiastic for the creation of an additional marine teaching facility and agreed with our assessment of need. Nearly all supported the basic philosophy of presenting an overview of marine sciences for undergraduates, though a few added research potential as a desired feature of any new facility. The only negative comment (and that in only three or four letters) concerned the difficulty of operating on an isolated island.

Dr. Philip Armstrong of Syracuse University, who was then the Director of the Marine Biological Laboratory, and I had a lengthy meeting in his office at Woods Hole. I pointed out that the proposed undertaking was the direct outgrowth of circumstances then existing at the MBL, that the two institutions should not be competitive, but rather that the Shoals introductory program should complement and perhaps feed into the MBL's advanced courses very well. Dr. Armstrong agreed, and wrote a strong letter in support of the Shoals idea. So did Dr. Bostwick Ketchum, associate director of the Woods Hole Oceanographic Institution, with whom I also met. His letter was even more specific on the desirability of a Shoals program because of his former association with the University of New Hampshire's earlier field station on Appledore Island. These letters and others like them were powerful endorsements, even in the eyes of an agronomist.

The matter of fiscal feasibility was more difficult. John Barlow, a member of the Brady Committee, and I reviewed in our minds all the marine stations scattered on American shores and chose three at the suggestion of the committee, for closer examination. The first of these was the Marine Biological Laboratory at Woods Hole for reasons already suggested. Additionally, its proximity placed it geographically in the same major student population as the Shoals might serve, and its detailed financial record, published annually in its journal, was readily accessible. A disadvantage was that it was a considerably larger business than the one envisioned for the Shoals, and it supported a major national research function, which would be mostly absent at the Shoals.

We thought it would be well to review a marine station on a remote island. The longest established (indeed the only) such station then was the Friday Harbor Laboratory of the University of Washington. This was too far distant to visit (i.e., Cornell wouldn't pay for one of us to go out there), but its director cooperated fully, sending us his statistics and financial details, and also commenting on specific difficulties of the island location. Problems in making a direct comparison with the Shoals related to the facts that the Friday Harbor Laboratory is state supported, and its island has a small public village where common supplies and mail service can be obtained.

The third institution John Barlow and I investigated, this time in person, was the Duke University marine station at Beaufort, North Carolina. Here we had a very good fiscal comparison: the size of the business was similar to that we proposed. As we would do, it operated housing and dining services as well as a teaching program. On the other hand, its mainland location meant it was not as isolated from supplies and communications as were the Isles of Shoals.

The director of the Beaufort lab, Dr. C. G. Bookhout, took John and me under his wing. He seemed delighted by our visit and anxious to further our mission. He opened his detailed fiscal record to our view without reservation and answered all our questions candidly.

John and I saw clearly what we knew already: that operating marine stations is distinctly a not-for-profit undertaking. On the other hand, the record presented nothing to discourage us from thinking that income from reasonable tuition, plus reasonable charges for board and room, could just about pay the full costs of an efficiently run ongoing program. It was equally clear, however, that such income couldn't build buildings, buy boats, or amortize the cost of capital improvements in any reasonable number of years, if ever. A bare-bones teaching program might reasonably be expected to pay for itself, but costs of capital improvements of any kind would have to be obtained either from the parent university, foundations, public granting programs, or from donors.

At the request of the Brady committee, Dr. Barlow and I went to Washington, D.C., in December 1965 to meet with representatives of the principal agencies that might be able to make grants to support the Shoals initiative. Our reception in Washington was less than enthusiastic. The most egregious lack of enthusiasm was expressed by Mr. Kenneth J. Ashworth, Office of Higher Education Facilities, U. S. Department of Education. He received us graciously and listened to our story. He then pointed out that all awards made by his program had to pass through an appropriate state agency on route to the grantee. He said he would have to obtain an opinion from his legal department whether he could even listen to a proposal from a semipublic, semiprivate New York State corporation (Cornell) possibly in partnership with a New Hampshire public institution (the University of New Hampshire) to construct an educational facility geographically in the State of Maine on property leased from a private Massachusetts corporation. We decided he needn't bother.

The possibility of funding through the State of New York was also complex. The state's regents had earlier decided that the State University of New York (SUNY) system should have a marine facility somewhere among its campuses to serve the needs of all the units in the SUNY system. Over the period of several years, this had worked down to a decision to build a marine research laboratory on the Stony Brook campus of SUNY which, apart from the N.Y. Maritime Academy in New York City, was closest to the ocean of all SUNY units. The problem was that Stony Brook did not then have any marine expertise with which to design and staff such a station. They needed a founding director to write specifications for a station and program, but they could not hire such a person until they found someone at Stony Brook who could write realistic specifications for advertising the director's position. This circle of tail-chasing inability lasted quite a while before it was finally broken.

The Star Island naturalist's lab initially occupied most of the ground floor of the building at the left (Gosport), and was connected to the main building by a one-floor section which housed the lecture room (Elliot Hall).

In the spring of 1966, SUNY told Cornell it would not even think of funding anything else until it had got its own program up and running, and although the people at Stony Brook were trying, they had no real idea when that would be. Whatever funding we needed, it appeared, would have to come from foundations or private donors.

The third requirement of the Brady Committee, to establish that the Shoals was the best of all locations for such a field station, was met by a critical assessment of all marine shores within a reasonable radius of Ithaca, from northern New Jersey to southwestern coastal Maine. Desired features were constant fully saline and clean ocean waters, rich diversity of organisms and habitats, good tidal range, direct accessibility to shores (no busing), control of accessibility by others (to protect the existing richness), and easy availability of supplies.

The Shoals location came out tops for all the above except supplies. Also there was no salt marsh habitat at the Shoals.

Inside the naturalist's lab.

For the latter, one of the nicest salt marshes in all of New England is within easy reach by boat just south of Portsmouth. For the former, if the Star Island conference center could do it, so could we.

So said the Brady Committee unanimously to Cornell's Director of the Division of Biological Sciences on June 3, 1966, just as several of the committee members went off to Star Island to present the initial offering of the Summer Program in Marine Science.

THE FIRST PROGRAM

While the Brady Committee was investigating and reporting, the Shoals faculty had rounded up in Ithaca a satisfactory supply of seasonally inactive microscopes and dissecting scopes, glassware, a good library, some educational marine films (including one by Cousteau, whose underwater photography is exquisite), and much else needed for teaching. The faculty knew that there were no stores on Star Island; we would have to think ahead and meet all our academic needs. A truckload of gear left Ithaca for Star

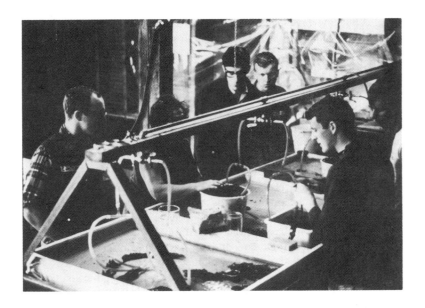

The sea table in use.

Island just before that first class was due to assemble in Portsmouth in early June of 1966.

Above all else at the Shoals, we needed a proper teaching laboratory, equipped with a sea table, up and going before the first class arrived. Was this possible? Easily. The island naturalist's teaching laboratory room, created the summer before, was available, but it lacked a sea table. A sea table is perhaps the most basic requirement of a marine laboratory. It consists of a large, shallow, tray-like, water-tight table supplied with running seawater through an array of plastic hoses, and a drain. Aquaria, pails full of collected organisms, trays, and bowls can be placed on the table and supplied individually with fresh seawater. In this way, organisms brought in from the field can be isolated and maintained in good condition while awaiting study, and various observations requiring live organisms can be made.

Providing a good, dependable water supply for sea tables is a serious and expensive problem for marine laboratories. Seawater is supremely corrosive. Laboratory systems that suck clean water from a good distance offshore, filter it, keep it from warming too much on its way to the sea table, and then dispose of the continuous effluent require sophisticated technology and nonrusting, nontoxic materials throughout.

Building a sea table for the naturalist's room proved no problem at all to island manager Harry Lent and the open-up staff on Star Island. Here's how they did it.

Because of the shortage of freshwater on these small islands, toilets are flushed with salt water. A plastic toilet supply line already ran right through the laboratory room. Tapping into it and building a capacious sea table were minor matters so far as the can-do people on Star Island were concerned. They had a sea table up and going in short order. The problem of the effluent was easily solved, too, by discharging the table into a nearby sewer line. The resulting unassuming but commodious sea table proved functionally to be one of the best I have ever used anywhere, including the sophisticated and massively more expensive ones at leading marine stations. It was ready when the class was, *and at no extra charge.* No engineering drawings, specifications, bids, requisitions, receipts, vouchers, reports, audits, or signatures were required, either. What would have been miraculous, grudging, over budget, and late at many academic places was routine, enthusiastically undertaken, free, and on time at the Shoals.

One other big problem remained that first season, the solution of which was to set a pattern for later days. Professor Hewitt wanted a way of getting students from one island to another so that the bird populations of the other islands could be studied. We had no boat, and the conference center in those days owned none suitable for this function. Tuition income from the first class of students would not suffice to allow buying or even renting a boat for two weeks. It just barely covered the projected direct costs of board, room, instruction, and expendable supplies.

Here's how he did it. Ollie Hewitt performed an impassioned sales job on Dean Charles E. Palm of the Ag College, his employer, representing that he had to be able to get students to the other islands to study the birds or half the value of the program would be lost! When he departed the dean's office, Ollie had a blank check for $200 to rent a suitable boat for the duration of the class.

Finding a suitable vessel was difficult. After hunting in all local marinas, fishing supply houses, and docks from Hampton to Kittery, Ollie finally located one reasonably priced vessel. It was home-made, intended for hand fishing, and looked like a barn door with a rectangular fish well in the center. The operator shared a cockpit at the stern with the outboard motor. This unlikely vessel had been made by placing a flat, overhanging deck (like an aircraft carrier), on top of a scow hull. About six students could sit comfortably and safely on the 17-foot deck with their feet and collecting gear in the central well.

How to get this craft out to the Shoals? Dr. Hewitt, never known for the inhibitions of prudence, rode it out across ten miles of open water triumphantly, after dickering for its rental for the two weeks for $75. Despite the peculiar appearance of this steel-gray wooden boat, she proved very useful in practice at the Shoals. She really had only one bad habit. If she caught a front corner of the deck underwater in a wave or took someone's wake over the bow while underway, she would immediately plane to the bottom, just like a submarine with the diving planes turned full down. Being wooden, and with some floatation pads that had been installed under the deck, she would come up again as soon as forward motion was stopped, but not until the passengers, and sometimes the motor, had been well-dunked seat-first in the cold waters of the Gulf of Maine. After having to bail her out once or twice with hats, boots, and collecting shovels, all hands soon learned not to let her take solid water over the bow. From that point on, she served students and staff admirably and faithfully.

A vessel with such obvious character required a proper name. Several possibilities arose. Dr. Gilbert came up with the one that stuck. He christened her the *Hesperornis* after a species of fossil bird noted particularly for being flightless. She carried that name proudly to her eventual grave on Appledore Island many years later.

The *Hesperornis* performed so well the first year it was abundantly evident that we needed to have her for future programs. The problem then became how to buy and own the boat. Buying her required money we didn't have, and owning her raised the question of what part of the complex university would take title—potentially a real can of worms.

If the boat were purchased by the College of Agriculture, using the dean's funds, it would be owned by, and have to be inventoried under the massive rules and regulations of, the State of New York, and its purchase would require prior approval from Albany. Would the College of Agriculture even care to own and inventory a distant, improbable barn-door boat? Who would license her with the Coast Guard (New Hampshire's practice at that time)—the State of New York?

Besides all that, how much did the owner want, and where would the funds come from? Dr. Hewitt was not sanguine of his chances for twisting the dean's arm to the extent necessary to solve all these problems. Again we found a way to use Cornell's complexity creatively to our advantage. Here's what we did.

Because the Shoals Summer Program was already using the services of the Summer School it came under the accounting supervision of the private side of the university. Buying the boat through the Summer School's accounts would avoid the special problems associated with state accounting. But there were other problems.

The only money available was the Dean's $200, $75 of which had already been committed to rent the vessel. If we used the rest of the $200, we would have to account for it somehow with a receipt acceptable to the State of New York. Beyond that, we had to convince the Summer School to own and inventory a boat even though it did not ordinarily "own" or inventory any property belonging to constituent summer programs.

The owner of the boat was asking $300 for a sale. Professor Hewitt, a master of charm and persuasion, dickered him down to a sale price of $225, including the $75 already paid. The owner, a typical Granite Stater, didn't care at all how the paper work went, only the cash.

In the end, the record of our transactions consisted of a bill from the owner for $200 for *rent* of the *Hesperornis* for two weeks (including the $75 already paid) which fully satisfied the accounting needs of the dean for his entire investment without creating any state inventory requirement. The actual bill of sale, made out to the Summer School, showed that we *purchased* the *Hesperornis* for $25 cash. Inventory is not strict on items costing only $25. The net effect of all this was that the Summer School now owned a very inexpensive boat, the exact physical possession of which (outside of any recognized academic department) was cloudy.

Creative bookkeeping, when done for a good and honest cause, can solve a lot of problems, and we took this lesson to heart for future reference.

The first Summer Program in Marine Science, June 1966, went extremely well. The selected students were able, enthusiastic, and ready to work hard to make the most of this opportunity. The faculty developed its own camaraderie. The biggest mistake I made in the entire program was housing Professors Anderson and Gilbert in the same room. One smoked cigars; the other hated them.

Let loose from the confines of the formal lecture room, faculty members sometimes let loose. Several of our group of faculty had been graduate students together and lacked the inhibitions of unfamiliarity. Professor Gilbert, over decades of practice in the large comparative anatomy course at Cornell, had developed an unusually smooth and polished lecture technique. Words issued forth in measured cadence not only in completely parsed sentences, but more remarkably, in fully formed paragraphs. Professor Hewitt took great pleasure in attending Professor Gilbert's lectures at Star Island and in interrupting the flowing paragraphs from time to time by loud vocal interjections of argumentative statements. Professor Gilbert rose to these challenges admirably and proved repeatedly that his learned paragraphs could continue flowing with aplomb despite abrupt changes of subject. The students loved it.

The open-up staff of the conference center was great, too. Cooperation and "here's what we can do" were the order of those two weeks.

Above: Hesperornis *under way.*
Below: Maintenance.

Some exercises were held outdoors. Here Dr. Gilbert conducts a laboratory exercise in shark dissection on the rocks behind the conference center buildings where the gulls were happy to do the cleanup when the class finished.

I remember one incident involving Lenny Reed, the conference center chef, that shows well the versatility of those island people. The supply boat (the original *Viking*) had just arrived from the mainland with his order. He needed something from it to prepare dinner. The island truck had gone down to the dock, loaded the chef's supplies, and was headed back to the kitchen when it died in its tracks.

The island vehicles, superannuated to begin, lead a rough life in seasonal use on Star Island's unpaved rock-ribbed paths (hardly roads), breathing salt air and ocean spray. Breakdowns are common. After grinding the starter for a while, the truck's driver departed, purpose unknown. Lenny Reed, watching from the kitchen window, could contain his frustration only so long. Soon he was down there, white cap, apron, and all, with the truck's hood up and his head buried in the interior. He soon got it started, drove it to the kitchen, and unloaded it unassisted. Then he resumed his usual functions. How many chefs at mainland hotels are willing to go to these lengths to put good food on the table on time —or would even know how?

The original in the series of Shoals ferries named Viking *(the copious bilging was characteristic of the old, original* Viking*).*

Given top-notch students, a great faculty, a supportive and creative island staff, and a magnificently rich environment, how could anything really important go wrong? Nothing did. The only criticism, if it was that, was that we were trying to cover too much academic material in too short a time. Nevertheless, the students left the island positively glowing. Something magic had happened.

Despite the difficulties of balancing a budget, assembling students, organizing faculty, scrounging and transporting a truckload of books and equipment from Ithaca to Star Island, and presenting a quality academic program on a remote offshore location, everyone involved recommended that we do it again next year. We wouldn't have bought the *Hesperornis* otherwise.

COURSE, YES; STATION, NO

The work of putting all this together just for a two-week period each spring, only to disassemble it immediately—carting microscopes, books, and materials back to Ithaca, New York (ten miles of water and four hundred miles of road)—made no economic sense. From before the first season we knew we should aim for a situation at the Shoals where we could present at least a full summer of courses each year. All faculty decisions concerning the summer program in marine science were made from the very beginning with that objective firmly in mind.

The word from students who had attended the first Summer Program quickly got around their home campuses. The program's reputation and the high number of applicants meant that we no longer had to argue with administrators whether such a program was needed or whether this kind of program could be educationally effective. These considerations had been demonstrated beyond even a skeptical administrator's ability to doubt. The next step, while planning the offering of another two-week program for the spring of 1967, was to keep at the matter of convincing Cornell University of the feasibility of building its own field station at the Shoals so that a larger, three-month program would be possible. The Brady Committee Report was just the start of that lengthy effort.

A number of thorny questions about new facilities needed definite answers. Always lurking behind the specifics was the fundamental query: How much will a new station cost and where will the necessary money come from?

In 1966 all of Star Island and most of Appledore Island were owned by the Star Island Corporation. When the Appledore House Hotel fell on hard times in the early years of the twentieth century, Appledore Island was subjected to a development scheme in which its land was divided into over 500 tiny lots. These lots were offered for public sale. Most of the lots with cottages on them, barely larger than the house itself, went into private hands along with a few of the unbuilt lots. In due course the Star Island Corporation bought the residual rights of ownership in the unsold lands and has since purchased private lots, with and without buildings, as they have come on the market and as its resources have allowed. The corporation now owns about ninety percent of Appledore. Its object in these purchases has been to protect the tranquility of Star Island, an important asset for the conference center.

The Star Island Corporation is a nonprofit organization chartered in Massachusetts for the purpose of owning and making available the land, buildings, and services necessary to run religious conferences on Star Island. Each conference, usually a week long, has its own management. The corporation's directors and officers are drawn from the Unitarian and Congregational denominations as they were known in the 1960s; now Unitarian Universalist and United Church of Christ, respectively. In the late 1960s, the 12 members of the corporation's board of directors included six former or current college educators. In fact, the president of the corporation at that time (Roland Greeley) was Dean of Admissions at the Massachusetts Institute of Technology. Hence the Star Island conference center board was not only sympathetic to our needs, but well acquainted with the contemporary educational scene.

After the hotel on Appledore Island burned in 1914, the island was left vacant for a number of years. In 1929 Professor C. Floyd Jackson, of the University of New Hampshire, started a summer field station for zoology in some of the cottages that had survived the fire. This undertaking deserves a history all to itself, which some day it will no doubt receive. The UNH program thrived for a decade and was terminated only when the Shoals islands were preempted for military purposes during the Second World War. That program's alumni, who call themselves The Barnacles, are among the most dedicated of all UNH alumni.

From the return of the island to civilian uses at the end of the war to the time of this narrative, Appledore real estate had been essentially abandoned, and the Coast Guard life saving station established on Appledore Island in 1920 had also closed. The island had gradually acquired a local reputation with boating mainlanders as a great place to camp, carouse, or have a beer blast. The two resident fishing families on the harbor side of the island could do little to keep vandalism of property under control. The boatless Kittery police were too far away to be an effective deterrent. Preventing island vandalism was not the Coast Guard's proper business. Leaving Appledore Island vacant and subject to vandalism did not serve the Star Island Corporation's purposes well at all. But they certainly didn't want a casino there, either.

Just as the Shoals fitted Cornell's needs well, so our ideas fitted the purposes of the Star Island Corporation. Cornell's senior administration, however, perhaps under guidance of the legal department, refused to consider purchasing land at the Shoals and told me so unequivocally. That was fine; the Star Island Corporation refused just as firmly to sell.

Quiet conversations disclosed this, but also suggested that Cornell could probably obtain a long-term lease to all of the corporation's land on Appledore and functional title to nearly all the remaining derelict buildings there, all for a realistic rent.

Considering that the University of New Hampshire had operated a successful zoological laboratory on Appledore Island from 1929 to 1941, an obvious question soon arose at Cornell: why had UNH not reopened the Appledore laboratory when the war was over?

The University of New Hampshire had indeed considered reopening its Appledore Island lab, inquiry disclosed, but had been unable to identify enough funds to do it. The buildings UNH had occupied before the war, already showing the problems of age when vacated, were generally in very poor shape after the exigencies of the war.

For UNH, the most likely source of funds to renovate buildings was a federal granting agency. When the UNH people went looking in Washington, they found that federal agencies would not pay for duplicating housing or dining within a certain crow's-flight distance of the home campus. Appledore Island was closer than those limits allowed. Like many federal fiats, reasonable on the surface, this regulation would not yield to special circumstances, such as the fact that ten miles of the distance between Durham, New Hampshire and the Shoals consists of difficult and sometimes angry open waters. Eventually UNH created the Jackson Estuarine Laboratory on Adams Point instead, where separate housing and dining facilities would not be necessary. In naming their new marine laboratory after Professor C. F. Jackson, founder and sole director of the Appledore Island zoological laboratory over its lifetime, UNH recognized the importance of its former laboratory.

Cornell University in Ithaca, New York, far beyond the federal crow's-flight distance limit, could seek funding from federal agencies for housing and dining facilities on Appledore Island if it wished. So much for federal logic.

Understanding why UNH had not rebuilt at the Shoals and that we were not to be so constrained by federal regulations, the top administrators at Cornell, who were now becoming aware of the Shoals initiative (Vice President Frank Long and others), just assumed that we would seek construction funding primarily from federal or state sources. They probably thought we might well be ultimately successful, even though our first efforts, as summarized in the Brady Report, were negative.

We were not alone in recognizing the need for increased marine educational facilities in New England. In fact, the spring of 1966 saw a surprising number of initiatives under way. The University of Maine was creating a marine laboratory (the Darling Center) on the Damariscotta River, and David Dean had just been appointed its first director. The University of New Hampshire had committed itself to construction of the new Jackson Estuarine Laboratory and named Galen Jones, formerly of Boston University, as its first director. Boston University itself, through the efforts of George Fulton, was working on creating a facility at Gloucester, Massachusetts, and Northeastern University in Boston was developing plans for one at nearby Nahant, with Nathan (Pete) Reiser as its founding director. All of these developments found themselves in the deep shadow of the Vietnam situation and its threat to federal granting budgets. Except for Cornell's initiative, the emphasis at these new facilities was on research, not instruction.

Galen Jones lecturing from the deck of the Jere Chase.

Shortly after the incandescent success of the first class at Star Island (July 1966), Dr. Morison presented the contents and recommendations of the Brady Report to the Executive Committee of the Division of Biological Sciences. The members of that committee (essentially his board of directors) were "virtually unanimous in concluding that the substantial investment in an offshore marine biology facility could not be given priority over the current building program of the Division on campus." Dr. Morison's personal opinion was, "All things considered, it looks to me that it might be some time before we can give any serious attention to developing a full-dressed station on the Isles of Shoals." He did, however, ask the six faculty members to keep on with the "excellent new course" there and present it again in the summer of 1967.

This was not satisfactory. After further exchange of increasingly heated but still diffuse memos between Director Morison and me, I decided to see if I could force the issue once and for all.

One of the things I had learned early in 30 years of toiling in the academic vineyard, and I suspect this is true in industry and politics as well, is that a resounding "no" is more powerful than any kind of "yes." Agreeing to an administrative proposal is nice and creates good feeling, but it rarely

56

forces a hard decision on the administration or resolves an important issue. On the other hand, a solid "no" often brings splendid results.

I reported to Director Morison that the six Shoals faculty members would not continue the Shoals program for 1967 in the absence of substantial positive action by Cornell toward creating a separate full-season marine facility there. Given the direct and hidden costs of assembling and presenting our program for just two weeks, then only to vacate the premises, was an unconscionable squandering of university resources and faculty time that should not be countenanced by any effective administration. We would not do it. *"No!"*

There was no reaction in the return mail.

COURSE, YES. STATION? WELL YES, I GUESS

The powerful momentum created by the success of that first class on Star in 1966 needed nurture, not negation nor yet neglect. Here's what we did to keep things moving at the Shoals while that little power struggle was working itself through in Ithaca.

In the summer of 1966 after the course had finished, Star Island Manager Harry Lent and I went across Gosport Harbor to Appledore Island with a few others and made a close inspection and inventory of the standing buildings, all in derelict condition. They consisted of the surviving cottages built during the later years of the Appledore House hotel (probably in the 1890s) and the buildings housing the Coast Guard Life Saving Service station (built in 1920).

When the Appledore House hotel burned in 1914, the fire started at its southeastern end. Strong easterly winds on that September day drove the fire quickly down the length of the main hotel buildings and into almost all the buildings to the northwest of it. However, the five hotel buildings located toward Star Island survived the fire and were still standing. These "cottages" had been built during the later years of the Appledore hotel era for long-time patrons who wanted private housing apart from the hotel itself, but with access to all its services. They were large, solidly built frame dwellings. Three of them, with permission of the owners, had been occupied by the UNH laboratory and had received basic maintenance from 1929 to 1940. The owners of the other two had mostly stopped using them long before the war and had let them deteriorate. By 1966, whatever their earlier history, all these buildings had been totally abandoned for a minimum of 25 years (some for perhaps 40 years) and had been subjected to heavy vandalism. On the day we visited, three of the five cottages were then owned by the Star Island Corporation.

The corporation also owned the land under the abandoned Coast Guard Life Saving Service Station house situated on the highest elevation of the island. Under terms of the original deed, ownership of the lot on which it stood had reverted to the corporation when the Coast Guard vacated the facilities after the war in one of those fitful moments of federal belt-tightening. After some investigation by Cornell's Washington office in late 1966, and with Cornell's active encouragement, the Star Island Corporation sought and obtained in 1967 a clear title to all U.S. Government improvements on Appledore Island. Like the cottages on Appledore, the Coast Guard house now was potentially available for marine laboratory use. But it was in only slightly better condition than the cottages.

In the summer of 1966 not one of the standing buildings on Appledore had a tight roof, or any windows or doors. Vandals had attacked all parts of these structures that could be easily reduced to firewood for camping fires or bonfires. All furniture, windows, doors (interior as well as exterior), bannisters, and stair railings were long gone. A good many shingles had been wrenched off the lower reaches of the shingled buildings. Rot had commenced in most of them and was rampant in some. Floors were soft and dangerous in some places and ceilings were falling, the plaster wet and decomposing. On our first close view the situation was pretty discouraging.

On the other hand, the roof lines were still straight, the chimneys standing, and the stone foundations sound. The buildings had been heavily-built. Studs in the late 1800s were full measure 2x4s or 3x4s, not the almost-fraudulent timbers that go by those names today, and they were placed closer together. All other framing timbers and the boards, too, were proportionately heavier than now. I calculated that these buildings could lose half their weight to rot and still have as much wood in them as a similar building built today. All of them had survived innumerable nor'easters and more than one hurricane.

In addition to three of the five derelict frame buildings and the Coast Guard house, the Star Island Corporation owned three other interesting structures on Appledore Island. One was the capacious Coast Guard boat house and marine railway at the head of Babb's Cove. It was perhaps in the best shape of all the Island's buildings when we visited that summer day. Dominating the southern end of the island was a seven-story pylon-like structure locally called the radar tower. This graceless but architecturally interesting military facility had been built during the war. Its dense and heavily reinforced concrete was built to withstand enemy shelling. Although its solid steel-plate doors had been dehinged by vandals, and some of the minor wooden framing of the slit windows had rotted, on the whole the radar tower appeared indestructible. What could one do with seven tiny,

Above: Coast Guard boat house (1967).
Below: Inside what is now called Laighton House.

damp, dark, nearly windowless rooms stacked on top of one another, with no stairs connecting the upper four? The excellent use we made of it will appear as this story progresses.

The third structure, also military in origin, was a large steel tank buried in an artificial hill on the northern edge of the waist of the island. Originally there had been a head house at the unburied end of the tank. Except for a piece of concrete wall encasing the exposed end of the tank, the wooden remainder of the head house was long gone. On casual inspection, the tank itself still looked sound.

Harry Lent thought he could find the old well, originally dug to supply water for the Appledore House, and now hidden in dense, almost impenetrable shrubby undergrowth in a valley at the north end of the island. After much challenge from a threatening tangle of bramble, poison ivy, and brush, topped by a cover of screaming, dive-bombing gulls, we eventually located it. The well was full of water and apparently in reasonable shape, though lacking a cover.

In the early summer of 1966, no responsible administrative office at Cornell had yet given its official blessing to the Appledore project. No money was available, no lease had been drawn up. Yet if the buildings were to be saved, clearly they needed tight roofs as soon as possible, and the window and exterior door openings should be closed. But nothing could be done in the brief time remaining in the summer of 1966.

The only real change in this picture occurred later in the summer when vandals burned the Coast Guard boat house at the head of Babb's Cove to the ground. The best of the remaining old buildings instantly became a total loss. This was a major step backward when we desperately needed forward motion.

At some point along the way, but not from Dr. Morison, I had discovered that he had a connection with the Star Island Corporation trustees and was already passing familiar with the Shoals. His ancestral home was in Peterborough, New Hampshire. I had invited him warmly, strongly, and repeatedly, to visit the Shoals in the summer of 1966 to see the teaching program in action for himself and to review the ideas for Appledore Island right on site. He procrastinated. The Summer Program ended without his presence, and the students left. I again put pressure on him to make a visit to the Shoals anyway, to see for himself what was possible on Appledore Island. No results. Eventually I gave up expecting to see him at all. Suddenly, at the very end of the summer, when students had long gone, the conference center on Star had closed, boats and docks had been hauled out of the water for the winter, and only a skeleton close-up crew remained on Star Island, word came from Ithaca that Dr. Morison had arranged to be aboard one of the very last supply runs of the ferry (the old *Viking*).

Garbage scow in foreground.

The only boat still in the water that was capable of going the mile or so from Star Island to Appledore was the conference center garbage scow, a worthy but aged, elongate, leaky, flat-bottomed vessel held together by infinite layers of sea-sick green paint. It was used exclusively for carting 50-gallon barrels of kitchen residue out to sea, as was the practice in those days. If the distinguished Professor Morison was to visit Appledore Island, he would have to be transported there from Star Island in the garbage scow.

And so, in the course of events, he was. I borrowed the underpowered scow when he finally showed up and took him across the intervening water, bailing occasionally.

Conversation was impossible. To balance the elongate vessel the passenger had to sit in the extreme bow while the operator sat at the noisy outboard motor in the extreme stern. When we arrived at the rocky shore of Appledore Island, I throttled back and proposed to land. Dr. Morison declined to get out and scramble across the seaweed. Instead we began a noisy but mute circumnavigation of the island, about three miles, and then continued slowly and raucously back to Star Island.

Dr. Morison was somewhat subdued on landing, but before leaving on the departing ferry, he asked intelligent questions about Appledore, details of our proposal, and what we had already done (without his explicit permission). Throughout, he gave no hint of his private thinking on the matter, nor of what he might do next. He could probably still have vetoed the whole thing if he had acted then. Especially at the administrative level is the power of a strong, unequivocal "no" greater than the power of a "yes."

Dr. Morison never did give us a strong "no," then or in the future. He was more given to the highly qualified "yes" when he enunciated at all.

Thus it was that in September after we had both gone back to Ithaca, and after his executive committee had recommended more or less against it, Dr. Morison capitulated gracefully and invited me to meet with him in his office to establish exactly who would be responsible for furthering each of the recommendations in the Brady Report. I left that meeting with personal initiative for day-to-day operations at the Shoals, subject to review by a committee he would appoint. This time the committee had no doubters aboard and it was so cooperative in succeeding years that it became nearly invisible in the workings of the laboratory.

More forward motion appeared in Ithaca in October 1966 as Director Morison undertook the initiatives he had agreed to do at our meeting. Principally, he conveyed the recommendations of the Brady Report to higher levels of the Cornell administration (to Vice Presidents Robert Sproull and Frank Long) and returned with their agreement that the Shoals construction project was worthy of further investigation, especially of funding possibilities—but with certain restrictions. No construction of any kind was to be committed at the Shoals until funds had been found by me and my associates to pay for it. No funds were to be sought from any potential donor or granting agency that might reasonably be expected to support Cornell's needs generally, or Cornell's needs in biological sciences specifically. We were to assume campus needs always had priority over those at the Shoals. I was further strictly instructed to "stay away from all Cornell Trustees."

The university's Development Office, which tries to exercise iron authority over Cornell's solicitations of its alumni, adjudicated that within the given restrictions, I could legitimately seek help from Cornell alumni with particular and clearly defined marine interests and Cornell alumni living in New England, ("who on the whole don't contribute very well anyway"). I was strongly encouraged to go after the general non-Cornell public any way I could.

In practical terms these restrictions meant the Shoals funding effort was barred from approaching any federal granting agency or major foundation because Cornell's general or specific biological interests would certainly have priority in those quarters. Similarly, funding from the State of

The radar tower in 1965.

New York could not be expected for the same reason, except perhaps from resources already clearly designated for support of marine science in the SUNY system. No general solicitation of Cornell alumni could be undertaken except in New England, nor could the support of one or two already-identified wealthy Cornell trustees with marine interests be solicited. So be it. There were still a few places where we could look for help.

We could have been a bit discouraged by these prohibitions, but the need for undergraduate instruction in marine sciences was still growing, and urging—even demanding—that the conscientious Shoals faculty members not give up. Here's what we did.

Chapter Four

INERTIA: APPARENT AND REAL
1967

SECOND PROGRAM AND CONSEQUENCES

The skirmish with Dr. Morison and his Executive Committee over, we planned a second Shoals program for summer 1967 and announced it with a
mailing to the same people who had received the 1966 mailing. Was the 1966
demand from a static pool or would new students apply? Undiminished numbers of applications for the second season proved the latter to be the case.

We gave ourselves the boost of an easily recognized trademark for
our letterhead and flyers. With no spare funds for printing, this had to be
accomplished as inexpensively as possible. A botanical illustrator at Cornell
took interest. Working in her spare time, Elfriede Abbe had attained a
national reputation as a woodcut artist, a reputation that has grown following
her subsequent "retirement" to Vermont. Would she be willing to render a
design of mine as a woodcut that could go directly into a printer's press? She
would, and she did, improving the design in the process by giving my stylized
bird the wings of a gull. A local printer took it from there at very little cost
and we had the first distinctive Shoals letterhead.

That was also the origin of the Shoals Lab logo. Its design was
intended to represent in a few sparse lines the land-sea-air interface. The
sinusoidal sea-land line also represented accurately half a tidal curve and

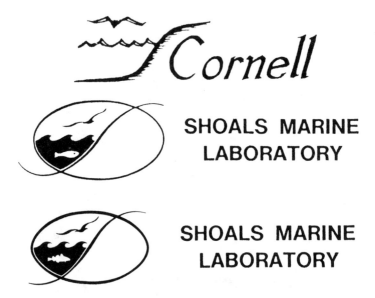

The progression from letterhead design to fish logo to codfish logo.

reminded one of the letter "S." Hank Gayley, of Cornell's design department, put the ellipse around the logo when it passed through his volunteer hands a year or two later. A fish appeared in the water. The original stylized fish evolved into a recognizable cod in 1984 when J.B. Heiser, an ichthyologist by profession, attended to it.

The inexpensive letterhead illustrates as well as anything the fact that, whatever their source, program dollars have always been spent as wisely, stingily, and productively as possible at the Shoals Lab, and they still are. Cornell can't touch its child in the frugality department.

In planning for the summer of 1967, two additional faculty members were added to the teaching staff. Dr. Morison had been impressed by the intensity of the teaching program on Star Island, and agreed that stinting on faculty was false economy. He used a small part of a grant he had from the Ford Foundation to allow the appointment of Dr. Louise Bush, of Drew University and Alicia Hills Moore of *Life Magazine*. Louise Bush had done research at the Shoals and added diversity to the instruction in invertebrates, warranted, as Dr. Anderson had pointed out on the basis of the 1966 collections, since invertebrate species at the Shoals were twice as numerous as marine algal species. Alicia Moore, a graduate of Radcliffe

College with advanced degrees in journalism and art, agreed to help students record their discoveries and experiences at the Shoals with their cameras. The Shoals summer program presented an unparalleled chance for each student to obtain a personal collection of instructive prints and color slides for use in later years. Alicia Moore, a professional photographer and editor on the staff of the leading photographic-essay publication of our times, had become enthusiastic and knowledgeable about invertebrates as a student at the Marine Biological Laboratory some years earlier. Her rule of thumb for good photography is still remembered: "Take lots of pictures; then put your thumb through the poor ones."

With a roster of eight teachers, the program now had a remarkable student-to-faculty ratio of almost four to one. Those people concerned with efficiency in education might demand at this juncture to point out that a student-faculty ratio of this kind is economically unsustainable without tremendous subsidy. At the Shoals Lab they would have been wrong. We didn't even spend all of Dr. Morison's money for faculty employment. Here's how we managed that rich student-faculty ratio without unbalancing the meagre budget.

Faculty members in the early years cheerfully accepted being seriously underpaid, and many of them even contributed their honorarium checks back to the construction project when that began. Because faculty members expect to make their real living during the nine months of the regular academic year, they often can be a bit adventurous with their summers. The Shoals program clearly offered some very special benefits to its faculty, such as placing them in a marine environment at an unequalled location and giving them the opportunity to teach carefully selected and highly motivated students in a setting of maximum pedagogical effectiveness. Besides, the Shoals program was a fantastic hunting ground for budding graduate students, for whom faculty members at research universities compete vigorously. These, and the island sunsets, were the rewards that kept the original faculty members coming back year after year; certainly it was not the pay.

The second summer program gave the teaching staff an opportunity to demonstrate its ability to deal with the unexpected. A three-day no'easter (usually transliterated 'noreaster' but pronounced 'no-eastuh' by the real old-timers) made it dangerous to continue scheduled field work outdoors and nearly drowned out the work inside as well. Lectures were particularly difficult because postwar attention at the Star Island Conference Center to a roof joint between the lectern and the first row of seats in the lecture room (Elliot Hall) had not been successful in stopping leaks. In fact, the leak there was so bad that the torrential rains of the no'easter created a curtain of water between the lecturer and the students. Forty-gallon garbage cans placed to catch the water filled in minutes and became too heavy to move. The resourceful Star Island carpenters instantly solved the problem of water removal by drilling four one-inch holes in the floor under the leaking roof joint. Water coming in now went out equally rapidly. It was fortunate that Elliot Hall is directly over the ground (no cellar). If you don't believe this story, go look. The four holes in the lecture room floor just in front of the stage were still there in the summer of 1990, although needed no longer.

When the storm subsided, we went outside and edged toward the windward shore to watch as the frenzy of the storm-generated mountains of water crashed onto the granite rocks. The cacophony of aqueous energy meeting immovable object made lecturing impossible there. The students, mostly in yellow slickers, just sat on the high rocks above the tumult trying to comprehend what it is like for an attached organism of the intertidal zone to be hit with this environmental fury. They were surprised to learn later that they had sat out there on the rocks for a full hour before the faculty dragged them in again; it had seemed like only a few minutes. What indoor classroom can produce a mute but totally absorbing lesson like that?

A high point of the second program (as well as the first, and all since) was the close examination of one particular invertebrate species, *Homarus americanus*, or American lobster. The Shoals area represents one of the richest lobstering grounds on the entire East Coast, and the lobster fishermen there readily supplied enough lobsters at wholesale to give each student one. We took delivery just before use. Consequently, these lobsters had been out of water only long enough to be measured and pegged.

Dr. Anderson gathered the class outdoors. Brandishing a lively specimen (as they all were), and with each student holding another, he proceded to demonstrate the external structure of a lobster, including such things as how to tell a male lobster from a female lobster—which is not common knowledge, even in mainland fish stores—and the relative proportion of left-handers to right-handers (crusher versus pincer claws).

Internal anatomy was left for close examination after the specimens had been prepared properly by cooking and were served with melted butter.

The lobsters were charged to Cornell on the Star Island bill for housing and dining. I worried that those who review bills in Ithaca might object to the apparent opulence of feeding lobsters to students. That problem was easily solved by asking the Star Island people to itemize the lobsters as "specimens of *Homarus americanus*." This they did, and no one at an audit desk ever noticed that students were eating lobsters.

Above: Storm watching.
Below: Lobster lecture.

The second program went at least as well as the first, and the 30 students left Star Island in 1967 with the same high glow as the 1966 class. Among them was John B. Heiser, who became director of the Shoals Marine Laboratory in 1979.

WHAT'S A VICE PROVOST?

Two important items of political and some practical consequence occurred in Ithaca in 1967. Of greater lasting importance to us was the creation of a new administrative position at Cornell, a vice provost with primary responsibility for planning and managing Cornell's complex relationships with the State of New York, particularly with the State University of New York (SUNY). The person chosen to fill this position was a professor of agronomy, W. Keith Kennedy, who was then associate dean of the College of Agriculture. Dr. Kennedy lost no time in looking into the Shoals Lab situation. He arranged to visit Star and Appledore Islands on a special run of the old *Viking* in October of 1967, and was accompanied by William K. Robertson, a trustee of Cornell University who had New England roots. Dr. Kennedy soon consolidated in his own hands the overall responsibility for the Appledore Island construction project. The academic functions remained mostly in the hands of Director Morison of the Division of Biological Sciences and Director William Smith of the Summer School.

Having a single clear administrative authority responsible for bringing about construction of the necessary facilities on Appledore Island certainly made life easier, but even more important, once Dr. Kennedy looked the situation over, he became an effective and enthusiastic advocate for the project, and he knew his way around the ivied halls of power at Cornell.

The second development of consequence that autumn was a round of high-level meetings. By 1967 the State of Maine had begun to react officially to the same burgeoning interest in things marine that had generated the Shoals initiative—high time, considering the role of Maine's coastline as that state's lifeline. Maine's Governor Curtis sought informal advice from Cornell. Dr. Kennedy arranged for some 15 of us (including himself) to fly to Maine in Cornell's DC3, *The Far Above*, for a meeting with the governor, his staff, and representatives of academic and state agencies with marine interests. We had a pleasant time in Augusta that December, but few conclusions were drawn.

To get the most out of this trip, Dr. Kennedy decided that we should stop also at the University of New Hampshire where Galen Jones, Eugene Allmendinger, and others had shown an early interest in our project at the Shoals. Further discussions in New Hampshire might advance the situation and would allow Dr. Kennedy to meet these people. The airport in Maine was in reasonable proximity to the meeting place with the governor, but Durham, New Hampshire, home of UNH, was a problem. Here's how we solved that problem—and the unexpected consequences.

Thinking about how best to get to Durham from Logan Airport in Boston, or the airports at Concord or Manchester, New Hampshire, which were big enough to take the DC3, it popped into my head that Durham was right next door to one of the world's largest landing strips—Pease Air Force Base. Why not try for a landing there?

Cornell, I soon found out, had no particular inhibitions against landing at an Air Force Security Air Command base. With somewhat more effort, I ascertained that Pease was open (reluctantly) to official governmental airplanes carrying the necessary permit. With a little further effort and some help from offices at Cornell, I was able to turn *The Far Above* into an official facility of the State of New York (New York State College of Agriculture), or close enough. After exchanging several letters with Pease, I obtained the necessary permit.

Coming south from Maine, our pilot radioed the Pease control tower as we approached. The tower seemed uncertain.

"Who did you say you are?"

"A DC3 aircraft operated by the New York State College of Agriculture at Cornell University."

"Where did you originate?"

"Ithaca, New York."

"We are not open to commercial or private aircraft."

"We are neither commercial nor private, and we have a permit aboard to land at Pease."

Silence.

Finally, we received landing instructions, stopped circling, descended over Adams Point (future home of the Jackson Estuarine Laboratory), and touched down at the western end of the only runway. After taxiing the length of the runway, which took us across stretches of the towns of Newington and Rye, we eventually came to the exit taxiway at its far end. A bus met us on the taxiway and loaded all of us, including the pilot and copilot, for transport to the control tower lobby. To the unhappiness of our pilots, Pease personnel insisted on parking the DC3 themselves.

After meeting with the people at UNH and staying overnight, we returned to the control tower lobby the next morning, having talked ourselves past the main gate at the base without difficulty. The person at the counter started tracking down where the DC3 was parked. He consulted some clipboards, but found nothing. He queried people standing nearby. No

The Isles of Shoals under the wing of Cornell's Far Above.

luck. He went into the office behind him, returning after some minutes no better off. He picked up the base phone and called here, and he called there. No one had heard of the DC3. He asked the control tower personnel to look for it from their elevation. They couldn't see it. Finally, after about a half hour of hunting unsuccessfully for Cornell's pride and joy, he called in the base bus driver and told him to scout around with us until we found the DC3. After an interesting tour of several off-limits areas of the base, we eventually discovered *The Far Above* nestled inconspicuously under the hulking wing of one of those behemoths the air force uses for in-flight refueling of its intercontinental bombers.

That winter a document entitled "Points for Agreement - Cornell and the Star Island Corporation," which I had drawn up at the vice provost's request, began shuttling between Keith Kennedy in Ithaca and Warren Witherell of the Star Island Corporation in Boston. Gradually they reached a consensus on each point and arranged to meet in Boston in early 1968 to consummate a lease. Before he went to that meeting, Dr. Kennedy made a necessary but fatal mistake. He asked Cornell's legal office to review the proposed lease. Inevitably the Cornell lawyers envisaged a thousand ways in which leasing an offshore island might get Cornell into trouble, and they started gushing caveats. In the end Dr. Kennedy and the Star Island people did meet and got along well, but ended up with a detailed letter of intent instead of a lease.

Cornell's legal office is, I suppose, typical of those at major universities. Its job is to foresee trouble and act accordingly. The attorneys don't take that responsibility lightly and their collective ability to foresee disaster in innocent situations is unparalleled. Whatever they do, it usually takes a great deal of time.

This characteristic could occasionally be put to good use. When some intractible problem came up that I wished to put off as long as possible, I would simply ask the legal office for instruction. In the absence of continuous agitation this was as good as putting it on ice for a year or so, and usually, in the nature of such things, the problem was long gone by the time the legal office rendered an opinion.

Once a visit to Cornell's legal office produced a surprise. Shoals questions at that time were handled by attorney Ralph Barnard, whose daughter had worked on Appledore Island for a while. I don't remember the exact nature of the problem on that particular visit, but we talked about it exhaustively without resolution. In the end, Ralph Barnard said something I had never heard from anyone in his office before (or since): "If it's educationally desirable, we should be able to find a legal way to do it." More power to Ralph Barnard (who is no longer with the legal office at Cornell).

In the absence of either money or authority to accomplish anything there, visits to Appledore Island, where we hoped to build, were disheartening. Expeditions went over from Star Island occasionally to check out particular matters as questions arose. On one such trip a mysterious open manhole was found deep in the underbrush near the old military tank at the edge of the central valley. Fortunately the circular opening, nearly three feet across, was spotted in the level terrain before anyone fell through it. We put some boards across the steel-rimmed pit opening to prevent a future accident.

For some years, that hole in the ground remained enigmatic. Even after it had been explored by ladder and flashlight its original use remained problematical. The manhole opened down into a beehive shaped cavity some 15 or 20 feet deep and about the same in diameter at the bottom. The pit was made of carefully laid brick walls covered inside with a thin veneer of concrete. An appreciable layer of muskrat skeletons covered the floor. The opening had obviously been a one-way exit from the world for hosts of Appledore Island's muskrats over many years.

Later, when the island freshwater system was under development, it seemed desirable to utilize the underground beehive for intermediate storage of water between the well and the pressure tank. When some students went down in scuba gear (to avoid asphyxiation in the gasses of decay) to clean it out thoroughly, they found a layer of sawdust under the muskrat skeletons. They also found some old ice tongs. Now its original use was entirely clear: the ice blocks cut from Crystal Lake on Appledore were stored in that cistern for summer refrigeration at the Appledore House Hotel.

A list of specific material achievements in 1967 toward building a new field station on Appledore Island would be discouragingly small. Those involved in the project were, however, not discouraged. Many academic and political minds had to be moved in the right direction before specific achievements were possible, and this process continued unabated, though mostly hidden, throughout the year. The search was on for money, too.

TEARS

A real vacuum was evident on Star Island when the second class of Shoals Program students departed. The let-down after the intense educational interaction of two weeks of daily work from dawn until the island generators were shut down for the night was almost palpable. Knowledge had been transmitted, enthusiasms kindled, skills developed, unrealistic dreams squashed, and true friendships engendered. Our total-immersion community had developed its own very special character. Clearly, many young lives were changed for all time.

It came into my mind at one such departure time that the Shoals summer program is like a whirlpool, owing its shape, structure, and very existence to those forces—from students, faculty, and staff—that set the water in motion and keep it spinning. On the day when that energy ceases, the whirlpool flattens and soon disappears into the background and into memory. There were, as usual, tears at the dock when the 1967 whirlpool played down.

Chapter Five

THE HAMMER SOUNDS
1968

GUESSTIMATES

By the end of 1967 enough momentum had been created both at the Shoals and in Ithaca to establish that the Shoals program was not going to die aborning. As it worked out, 1968 was one of the busiest years in all of the Lab's history. Here are some of the more vivid memories of that year.

The Lab's first Boston Whaler was delivered to Ithaca right at the beginning of the year. Although the wooden *Hesperornis* was great for landing on rocky islands, we knew we needed to be able to carry more students on the water at one time, and also we needed the greater margin of safety a more stable, unsinkable vessel would give for routine all-weather interisland transport. The Boston Whaler had been on the market only a short time then. We studied its specifications, compared it with other fiberglass boats, and chose it over the others. That winter, using funds from Dr. Morison's special grant to the program, and taking full advantage of the special discount the Johnson Outboard Marine Company was giving to educational institutions (greater than its dealer discount) for large outboard motors, we bought this excellent craft, which the Lab still owns, maintains, and uses heavily even to the present day (25 years as I write).

The Boston Whaler.

Despite this longevity the Whaler never received a special name. After overcoming some difficulties arising from the fact that the office of my home department at Cornell mistakenly put our boat registration sticker on its carryall vehicle, Phil Sze (then a graduate student of mine, now a regular Shoals Lab core faculty member) and I had the pleasure of trying out the new boat and a depth sounder in seemingly bottomless Cayuga Lake before hauling it to Portsmouth.

The prohibition against approaching any Cornell trustee about funding construction on Appledore Island applied to me personally, but did not seem to bind the vice provost. Keith Kennedy arranged for four trustees (not including the marine-oriented one I knew of) who were on campus for the regular April board meeting to meet informally with himself and me in a quiet corner. We presented our vision of the unsatisfied demand for marine biology in undergraduate education and the unusual possibilities at the Shoals for meeting it. All four trustees appeared initially unmoved. Three of the trustees remained so, but one, who requested anonymity, sometime later told Cornell President Dale Corson, who had succeeded James Perkins, that he would put up $50,000 if someone else would match it or do better. This monetary act of faith was a great boost to morale!

Dr. Kennedy figured the time had come to find out exactly how much it would cost to build a suitable facility on Appledore Island. The quickest way to do this, he thought, was to get a group of contractors to provide estimates on some specific projects. He asked me to calculate what the student and staff size on Appledore Island would have to be to pay for a reasonable housing and dining facility while at the same time not overloading the fragile ecology of the island's natural populations. Then I was to estimate the square footage of space required to meet the academic and housekeeping needs of such a population.

One of the conclusions from the Brady Committee study had been that a class size of about 60 paying students would be needed to make the kitchen self-sustaining. Needs for staff, faculty, assistants, and the occasional research investigator brought the eventual total island population to a projected minimum of 85. The Brady Committee felt that if the population went beyond one hundred, it might put damaging pressure on the richness of the island's natural resources.

Those numbers served as the basis of projections for the space needs for housing, dining, and instruction. I also added a list of requirements for docks, roads and paths, generators, a power distribution system, salt water and freshwater distribution systems, and a sewage system that could meet the requirements of the State of Maine, which were then among the toughest of all coastal states'. These, expenses, too, must be included in any realistic estimate for the project. The resulting four-page document was entitled *Information for Contractors, Proposed Cornell University Field Station, Appledore Island, Prepared for Trip to Appledore with Contractors, May 22-23, 1968*. It was reviewed and signed by Keith Kennedy, Warren Witherell for the Star Island Corporation, and myself.

What contractors would be willing to come out to Appledore Island? Two possibilities were Dick Soule, who had worked for the Star Island Corporation off and on for many years, and Dominic Gratta, who was working for the corporation then. We spread the word widely in seacoast New Hampshire and southern Maine. Three additional local contractors, one of whom had built the Dement Infirmary on Star Island, expressed interest.

Normally, of course, Cornell would have hired architects and engineers; drawn, revised, and eventually approved detailed building plans suitable for bid; and only then invited interested bidders to tour the site at their convenience with a thick document of specifications and caveats in hand. That protocol was not possible on Appledore Island. We provided no plans—only a statement of square footage needs for various functions—and we could not show the contractors the site one-by-one. It would have been too expensive to arrange separate trips out. They had to come together.

Rosamond Thaxter and the author in front of her cottage on Smuttynose Island (1968).

Thus it happened that Dr. Kennedy, who had arranged with Captain Arnold Whittaker for the M/V *Viking* to make a preseason trip to the Shoals, gathered with the contractors and the rest of us on the dock in Portsmouth and we started out. To my great pleasure, Rosamond Thaxter came along. Miss Thaxter, who lived at Champernowne Farm on the shore in Kittery Point, was a lineal descendant of the Laightons who built and operated the Appledore House Hotel. In many ways she was then the grande dame of the family and the keeper of its historical artifacts.

The five competing contractors eyed each other suspiciously, and conversation was minimal on the hour-long trip out. As we scrambled over the rocks onto Appledore Island, I wondered whether this coolness would mark the rest of the day.

The derelict buildings solved the problem. A vigorous argument soon developed among the contractors as to whether it would be better to renovate the old buildings or build from scratch. There were strong proponents on each side of the question. The vice provost and I learned a good deal about island realities by listening closely to the give and take.

Our competing contractors never did resolve the question. They remained stubbornly divided as to the least expensive approach. All five were reluctant to make any kind of estimate as to total cost. Dr. Kennedy told them we would be satisfied with nonbinding, nonembarassing, entirely confidential guesses. That was, apparently, the most we could hope for. The discussion continued vigorously aboard the *Viking* on the way in and ceased only as the contractors parted to go home. Each said he would provide a recommendation and an estimate of cost later. They understood we had no funds in hand and would have to decide whether to go after funds or abandon the project on the basis of the figures they provided.

Only three of the contractors submitted figures. They varied quite a bit. Keith Kennedy took the average and then inflated it substantially (30 percent, if I remember correctly) on the grounds that contractors' estimates were rarely high enough as demonstrated repeatedly on the Cornell campus. His resulting projection for constructing on Appledore Island the basic essentials was $350,000. To me he said, "Go get it!" But not from major foundations, granting agencies, or Cornell donors outside New England, and I shouldn't expect much help from Cornell University itself.

Someone took a classic picture of Rosamond Thaxter on that trip or another at about the same time. She was seated by herself on the bench just below the windows of the wheelhouse of the old *Viking,* with a ring life preserver above her head like a halo, looking very much the island matriarch. With some trepidation I sent her an enlargement of that portrait. She wrote back a most friendly letter, thanking me for my interest. As for the figure in the portrait, her comment was, "As the fishermen say, it don't pretty up none with age!"

Two months before the contractors' expedition to Appledore Island, three important people from the University of New Hampshire had come to Ithaca to meet with their approximate counterparts. They were Galen Jones, first director of the Jackson Estuarine Laboratory at Adams Point; Eugene Allmendinger, of the Marine Center in the Engineering College; and Vice President Jere Chase. They told us that a contract had been let for the construction of the Jackson Lab and presented Gene Allmendinger's powerful concept of the two universities forming a "corridor to the sea" by cooperative use of the home campus in Durham (on navigable water), the Estuarine Laboratory at Adams Point on Great Bay, the UNH shore facility at Odiorne's Point, and the open water field station Cornell was contemplating at the Shoals, where Professor Jackson had been so successful decades earlier. This concept was pregnant with vast motivating power in New Hampshire and had tremendous political potential.

This meeting led to the first of several written agreements between Cornell and UNH, the terms of which were never fully met on either side in the exigencies of construction, politics, and reality. Among the realities was the fact that, on the whole, all marine-interested persons cooperated well whatever their affiliation. Formal agreements were almost superfluous at the operating level. They just made the administrators feel good.

The SUNY Stony Brook marine situation also gelled in the spring of 1968 with the appointment of Dr. Donald Squires as the founding director of the New York State Marine Sciences Research Center there, long proposed in the state's regents scheme. Don Squires, then at the Smithsonian Institution, had received his Ph.D. at Cornell (in geology) and did not need to be specially educated about our faculty and its marine interests. His appointment was effective in September 1968, but he began thinking about his new job well before that.

Another development in the spring of 1968 also was to have considerable importance for the Shoals operation, particularly the fund-raising. On the occasion of its centennial observations in 1962, Cornell had mounted a massive capital campaign. This was put in the hands of one of the major national consulting agencies that conduct such efforts for a healthy fee. The campaign was satisfyingly successful, but had required a large expenditure by Cornell both in funds to pay for the consultant services and in time to educate the consultants about the peculiarities and characteristics of this hybrid institution. Someone in Cornell's administration decided that the university would be better off in the long run by spending the same funds to conduct future campaigns itself. Out of that decision came the creation of a number of Cornell regional offices across the United States, one of the first of which was set up in Boston and given responsibility for relating to Cornell's alumni in all of New England. Richard C. B. Clark was named its first director. Rik soon took hold of the Shoals project as an item of major interest to New England alumni (and himself). He made many things easily possible, especially those related to fund-raising, that would have been difficult for me to do by myself in following years.

One development that seemed at first to have great potential for the Shoals project turned out not to. That was the Sea Grant Act. As eventually passed by the Congress under the leadership of legislators from Rhode Island, which already had such things, it contained no funds for marine facilities or for undergraduate education in marine sciences. Indeed the Act itself contained a specific prohibition against using its funds for boats or buildings. The Shoals project did not fit Sea Grant objectives well at all.

The flyer for the third Summer Program, June 1968, was prepared, printed, and mailed early in the year. Applications again came flooding back. The program, presented by the same faculty as before with the exception of Professor Hewitt who was on sabbatical leave in Africa, was again eminently successful, but we were reminded forcefully of current events in the outside world when two of those admitted were drafted into military service before they could attend. They were instantly replaced from the top of a long waiting list.

That spring we found ourselves better able to meet requests of admitted students for financial aid by the help of a grant from the Link Foundation of Binghamton, New York. Marilyn Link, executive secretary of the Link Foundation, took a personal interest in what we were doing and came out to Star Island that summer to see the class in action. The Link Foundation supported Link Fellowships at the Shoals for several years following. That constituted another vote of support for what we were doing, and it was immensely encouraging.

SIX HUNDRED DOLLARS AND "GO"

The deteriorating buildings on Appledore Island, like a decaying tooth, kept nagging at me. I could almost feel them softly eroding away, and I talked to anyone who would listen about an opportunity being slowly lost. Herbert Everett, Director of Resident Instruction of the College of Agriculture was keeping in touch with developments. That spring he found in his budget $600 that he could break loose for an effort to do something about the deteriorating buildings on Appledore Island.

How far could $600 stretch? It certainly wouldn't go very far if paid to a contractor off the top. In fact, what sane contractor would undertake to do anything at all for our project given the island location and a $600 budget? The question really was how to establish a construction foothold on an uninhabited island such as Appledore was then, with absolutely none of the amenities one takes for granted on the mainland. Here's how we did it.

Student power was the answer! Five of the students in the Summer Program in Marine Science volunteered to stay on for a week after the conclusion of the program in 1968 and work with me on Appledore Island in return for board and room on Star. Dom Gratta, then at work on Star Island, who had looked over the derelict buildings during the contractors' visit to Appledore Island, gave his detailed opinion as to what should be done first. The highest priority was to keep the Appledore buildings from deteriorating further. A second urgent need was to create passable living accommodations for future construction workers on that island. We chose to work on the Coast Guard building as the best bet for our limited time and resources.

What the students lacked in experience and resources they more than made up in enthusiasm. Using tools and equipment borrowed from Star Island, we opened a trail from the shore landing site (a little farther up

Babb's Cove from where the dock and float are now) up the hill past what is now called Laighton House, continuing on more or less directly to the Coast Guard building. That distance through heavy brush, poison ivy, brambles, and a small marsh where a few wild cranberries grew seemed a lot longer then than it does now! The goal at the Coast Guard building was to patch the roof and make it tight; to make and install plywood covers for all exterior windows and door openings (the building had five exterior doors!); to paint the exposed trim, which was weathering badly; to clean the building of the debris accumulated over 20 years; and to remove all the plaster from walls and ceilings, most of which was wet and decomposing.

It rained off and on all week. That didn't slow down the inside cleanup and plaster removal, but it made the roof patching difficult and trim painting nearly impossible.

I did the roof patching myself. It was basically a simple matter of clearing the leaky areas of old cedar shingles that had deteriorated and piecing in new ones. Fortunately these leaky spots were few and mostly small, but the effect of moisture on a gull-inhabited wood-shingled roof is to make it supremely odoriferous, greasy, unpleasant, and very slippery. Proper staging would have helped, but none was available on Appledore Island. The work got done anyway.

In August another volunteer group assembled to complete what the rain had prevented in July. That group consisted of three faculty members, one student, and their assorted relatives working on the same unpaid basis as before. At the end of this second work week all the summer's construction goals had been achieved. We even painted and erected some signs warning off trespassers. How much did all that cost? We still had about $200 left when all costs of materials and board and room had been paid. This we used to purchase a small portable generator to make possible the use of electric hand tools or a few electric lights in the future.

With a jury-rigged outhouse made out of the old paint locker at its rear, the Coast Guard building was now at the camp-out level of housing. Several graduate students lived in it from time to time over the next three years, carting their drinking water and food supplies from Star, while working on ornithological research projects under Dr. Hewitt's supervision. Sponsored by the American Museum of Natural History, Cornell, and the University of Michigan, the studies dealt mostly with the habits of the cormorants, gulls, and herons. With students living in it, the Coast Guard building began gradually to accumulate the minimum needs for housekeeping.

In July 1968 the Executive Committee of Cornell's Board of Trustees quietly approved the Appledore Island project, conditioning its

Above: Coast Guard building before attack.
Below: Students Jeff Prince, Frank Sun, Pat Stanley, and Howard Cooper.

Above: Painting trim; Cliff Rice in gutter.
Below: Second group of volunteers John Kingsbury, John Anderson, Oliver Hewitt, and latter's son-in-law.

approval on the provisos that had already been enunciated by Vice Presidents Frank Long and Robert Sproull about having funds in hand before making any commitments. This approval vouchsafed retrospective validity to some actions we had already taken and removed inhibition from some contemplated future actions.

Like the first two programs, the third in June 1968 sent forth into the world another 30 highly motivated students who knew that one of the most important events in their academic lives had just taken place. With experience, setting up, presenting, and cleaning up after the programs was becoming easier, but it was still a lot of work for just two weeks of class. Hammers had now sounded on Appledore Island for the first time in furtherance of a new field station, but opening one there was obviously still several years away.

SHOALS LAB TOWN MEETINGS

If you were now to search office and archive files throughout the whole of Cornell University, you would find no document or letter from anyone ever appointing me as Director of the Summer Program in Marine Science or of the Shoals Marine Laboratory that arose from it. The reason is simple: none exists. The title actually developed from the need of the Cornell News Bureau to call me something other than associate professor of botany when it began to publicize the Shoals. After seeing "director" in print a few times, I began to use it under my name in correspondence. Nobody said I couldn't. In fact, I doubt that anyone at Cornell ever realized that the university never gave me that title. Even the administrators began using it.

The only actual authority I had in this matter from 1965 through 1968 was that given me by Dr. Morison when he put me in charge of the committee of faculty members he set up to supervise the Shoals project. I reported to that committee (which was comprised essentially of the Cornell members of the Shoals faculty) the fiscal results of each year, and together we worked out the staffing and program for the coming year, its budget for presentation to the Summer School, and the text of the annual flyer.

As the program gained momentum and increasing national notice, and as the first hammer sounded on Appledore Island, I felt a need for stronger administrative backing at Cornell. Under regular circumstances I would have reported through the head of some college department to a dean, and thence to the central administration. As it was, reporting through the Summer School, no regular department head or dean was involved with creating or approving our budget, and it was not at all clear to me just how much personal risk, financial and otherwise, might be devolving on the associated faculty members in this situation. Taking students into the marine environment, with the slippery rocks of the shore and the special hazards of boats, scuba diving, and snorkeling, is not to be done without some thought to the possible consequences of a serious, even potentially fatal, accident. The university legal department was of little help. Their summary advice was simply, "Always be prepared to look good in court."

Because no department or dean would have us, I decided to take the initiative and reverse the normal procedures. I invited the deans and department heads who should have been involved in our administration to a Shoals annual meeting to listen to our summary reports of finances, programs, and facilities and to comment if they wished. I took the position that if they didn't come they had no grounds for complaint, come what might. Thus was born, in 1968, the Shoals Lab Annual Meeting, patterned after a New England town meeting, at which all who had anything to do with the Shoals program, including students and donors, were welcome and had both voice and vote. Some of the important administrators did come regularly in those early years, including faithfully the director of the Summer School and the vice provost.

A review of the annual reports prepared for these meetings will show that the Shoals program always ran in the black, or so close as not to matter. Our projection that a competitive charge for tuition, board, and room should be able to pay the costs of housing, dining, and academic program held well. We were fortunate to receive small amounts of special moneys from time to time (like the $200 from the dean of the Ag School for the *Hesperornis*) that helped with unusual situations or demands and also a number of grants for scholarship support over the years from the Link Foundation, the Dyson Foundation, and the Jessie Smith Noyes Foundation. Dr. Morison continued helping with some honoraria for extra faculty and other kinds of support from his Ford Foundation grant.

ON SHOOTING ARROWS

Presenting each summer program was a lot like shooting an arrow from a drawn bow. First you pull back the string as tautly as possible by organizing the program carefully, assembling faculty, admitting students, providing supplies and equipment, and arranging to provide board and room. When all of this but the students was assembled on Star Island, the bow was fully drawn. To that point one had a good deal of control during which the target could be perceived and aim carefully taken. Then the students arrived and the program started. The arrow was suddenly released. How fast and far it

A whale spout seen from the islands instantly changes the day's program.

would go, what its exact trajectory would be, and where it would land were no longer under control. Funds were spent rapidly, almost wantonly, as required by a fully functioning program the conduct of which was determined daily at breakfast by staff decisions on how best to relate activities to time, tides, and weather, and who was on the island to lecture. The arrow was buffeted by the winds of chance. An unexpected trawler at the dock, or a whale spouting off the shore, or a prosaic sprained ankle immediately overrode whatever was planned. Only when the program ended—the nearly spent arrow had hit the target or fallen to the ground—could we see where it had gone, what it had achieved, and how much effort it had cost. The annual excitement of drawing that bow, aiming that arrow, and releasing it remains in my blood to the present day.

A simple method of controlling our spending worked well in keeping us within budget year after year. All who obligated funds, meaning nearly all members of the faculty and staff, agreed at the beginning of each season to spend stringently only for what was absolutely necessary to present a good program. At the conclusion of the teaching season we would tally up. If there were any unexpended balance, we would agree by consensus how best to spend it. The incentive of a reward up for grabs at the end of the program was surprisingly powerful in keeping the regular costs down.

It is worth perhaps brief note that the situation in which everyone gives up a bit of a common resource in order to enhance his access to a larger kitty in the end is approximately the reverse of what Garrett Hardin has called "the tragedy of the commons." In utilizing the old New England commons, each farmer gained personal advantage to the degree he could place the most animals on the common resource successfully. In the commons situation, the resource is inevitably destroyed by conscious overuse. In the Shoals program, the resource was increased and maximized by conscious underuse.

The program was not without change over the early years. Perry Gilbert left Cornell to become director of the Mote Marine Laboratory in Florida, though he returned to the Shoals when he could. Edward Raney retired from Cornell to set up Ichthyological Associates, a private consulting firm. At Perry Gilbert's instigation on arrival there, Cornell and the Mote Marine Station signed an agreement of affiliation in 1968. Despite the best of intentions, the actual relationship never became very strong, although Cornell classes occasionally went to Sarasota and found a warm welcome.

Another significant event occurred in the summer of 1968. Rosamond Thaxter, the grande dame of Champernowne Farm in Kittery Point, instructed her financial people to provide a grant to Cornell from the Rosamond Thaxter Foundation to establish the Thomas B. Laighton Fund for support of the Appledore Island construction project. This was the start of many such annual contributions from the Foundation and one of the earliest infusions of actual spendable money.

Some years later I discovered a direct, personal relationship with Rosamond Thaxter, and particularly with Katharine Thaxter, her first cousin. It goes this way: Following Asa Gray, who was the first professor of botany at Harvard University, the subject divided into specialties, one of which was cryptogamic botany (lower plants). The second professor of cryptogamic botany at Harvard was Roland Thaxter, the son of Celia Laighton and Levi Thaxter. Celia was, in turn, the daughter of Thomas and Eliza Laighton, the founders of the Appledore House Hotel.

At Harvard, Roland Thaxter was succeeded by William H. Weston who, in his later years, was my graduate doctoral adviser. In a sense, Celia Thaxter thus was my academic grandmother.

Celia Thaxter was actual grandmother to Rosamond and Katherine Thaxter through her sons John and Roland respectively. In my graduate student days, I had heard stories about the Roland Thaxter household from my major professor who apparently visited it frequently as Roland Thaxter's student. Years later, after I had made the Shoals connection, Katherine Thaxter told me stories about young graduate student Weston and his visits to her home. All of this gave me a personal feeling of closeness to Rosamond and Katharine and the Thaxter family generally. It probably had something to do, too, with the reestablishment of Celia Thaxter's garden on Appledore Island. More about that later.

Chapter Six

MONEY
1969

NEW INITIATIVES

Relationships with both the University of New Hampshire and the State University of New York deepened in important practical ways in the fall and winter of 1968.

Don Squires visited the Shoals very soon after he took office as the first director of the Marine Sciences Research Center at SUNY Stony Brook. He wrote later "Now that I have seen the opportunities presented by the planned program for the Isles of Shoals, I think that I can speak for all those in the State University who are interested in a marine program that they are indeed fabulous and we would welcome a joint program there with Cornell."

Galen Jones and others from the University of New Hampshire attended the Shoals program's first annual meeting in Ithaca in the autumn of 1968, as did representatives from SUNY Stony Brook. The UNH contingent presented a proposal, coming from a deepening interest in the Shoals program, that it be expanded to four weeks in length. They proposed to do this by moving it to the UNH campus at Durham for two more weeks after the first two weeks at the Shoals. In justification of the added length,

Arthur Borror.

they noted that the two-week program, crammed full even at its first presentation, was nevertheless experiencing accretion year by year, that some good faculty members who wished to participate had not been able to squeeze in, and that certain kinds of subjects and activities could be supported better in Durham or at the brand new Jackson Estuarine Laboratory than on Star Island. Their proposal was well received by all, and planning began for doubling the length of the program.

The flyer for the 1969 program, showed what was worked out. The summer program was enlarged to two courses. Cornell Biology 374, *Field Marine Biology,* was presented on Star Island for two credits, followed immediately by UNH Marine Science 774, *Introduction to Marine Science,* presented in Durham, also for two credits. Both parts had to be completed for a student to receive credit for either one. The Star Island faculty remained much the same as before, but the Durham course added 16 new names to the faculty roster. Among them was that of Arthur Borror, whose intimate association with the program was to become the longest of any member of the Shoals faculty, covering the full span from 1969 almost to the date of this book. Galen Jones was named the director of the Durham segment. He raised and administered a separate budget for his part of the program.

In terms of building on Appledore Island, 1969 would seem at first like a lost year. No building happened, not even any attention to the old buildings there. No hammers sounded anywhere on Appledore Island that summer.

That is not to say that nothing was happening. On the contrary, actions of great significance took place in 1969. The most important was, of course, the first presentation of the new four-week Summer Program in Marine Science to a group of 30 students, carefully selected as always. This doubling of the duration of the program required not only adding UNH representatives to the admissions committee, but also an enormous effort at Durham in planning, funding, and arranging for credits and facilities at UNH, in presenting the new course, and in summarizing the results for the second annual Summer Program town meeting in Ithaca that autumn.

On a technical level all went surprisingly well and smoothly. What the students experienced in Durham the second two weeks was well thought out, well integrated with the first two weeks, well organized, well presented, and well received. But the Durham campus itself and a return to dormitory life was definitely a let-down after life at the Shoals. If we could have done it the other way around, with Shoals last, our success would have been total, but the realities of college and Star Island calendars prevented that. Nevertheless, the program was excellent by any academic measure and all those faculty members involved in the presentation were enthusiastic to continue with another four-week program along the same lines in 1970.

SINE QUA, NON

The other major effort of 1969 was, bluntly, the commencement of high-powered fund raising. Without money, no building could be done. Unlike many of my academic colleagues, I lack inhibition when fund-raising is necessary to an important educational goal.

In January Cornell's Development Office designed a brochure, *On a Significant Frontier,* to support the fund-raising effort. Cornell University, the State University of New York, and the University of New Hampshire were listed on its cover as project cooperators. The Cornell address on it, "Water Resources and Marine Sciences Center, Hollister Hall," reflected a brief period during which the Shoals program tried to make that corner of the Engineering College its administrative home because the biology departments would not have us. The impressive brochure contained a map showing seven buildings on Appledore Island. Two of those were identifiable by location as the existing Coast Guard building and the radar tower. The new utility building (now Grass Foundation Laboratory) and the commons building (now Kiggins Commons) are shown in it about where they actually were later built. The other three buildings were entirely hypothetical and located on the map in such a manner that the decision whether to renovate the old buildings or build new remained entirely for the future.

What was reasonable to expect from alumni for financial support? Cornell's Development Office was the authority on that question. It was also the traffic cop who determined which alumni or foundations could be approached and in what way. Despite evidence that readers of this book who are college graduates may believe they have to the contrary, their alma mater does not ask for money indiscriminately nor continuously. There *are* rules.

On its record, Cornell's Development Office is one of the best in the country. It encouraged us that raising the needed funds was possible, but warned that it would be difficult. What alumni would the Development Office allow us to solicit? Certainly not all of them! Not ever! Everyone seeking funds in the name of the Shoals Lab was informed of the earlier restrictions that had been placed on our fund-raising and honored them from the beginning.

In February of 1969, the monthly *Cornell Alumni News* ran a major article about the proposed new facility on Appledore Island. Entitled "Lab in the Ocean," it was distinguished by stunning photographs taken by Shoals faculty member Alicia Hills Moore of *Life Magazine*. Through that article many alumni became aware of the Shoals project.

I began seeking opportunities to tell the Shoals story to the general public: the need, the success of the teaching on Star Island, and the opportunity to expand to new facilities on Appledore Island. With the help of Cornell's Office of Alumni Affairs, which supports Cornell Clubs across the country and around the world, and of the new Northeast Regional Office, invitations began to appear. Interest began to materialize also in the Portsmouth area and the broader seacoast region, which led to further invitations there.

Thus began a series of meetings or slide shows in auditoriums, at dinner meetings, in colleges, churches, Cornell Alumni Clubs, service clubs, and homes that lasted several years. In the Portsmouth area, Dr. Henry Saltonstall and his wife, Cecilia, gathered a small group in their lovely home in Stratham. James Barker Smith, a loyal alumnus of Cornell's School of Hotel Administration, and his wife, Margaret, scheduled a large public dinner meeting and slide presentation in the auditorium at their resort hotel, Wentworth-by-the-Sea. That dinner was graced by the presence of Dr. Jack McConnell, recently President of the University of New Hampshire and before that a professor and dean at Cornell. The after-dinner slide presentation was enlivened by a swooping bat that became quite active, much to the agitation of the audience, when the cavernous auditorium was darkened for the slides.

Rik Clark's services in gathering groups, identifying potential donors, finding convenient places to meet, and sending out publicity from the Cornell Northeast Regional Office in Boston (later at Wellesley) were invaluable and never-failing. He would even volunteer advice on what to do next and straighten my tie before I stepped on stage. In a very real way, the Shoals Lab owes much to the imagination and persistent efforts of Rik Clark and the Northeast Regional Office.

Over those same years I appeared before every Cornell Club in New England at least once and at meetings of nearly all of the Cornell Clubs east of the Mississippi. I addressed the large Boston club annually. Appearances before Kiwanis, Rotary, and other civic and service clubs were numerous, too.

The understood rules of the game did not allow an obvious pitch for funds at public meetings. My mission was, rather, to describe to audiences this unusual Cornell project and how it was going. Yet the real need for funds inevitably came through vividly. Frequently people would come up to me afterwards and ask how they could help. Once spontaneously asked, I was free to respond as I saw fit. The Development Office rules were superseded in such circumstances.

Those meetings, and the opportunity to meet and know a whole spectrum of people, left many warm memories. Occasionally the memories weren't so warm after a particular meeting. One alumni dinner meeting at Chatham, Cape Cod, for example, not only aged me considerably but cost quite a lot of undeductable personal expense. Here's how that happened.

One does not go around in a business suit on Appledore Island. This is true now and was especially so during the early construction years. But I kept a presentable blazer and slacks on the island for off-island events, as well as a tie and proper shoes. A day before the Chatham meeting I went ashore aboard the *Wrack* (the laboratory boat). I made sure to take with me my good clothes and shoes, carefully preserved in a waterproof garment bag. The trip was rough and wet, and just to be extra safe I put the garment bag below deck. For some reason I don't now remember, the docking at Frisbee's was hurried. I tossed my suitcase, the briefcase, the slide projector, and the carousel of slides ashore, got in my car, and drove to the family summer cottage on Cape Cod for the night. When I began to get things ready for the meeting the next evening, I discovered I had left my good clothes aboard the boat. I could *not* appear at Chatham in my island clothes.

A quick trip to two men's stores in Falmouth was without success. Nothing they had was suitable without further fitting and there wasn't time for that. In the third store I found a green blazer, identical to one I already had except that it didn't fit quite as well, and a pair of slacks that barely touched the floor if I hiked them up high enough. These had to do —and did— but at the cost of much equanimity and all my available cash. Besides that, I was late to the meeting.

I like to arrive early at meetings to set up, check out the slide projector, and survey the room, lest something as simple as turning off the lights develop into a major problem. I remember one occasion when we were forced to twist out the fluorescent tubes in the overhead fixtures to darken a room when no one there could find the light switch.

I thought I knew Chatham pretty well, but discovered when I got into the downtown area that the meeting was not anywhere there. Instead it was at an obscure location quite a ways out of town toward Orleans. A brief session with my CB car radio produced proper directions and I arrived just as the dinner was starting. Fortunately the lecture setup was quick and easy and the light switch obvious, but the personal stress level had been immense that day.

Later that summer, trying to explain to my wife why I suddenly had two identical green blazers was a further reminder of my Chatham difficulties.

SYMBIOSIS, INSTITUTIONAL AND DONOR

Along the fund-raising path, administrators at the University of New Hampshire did a truly remarkable thing. Deciding that the Shoals project was worthy of UNH support, they permitted UNH alumni to designate their contributions for the construction of facilities on Appledore Island. Given the usual competition of academic institutions for funds, and the normal institutional chauvinism of alumni, I believe it would be difficult to find another example in the whole of the United States where one major university has actively encouraged its alumni to support the construction of facilities owned by a different major university. Moreover, UNH accords its alumni who contribute to the Shoals project the same recognition as the ones who contribute directly to its own budget. This remarkable situation has continued to the present, though sometimes fitfully as administrators come and go.

Alumni of Cornell and the University of New Hampshire, and people of the seacoast area, and those with special Shoals connections have been generous to the Shoals Lab. Those people didn't come to public meetings to have their pockets picked, but in those early years anyone hearing about and seeing the island hardships and the students' motivation, needs, and accomplishments, could hardly escape the conclusion that this cause was worthy and money would help. By bits and pieces significant funding began to appear.

But in several respects it was uphill work. Those were the years of the Vietnam War and campus ferment. Many older alumni did not like what they saw in the national press concerning protests, building occupations, intimidation of administrators and faculty, and forced closings at universities, Cornell included.

In the matter of attracting significant donors, the Cornell Development Office had a little litany, often recited. It was "awareness, interest, involvement, commitment." That path, they said, usually takes a year or more to result in the emergence of a significant donor. Furthermore the attrition along the pathway is great. As a rule of thumb, they said, it takes a thousand persons entering at the awareness level to yield one committed donor. That observation was discouraging because the average alumni club meeting brought out only 20 or 30 people. But of course the Shoals project was hardly typical, and special enthusiasms and devotion sometimes developed almost instantly when a certain kind of person found out about us.

Donors, as I see it, divide largely into two major categories: those successful, wealthy people who wish to leave their mark on civilization in the form of a named building or similar titled recognition; and those donors, also successful and with resources beyond their needs in later years, who wish to put the surplus to work accomplishing something really useful whether or not it brings special recognition. While funds from both kinds of donors are truly welcome, a special relationship can develop with the latter. Such people have the resources to accomplish something, but not the ability. Those like me, involved in a project, know how to get things done, but don't have the necessary financial resources. Under such circumstances a serendipitous marriage of abilities and resources can bring great joy to both partners. The Shoals project has been graced with a number of this kind of donor. Nothing in my life has been more satisfying than seeing the pleasure those donors get from participating actively in the use of their funds and experiencing firsthand the results of such philanthropy in the lives of students.

Willard Kiggins was a donor of that kind. A graduate of Cornell, he was devoutly devoted to his alma mater. When the new library was proposed for the Ithaca campus he funded the Willard and Kathryn Kiggins reading room in it. One spring, on their annual migration from Placida, Florida to Londonderry, Vermont, he and his wife, Kathryn, detoured through Ithaca and asked to see the Kiggins Room in the new library. Unfortunately no librarian then on duty knew anything about the Kiggins Room. Willard was not surprised, but he wasn't particularly pleased either. His displeasure

Willard Kiggins, Kiggins Commons basement lecture room, 1976.

increased markedly soon thereafter during the campus unrest of the late '60s and early '70s. Those Cornell students making national headlines and achieving noteriety in the *Cornell Alumni News* were not behaving as Willard thought proper for Cornell students. He wrote the university that in good conscience he could contribute to his alma mater no longer.

Rik Clark in the Northeast Regional Office learned of this. Finding himself not too far from Londonderry one summer day, Rik decided he had nothing to lose by showing up unannounced at the Kiggins estate. On arrival he found himself between Willard, returning from a pasture, and the house. Willard met Rik cordially, if unavoidably. Rik soon turned the conversation to what some Cornell students were then doing just off the New Hampshire shore. Willard and Kathryn Kiggins took interest, came and visited the Shoals, and became major contributors to what they saw. This marriage of resource and result allowed Willard to regain the faith in college students generally and in Cornell particularly that he had lost so painfully earlier.

Chapter Seven

HAMMERS RESOUND
1970

CRIPPLED FLYER - I

By spring of 1970 the analysis of the fiscal and academic success of the 1969 four-week summer program on Star Island and in Durham had been presented at the annual meeting and decisions for 1970 had been made. A flyer had been mailed, students admitted (again to capacity), course needs assembled, and the program was ready to go once again. Funds for construction on Appledore Island were accumulating, and construction goals were becoming more and more solid. So far no major administrative or other kind of block to progress had appeared.

There were quite a few minor problems, however.

One unexpected snag had surfaced the previous year when copy for the 1969 flyer had gone to the Cornell print shop with the expectation of the usual rapid turnaround. But the printer said he was no longer allowed to accept copy unless it had the initialed approval of the Cornell publications office. Apparently the university, embarrassed by the poor quality and excessive cost of certain departmental efforts, had decided to impose stylistic and production controls on everyone. No one had told me! While I had no quarrel with these objectives, the newly required design and contract procedure would add at least two weeks to our very tight production schedule. Ideally, the flyer should be in the hands of students so they could talk things over with their parents during the midwinter break between semesters. Flyer copy could not be created until after the decisions of the Shoals annual meeting. The Shoals annual meeting could not be held earlier because we could not assemble a final picture of finances until the straggling bills of the summer had been chased down and settled. That took more than a month, sometimes two, after the start of the autumn semester. Adding two more weeks (and extra cost) to the production schedule for the flyer was just not acceptable. Here's what I did.

I called the publications office immediately from the printer's office (late in the afternoon). The person whose initials I needed was not there, and I learned that his office would not open the next morning until nine. University offices are supposed to open at eight. I announced that I would be on his doorstep promptly at eight the next morning and would camp there until I had the initials on the flyer copy that would make it acceptable to the printer that day. I was furious at the unexpected delay and would not tolerate it.

The head of the publications office appeared at his office shortly after eight, probably an hour earlier than he normally did. I stated my case, he scanned the copy and initialled it—but only on the condition that flyer copy would be prepared earlier and sent through the new regular procedure the next year.

With extra effort and expensive long distance calls to run down unsubmitted bills, copy for the 1970 flyer was ready early. I sent it to the publications office and let the process run its course as a test. As expected, it took a full two extra weeks to get the flyer back from the contracted printer (who was located out of town and out of our control). The resulting professional flyer seemed to me less attractive from a student's point of view than those earlier flyers we amateurs had produced more quickly. The distinguished botany department artist, Elfriede Abbe, agreed with me. By the time the design fee had been paid, any savings in production were more than used up.

Armed with those facts I wrote a memo to the Cornell vice president who supervised the publications office. The memo pointed out that the Shoals project employed an editor who was probably as experienced professionally as the average editor in the design office and a designer (Elfriede Abbe) who was listed in *Who's Who of American Women*. We did not need the services of the publications office and could ill afford the time delays or extra costs involved in using it.

In his response the vice president cleared me from having to get editorial or design approval in the future. Thus in 1971 we resumed producing our flyer ourselves and having it printed quickly on campus.

Another minor problem was not so easy to resolve. It had to do with bookkeeping in relation to the increasing inventory of Summer Program equipment. Some items like the Boston Whaler were fairly major. The government surplus property we had begun acquiring also included some big-ticket items, though the funds we invested in them were minor.

Program operating funds were handled comfortably through the Summer School Office as described before; equipment ownership and inventory was the problem. There being no other clear option, funds for equipment began to flow in channels paralleling my paycheck. My professorial appointment at Cornell was in the New York State College of Agriculture. Initially I was in the College's Department of Botany. The creation of the Division of Biological Sciences just before the Shoals Program got going and the resulting reorganization had shifted my position to the Division's Section of Genetics, Development, and Physiology (whose title didn't represent even slightly my professional interests). When funds were allocated for Shoals use by either the dean or the director of resident instruction of the College of Agriculture, or by the director of the Division of Biological Sciences, they tended to pass from the originating accounts to ones in the hands of the Section of Genetics, Development, and Physiology.

Remember, I was then just an ordinary professor at Cornell, never released from any of the usual professorial responsibilities in Ithaca. I received no special pay for the Shoals effort, and no Cornell administrator was prepared to supervise my work at the Shoals. This administrative anomaly, together with the accumulation of Shoals inventory under my name in the Section of Genetics, Development, and Physiology, began to cause accounting problems which soon were magnified. The funding irregularities, long the source of increasingly irritating little day-to-day problems, were now becoming seriously difficult. To the Shoals faculty in 1968 I wrote, "As a nonsectional anomaly obtaining its present mandates from two of the greater of the Cornell anomalies, namely the Summer School and the Division of Biological Sciences, confusion now reigns supreme in the bookkeeping of the Program." I kept nagging the administrators for a solution but nothing happened. The problem was not solved in 1970; indeed it just got worse over the next several years.

On the other hand, some of the early fund-raising enthusiasm infected even Cornell administrators themselves. Herbert Everett, Director of Resident Instruction for the College of Agriculture, and Director Morison, of the Division of Biological Sciences, each produced $1,300 for the Shoals Program operating budget in 1970.

Martin Sampson succeeded William Smith in 1970 as director of the Cornell Division of Summer and Extramural Programs. Once he had

Martin Sampson, Louise Kingsbury, and Gary Boden (1976).

figured out what was going on, Marty became even more sold, if that was possible, on the Shoals project than Bill Smith had been. He and Mrs. Sampson were among the first personal contributors to the Shoals Lab construction campaigns.

The first issue of our newsletter, initially titled *Marine Laboratory at the Shoals,* appeared in April 1970. It was intended as a bimonthly publication to convey information about the Shoals project. It was frankly promotional, and made no secret of this.

OSPREY, BARGE, AND EVENTS OF 1970

Of the steps forward in 1970 the most visible was a second major volunteer project on Appledore Island to improve the condition of the old buildings and get ready for serious new construction in 1971. Cornell came up with an extra $1,000 to pay for three weeks of work by student volunteers. More students volunteered than we could handle, but in the end 17 students devoted over 25 man-weeks of labor to manual work on Appledore Island in

The Osprey *off White Island.*

July and August. They not only worked for free, but even raised a $50 contribution from among themselves to help support the work.

During the presentation of *An Introduction to Marine Science* each spring on Star Island, Professor Hewitt had felt an increasing urge to get a larger vessel than the *Hesperornis* or the Whaler for field trips. I, too, wanted a suitable vessel for trips from Star Island to Appledore Island and Portsmouth in support of the construction project. The volunteers headed for Appledore Island needed more freight capacity than either the Whaler or the *Hesperornis* could provide. At the very least, we needed something capable of towing a small barge.

Dr. Hewitt, through his ornithological connections, learned that the *Osprey*, a Jonesport-type lobster boat owned by the Massachusetts Audubon Society and used for several years by Dr. William Drury for his work with gulls, was for sale. The price seemed reasonable and the condition basically sound. Dr. Hewitt and I bought the vessel fifty-fifty. Thus the privately owned *Osprey* started work for the Shoals project for free and uninventoried.

One of the first necessities was to open up some of the old roads and paths on Appledore Island, and to cut a trail to the island's main well.

Scythes and brushcutters were useful to some extent, but the undergrowth was so thick along the old roads and paths that to clear all of them by hand would have taken an immense investment of hours and muscle. Besides, few students knew how to handle a scythe safely. Here's how we licked the clearing problem.

My brother, Edward Kingsbury, had an old but functional Ford farm tractor with a rotary brush cutter mounted behind. It was located in northeastern Massachusetts. He was willing to loan it to the project if we could get it out to Appledore Island and back. Why not build a barge right then? The project would need one eventually, anyway, and it could be used as a floating dock at Appledore Island when we were not dragging it back and forth from the mainland.

Any barge built that summer would have to be very inexpensive because the proposed reroofing of Laighton House itself would use up most of the limited budget. The Star Island Corporation agreed to participate in the construction of the barge if we would let them share in its use. Harry Lent, the Star Island manager, and my brother, an engineer, whose tractor would be at risk on it, worked on designing a practical and inexpensive barge. On an early summer weekend in 1970 they figured out a deck and framing understructure that would enclose eight 250-gallon second-hand oil tanks (the kind used in home basements for fuel-oil storage) as floats. The deck would measure 14 by 22 feet, and if the calculations were right, should be able to carry almost five tons before going underwater itself.

The design was somewhat complicated. The lumber yard in Portsmouth, however, was willing to cut all the framing lumber to size at no extra cost. Harry Lent took the sketch plans and list of materials in to the lumber yard and ordered the lumber for delivery to the ferry dock. Unfortunately, he then hit the road out of Portsmouth for a brief vacation in his home Down East. My brother also went ashore. Thus, when the pile of wood was thrown off the ferry with no accompanying plans, there was no one left at the islands who had helped with designing the barge. We sorted the pieces into various lengths, but to make a barge from them was something like doing a picture puzzle with blank pieces.

Star Islander Clifford "Pop" Bourne, a carpenter by trade, after standing by the lumber pile and giving it much quiet thought, announced he was willing to give it a try.

As it happened, Star Island was replacing its six oil tanks with larger ones that summer. The old ones were still sound. Scouts ashore found two more in the Portsmouth area that we could have for free or close to it. These were horsed to the dock in Portsmouth, put aboard the ferry, and heaved overboard into Gosport Harbor from the deck of the old *Viking* just before

Volunteer students on new barge (decking planks not yet trimmed) with tractor and brushcutter; Edward Kingsbury with beard.

she docked at Star Island. Handy students swam out, climbed aboard the tanks, and paddled them ashore on Star.

In a surprisingly short time the barge frame was assembled, the tanks painted with antifouling paint, the deck spiked on, and all wood treated with creosote. This work was done at the edge of the beach on Star Island. At high tide the *Osprey* backed in cautiously, took the barge in tow, and headed out into the harbor to see how a hull composed of eight oil tanks would behave under way. No problems.

The new barge soon went ashore on its maiden voyage to fetch the tractor. We loaded from the beach in a quiet backwater of the Piscataqua River near the road to New Castle, tied the tractor down securely for the voyage, got the barge successfully in tow in the strong river currents, and headed out to Appledore Island. Still no problems. Near Babbs Cove we transferred the tow to the Whaler and ran the barge to the head of the beach there. After a little excitement with the tractor sliding and plowing over the loose rocks at the head of Babbs Cove, which were like ball bearings under the wheels, we got it ashore. At that historic moment it became the first self-propelled vehicle on Appledore Island since the demise of the Coast Guard truck two decades earlier.

The first job for the tractor and its six-foot brushcutter was to open the original back road to the Coast Guard building. Until that was done, everything needed for working or living there had to be carried by hand across nearly the full width of the island, through the brush and poison ivy and across a perennial wet spot where a few precarious, gull-slurried walkway boards had been thrown.

The old Coast Guard road went along the north side of the cut through the waist of the island, then across that cut just inland of Broad Cove beach, then teetered on the edge of the cliff up the hill, then followed the high shore edge for a way, and eventually turned inland and wandered along as level as possible to the back side of the Coast Guard building. Following it to the point where it turned inland was relatively easy because the shore vegetation had been kept somewhat in check by winter storms and the gulls that occupied it nearly shoulder to shoulder during the early season nesting period. The tractor's progress along that stretch could be marked from anywhere on Appledore Island by the cloud of gulls shrieking overhead.

Following the trail after it turned inland into the dense shrubbery was not easy. Disaster threatened if the tractor got off the original trail because the uncleared ground under the brush was studded with both jagged fixed and unstable pieces of granite. Running into them unawares would result in a dented tractor, a broken radiator, a hung vehicle, or a mangled rotary cutter.

To keep the tractor on the old roadway, here's what we did: Dave Pierson, who swore he was immune to poison ivy, struggled through the head-high cherry, sumac, and poison ivy, prodding with a pitchfork to locate the larger irregularities underfoot. Another volunteer rode on the front hood of the tractor, peering closely at the terrain for the presence of loose rocks as the brush was forced forward and under by the tractor's front axle. The tractor itself crept ahead as slowly as its gearing allowed, crashing down the higher brush and grinding everything up behind it. Under a cloud of gulls this was all very exciting!

Even with these precautions the tractor went off the roadbed a couple times. Fortunately, no damage was done, but getting back on the track was quite a job. After much sweat, tears, gasoline, and some blood, the tractor eventually emerged from the sea of brush at the Coast Guard building. On the return trip, the width of the trail was enlarged. Here we encountered the only serious accident to equipment of the entire summer. We found the old Coast Guard truck right where it had expired through the

Above: Brian Rivest building Brian's Bridge.
Below: Lucy Palmer following a pipe to open a trail to the well.

Volunteers moving building materials onto Appledore Island.

misfortune of running the back wheel of the Ford tractor onto a protruding leaf spring of the truck skeleton and puncturing the tractor tire before we saw the truck's bones in the vegetation.

That stopped everything. The tractor had to be jacked up, the wheel removed, rolled by hand with great difficulty down the stubbled path to the beach head, loaded aboard the *Osprey,* and taken ashore for tire repair. Then the process was reversed and the wheel remounted. This was backbreaking work, but we did it, and in a few days the tractor was back at work. We used fulcrum and lever or block and tackle where we could, but most of the heavy work on Appledore Island in the summer of 1970 was done by direct application of human muscle. Before summer's end the tractor also mowed down the dense sumac growth where the lawn of the Appledore House Hotel had been—the first step in reestablishing that grassy vista.

That summer we also had to open other roads and paths and build an essential bridge over a small ravine (just to the side of what is now the University of New Hampshire building). A student, Brian Rivest, made the bridge his personal project. Brian's Bridge, built of salvaged lumber in 1970,

Volunteer students 1970; lunch break.

lasted until 1983 before it finally had to be replaced. Brian himself is now a professor at the State University of New York at Cortland and is a regular member of the Shoals Lab faculty.

PIRANHAS AND ARTISTS

The first major construction project was to reroof one of the cottages. Roofing on an offshore island takes a bit more thought, skill, and attention than on the mainland. Here's how we did it.

Of all the buildings we thought we could salvage, Laighton House (earlier the main teaching building for the University of New Hampshire Zoological Laboratory) was in the worst shape. It needed a new roof badly. Another year or two of porous conditions would have finished it.

We began by removing entirely a squarish recent addition to the back of the building; it had housed a generator in UNH days, and was now thoroughly rotten. Uninhibited students attack such demolition jobs like piranhas in the Amazon, and the structure was down almost instantly. The next job was to take off what remained of the roof's old asphalt shingles. We did that. Underneath we found that only about a third of the roofing boards were still sound enough to hold nails. Two-thirds of them had to be removed. We did that.

Under the roof boards we found more rot. About a third of the rafters were eroded or softened to the point where they wouldn't hold nails or provide a plane surface for the new roof boards. Thus, to replace the shingles, we had first to replace or repair about a third of the rafters and two thirds of the roofing boards. This was something of a bad surprise. Even the plate (the timber on which the rafters rest) was seriously rotted in a few spots. This was beyond our powers to deal with properly. They built right in the old days, carefully mortising the upright, full measure 3x4-inch studs into both the plate above and the sill below. Replacing a section of rotted plate was not a simple matter.

So far as we could, we replaced rafters with similar timbers that had been salvaged from under the sagging front porch, which would have to be entirely rebuilt anyway. That way we matched the full measure dimensions of the original rafters. Rafters that were only slightly rotted could be sistered with modern measure 2x4s or 2x6s to provide a good nailing surface. Sistering is done by nailing a new timber to the old alongside the damaged area.

Matching the roof boards was a bigger problem. Few good full-measure boards were available by salvage. New boards were significantly thinner than the originals (and also narrower). Unless we paid for special custom sawing, they would have to do. They did, and if you look at the Laighton House roof closely, you may still be able to notice places where the surface drops by about a quarter of an inch between the old and new roof boards.

Slowly, the new roof took shape. A cosmetic dormer was removed. The two chimneys were taken down below roof level and the holes boarded across. This eliminated the need for complicated flashing. The day soon came when the roof deck was complete and a tarpaper covering was nailed down. Then came the new asphalt shingles. We chose black (the same as the previous shingles) on the theory that black can always be matched, and we lapped them with only four inches exposed to the weather rather than the five inches they were designed for. In all, more than a ton of shingles were nailed onto the Laighton House roof.

Proper staging did not exist on Appledore Island, but safety was always paramount in everyone's mind. Each student who went out on the roof wore a rope tied around the waist. These ropes passed over the roof ridge and were fixed to some solid structure on the other side. If the students fell, they wouldn't fall far. None did.

Above: The addition to the rear was rapidly removed;
Below: ...leaving a hole.

Above: The new roof slowly took shape;
Below: ...and was shingled. Abby Machamer and Jim Smith at work.

Abby Machamer at day's end.

Boards, framing lumber, tarpaper, seemingly unending bundles of shingles, lunches, drinking water, first aid, fire extinguishers, ladders, wheelbarrows, tools, and rigging all came to the rocks of Appledore Island (much of it borrowed from Star Island) on the Whaler or the *Hesperornis*, and went ashore across the slippery intertidal seaweeds and the sharp barnacles and then up the hill, through the brambles and poison ivy to the building on the backs of sweating, unpaid students.

That student-laid Laighton roof lasted a full 20 years, which is really very good considering what the gulls and the weather do to roofs at the Shoals.

At some time before 1970 another unexpected but strong Cornell connection with Appledore Island came to light. Many of the distinguished oil portraits of early Cornell luminaries that hang in halls and fraternities throughout the university are signed by Olaf M. Brauner. Among them is one of Professor Benjamin Freeman Kingsbury, an early histologist at Cornell, which hangs in the main floor of Stimson Hall. That attracted my attention to Brauner shortly after my arrival in Ithaca in 1954. Many years later I discovered Olaf Brauner's connection with the Shoals.

Above: Laighton House before volunteers (rear).
Below: Laighton House after volunteers (front).

Professor Brauner spent his productive lifetime at Cornell—52 years to be exact. He was the first professor of art and a founder of the Department of Fine Arts, which he served as head from 1896 to his retirement in 1939. Olaf Brauner came to American shores with his parents from their native Norway at the age of 14. In a few years his natural artistic talents led to formal instruction at the Boston Museum of Fine Arts. There he undoubtedly learned of the summer gathering of artists and writers then thriving under Celia Thaxter's influence at Appledore Island. As a youthful aspiring artist, Olaf Brauner spent several summers at the Appledore House Hotel near the turn of the century.

While Olaf Brauner was painting on Appledore Island and continuing his education informally among the artistic greats assembled there, he was attracted naturally to a young maiden of Norwegian upbringing then living at the Shoals. Celia Thaxter's brother, Oscar Laighton, in *Ninety Years at the Isles of Shoals,* tells the story thus.

"An old Norwegian sailor, named Ben Berentsen, who was working on Appledore Island, was ever telling us of his family he had left in Norway. We advanced some money and he sent for his family. The Haley Cottage on Smuttynose Island was vacant, and we let Ben have it with some furniture to make the place comfortable. Their meeting was something beautiful, though we could not understand a word they were saying to each other. My mother (Eliza Laighton) at once made arrangements for the two eldest girls to stay with her. They proved a great help and delight to mother. Olaf Brauner, a young Norwegian artist, who was painting at the islands, fell in love with the youngest sister, Nicolina, and they were married when she had grown up."

The marriage took place in 1895, the year after Celia Thaxter's death, and just as Olaf Brauner received his first appointment at Cornell. The young couple set up housekeeping in Ithaca, New York.

Among the artists Olaf Brauner met on Appledore Island was the American impressionist Childe Hassam. Noted in Brauner's faculty memorial statement is the observation that the most complete exhibition of the works of Hassam (up to then) had been gathered at Cornell University. That this was so undoubtedly traces to a relationship established between these artists at the Shoals.

Although the university owns many of Brauner's portraits, the holdings of the many seascapes he painted is meager. One in the collection of the Herbert F. Johnson Museum of Art at Cornell is entitled *Noreaster* and appears, from the lay of the rocks depicted, to have been painted at the southeastern corner of Appledore Island. A number of others are still in the possession of Brauner's descendants.

It will come as a surprise to many Cornellians to learn that the existence of the Herbert F. Johnson Museum of Art itself traces in a real way back to that Norwegian maiden who was uprooted from the Shoals to live out her life in Ithaca. Here's how.

Olaf and Nicolina Brauner raised a large family in Ithaca. Among the children was a daughter, Gertrude, known as Daupho (a nickname derived from Dauphine). Daupho married Herbert F. Johnson. Their son Samuel Johnson, the grandson of Nicolina Berentsen Brauner, was the principal benefactor of the Museum of Art at Cornell, which, fittingly, is named after his father. Had it been named after his maternal grandfather, it would now be the Olaf M. Brauner Museum of Art.

SUPERSCROUNGING

The value of governmental surplus had become clear back in 1968. A little investigation at that time showed that Cornell knew where the surplus items were and how to obtain ownership. The general route was through state warehouses. As I remember, there were three of them in New York: one at Canandaigua, one near Albany, and one on the western extremity of Long Island. State purchasers watched the lists of property being written off by federal agencies, including the military. When they saw something they thought would be useful to state agencies, they requisitioned it and had it moved to one of the warehouses. If no federal agency put in a prior request for the item, the state took possession at no cost. The state then assessed a few cents for the inevitable paperwork and the further costs of moving it to the state's warehouses. Educational agencies, especially the school districts throughout the state, made good use of those warehouses. The average final cost of goods going to educational institutions in this fashion was quite a bit less than ten cents on the dollar of assessed value.

One big advantage of the state warehouses was that seekers could see what they were getting, and when they found something really useful, nail it on the spot. We began scouting the warehouses whenever there was spare time to go to Canandaigua (the closest) or Albany (stopping on the way to or from the Shoals). We got some great things that way. I remember reels of suture thread, navy chart dividers, a dental light that worked just as well over dissection trays as over patients, and much more of a similar eclectic nature. My first visit to Canandaigua yielded items inventoried on the federal lists (conservatively) at $550 for which I paid $25.

We called it scrounging and we became very good at it during the construction years ahead.

For a brief time our tenuous affiliation with the federally funded Water Resources and Marine Sciences Center at Cornell gave direct access

Telephone poles at Appledore; not yet hauled out.

to the federal surplus lists even before the state got them, for the simple reason that federal agencies had first grabs. The Water Resources Center was federal enough to qualify. Shopping from the federal lists had the advantages of first access and especially low prices (often as little as a penny on the dollar for the paperwork), but it also carried the distinct disadvantage that, except by travelling to the federal agency where the surplus happened to be located, we couldn't see the items first. For those low rates we took chances on the reliability of the condition report, and sometimes even on exactly what it was that was hiding behind the federal acronyms or abbreviations.

We were sometimes surprised when the goods came. One such time, "25c Paint/lac, rustproofing" appeared on the list. I thought the "c" probably meant gallon cans. The quoted charge would have made 25 gallons of rustproofing paint dirt cheap and rustproofing was always of interest on Appledore Island, whatever the color. When the paint came, it turned out that the "c" meant five-gallon pails. We suddenly had 125 gallons of fast-drying, rust-colored lacquer on our hands. For several years we used it for everything possible on Appledore Island, even as floor paint on the seriously weathered floors in the old buildings. It was eventually gone.

Another memorable time "poles, wood pres" were listed. Thinking they were probably larger than fence posts, we had them shipped direct to Kittery in care of Warren Delano, who had taken a personal interest in the project. They turned out to be about the largest possible pressure-treated telephone poles. Mr. Delano had to cope with them entirely by himself when they arrived —all Shoals people were back in Ithaca. He took delivery on the town dock (Frisbee's), rolled the poles into the water one by one with a log-roller's peavy, chained them together with a come-along, and diverted the old *Viking* into Kittery Harbor (Pepperrell Cove) to take them in tow. They arrived successfully at the islands, although Captain Arnold Whittaker complained that they yawed about wildly at any decent speed. Eventually the poles were hauled out on the Star Island beach on a high tide. Later that summer we towed them over to Appledore Island and returned the chains to Warren Delano. How the telephone poles were used on Appledore Island where wind is a problem and consequently where all power and communications cables run under ground where possible or on the granite rocks where not, is another story.

Unfortunately our direct access to federal surplus didn't last long. After a year or so of very happy hunting (nonrusting magnesium bomb trailers, commercial life rafts, several generators, a powered life boat, a tool kit valued at nearly $1,500, and the like), a sharp-eyed federal auditor noted that the Cornell Water Resources and Marine Sciences Center received federal funds for work only in fresh waters, and some of the requisitioned items were appropriate for use only in salt water. This distinction had not occurred to anyone in the Water Resources Center, but it caused a federal query and we were no longer able to receive federal surplus by this route.

Unfortunately, no other part of Cornell University was then receiving federal funds in support of marine sciences so there was no substitute for the Water Resources Center in getting us access to items on the federal surplus lists. We had to go back to the state warehouses, lower on the scrounge pecking order and somewhat more costly. At least we no longer got 125 gallons of paint when we expected 25, and we could more easily check out the condition of a generator before committing ourselves to moving the brute. A dog is a dog, no matter how low the price, and a dog on Appledore Island is twice the dog it would be on the mainland.

Loss of direct access to federal surplus lists was mitigated in some measure by getting to know Dr. Peter Beck, ophthalmologist, of Portsmouth. Dr. Beck's powers of accumulating good merchandise at ridiculously small costs were second to none. A visit to his home basement or accumulating-barn was a rare treat and an awe-inspiring experience. We began calling Dr. Beck "Superscrounge" and utilizing his services to Shoals's advantage.

LAYERED ACCOUNTING

On June 30, 1970, Robert S. Morison, founding Director of the Division of Biological Sciences, retired from that position. He was replaced by his second-in-command, Dr. Richard S. O'Brien of the Division's Section of Neurobiology and Behavior. On taking command, Dick O'Brien made a valiant effort to bring some administrative order to the Shoals anomaly. He appointed a committee headed by myself to study the situation and make recommendations. The committee was large and broadly representative of the unusual range of marine interests at Cornell, including some that conflicted, or at least competed, with each other.

In 1970, Professor Gene E. Likens, who was on the new committee, published a summary of Cornell's academic resources in aquatic sciences (freshwater and marine). In *A Program in Aquatic Studies at Cornell University* he listed 39 faculty members with interests in almost as many discrete aquatic subject areas and 54 credit courses dealing with the aquatic environment in some way. Realization that Cornell, by itself, had a greater number and broader range of faculty members with experience and research interests in the marine sciences than possessed by any other single university in New York State came slowly. That this was true of an inland university was surprising , but is a large part of the reason why inland Cornell became an equal organizing partner with the State University of New York to form jointly the Sea Grant Institution for New York State. The political power of New York's large population and the fact that it is the only state in the union possessing open shorelines on the ocean and two of the Great Lakes, made eventual Sea Grant status for some New York academic institution almost inevitable.

Given the size and range of watery interests at Cornell, it is not surprising that Dr. O'Brien's committee was unable to reach any firm recommendations for how the diversity of marine interests should best be gathered and administered, or even for the future organization of the Shoals initiative. The committee didn't really try very hard. Even if it had made some solid recommendations, the administration would have probably wanted something else.

Accounting at Cornell, especially in 1970 when computers were still spotty, was multilayered. In order not to go over a grant budget, individual professors often kept close track of what they were spending. Their departments certainly did. Departments also kept close track of the teaching costs professors generated, so as to keep within account authorizations and out of trouble with the dean or the business office. The contract and

Jay Freer pouring; others, all from UNH, are Robert Correll (plain shirt), Arthur Borror (plaid shirt), and Charles Walker (striped shirt).

endowed business offices also kept track, item by item, of all bills and payments in the separate state and private parts of the university, and the university auditor reviewed both accounting systems continuously for purposes of detecting fraud or other moral lapses. The treasurer of the university required yet another accounting for his summary purposes. Each of these layers of accounting usually took weeks to function, and awareness of budgetary consequences could easily lag six months or more behind the actuality of spending. This could lead to definite problems in the originating departments.

In self defense we had to know at all times and from our own records that all money spent for Shoals programs, scattered as it was through several spending authorities within the university, remained within budget, even though this primary accounting would be duplicated two or three more times up the ladder. Until this point I had done it myself with the help of Marge Van Ness in the Summer School Office and Esther Spielman in Genetics, Development, and Physiology.

Accounting through Genetics, Development, and Physiology was fraught with possibilities of error because the office staff couldn't always guess just which of my accounts a particular bill was meant to obligate. Should they charge the two reams of mimeograph paper against courses taught in Ithaca, research in algae, botany extension, or the plant toxicology I was responsible for in the New York State College of Veterinary Medicine? Or should they forward that bill to the Summer School Office for payment?

The point of all this is that the growing and shifting Shoals anomaly had developed into a major accounting problem. Fortunately, Dr. O'Brien, as recommended by his marine study committee, came to the rescue. In September, 1970 he provided funds for a half-time position of bookkeeper to the Shoals project. This was the first continuing salary support received by the Shoals from Cornell, and Jay Freer was the first incumbent. Jay, with an MBA from Cornell after an undergraduate major in botany at the same institution, was well positioned not only to bring fiscal order to our records, but also serendipitously to understand what we were doing. Like most other Shoals employees since, he even cheerfully provided physical labor on Appledore Island occasionally. Jay's services were invaluable when I had to make command appearances in the office of the university treasurer, as will become apparent soon.

Contractor Dominic Gratta had been working on major repairs and miscellaneous new construction projects for the Star Island Corporation during the first years of our Shoals program there. In 1969 he was awarded the contract for constructing the Brookfield Center and Rutledge Naturalist's Laboratory on Star Island, and began work on this major building early in the spring of 1970. By then Cornell (meaning Dr. Kennedy and I) had pretty well settled on Dominic as the best contractor for the renovations and new construction we contemplated for Appledore Island. Of the three contractors who had submitted project "guesstimates," he seemed to have the most realistic idea of what was needed, the best concept of how to do it, the fullest understanding of the importance of getting the most out of each available dollar, and the greatest enthusiasm for the Appledore project. Dominic expected to be done with the Brookfield Center in the fall of 1970 and ready to go to work for Cornell as soon as weather allowed in the spring of 1971, despite Star Island Manager Harry Lent's loud complaints that Cornell was stealing Dominic from him. At first Dominic even thought he might be able to establish a foothold on Appledore Island in autumn of 1970 if the Brookfield project went well and the weather held. It didn't bother Dominic in any observable way that we did not have enough money in hand to begin, or even to get Cornell to approve beginning. Dominic had faith that it would all happen in good time even if he jumped the gun, and he maintained that immense faith throughout the entire project.

Dominic's faith was built entirely upon watching the effect of our Star Island program on our students. He wanted to be part of that effect.

The Brookfield Building, containing the Rutledge Laboratory, front-center.

As we will see, it didn't work out quite as hoped. Getting from those early, naive decisions and inadequate resources in 1970 to the actual opening on Appledore Island in 1973 involved vast amounts of blood, sweat, and tears and might well never have been attempted had anyone been able to see all that was ahead.

Chapter Eight

FOR REAL
1971

WHAT A DIFFERENCE A WEEK MAKES

A number of decisions affecting 1971 were made in the autumn and winter of 1970.

The regular annual meeting had endorsed some momentous changes in the teaching program to take effect the following summer. The Star Island Conference Center calendar, it turned out, would run a full week later in 1971 than before in relation to the end of the regular college season. This meant we could have three weeks on Star Island instead of the usual two, and needed only one more in Durham to complete the four-week course. To take advantage of this seemingly minor calendar event, however, meant merging two two-credit courses at two different universities into one, getting the unified course recognized for four credits by the diverse faculties of both Cornell and the University of New Hampshire, bringing a number of UNH faculty members out to live and teach on Star Island, and integrating the two separate budgets and accounting into one. Jay Freer had appeared just in time!

The teaching program changed even more when the Marine Sciences Research Center at Stony Brook, acting for the entire SUNY system, bought into the Shoals program early in 1971. In return for representation on the Shoals admissions committee and consideration of SUNY faculty members on an equal basis with those of Cornell and the University of New Hampshire in staffing courses at the Shoals, the Marine Sciences Research Center agreed to provide $15,000 a year to the capital budget of the Appledore Island project for ten years. Drs. John Storr (SUNY Buffalo) and Peter Weyl (SUNY Stony Brook) were among those immediately added to the regular program faculty. Jack Storr had just stepped down as president of the American Littoral Society, and Peter Weyl's major college text on oceanography had just come off the presses. We felt honored.

Fund raising and scrounging had both had good success by late 1970 (as we judged things then and in dollars of that time). In December Jay Freer's records showed $201,000 in cash and pledges toward the $250,000 Cornell required before building could begin. We had counted SUNY's pledged contribution as $125,000 of that, capitalizing it not quite fully in consideration of inflation and other unseen dangers of the future. The $30,000 worth of surplus property we had accumulated was not included in the totals, but kept in reserve as a final "kicker" if one were needed. Clearly, if the early spring season of 1971 brought $25,000 more in regular contributions as hoped, we should be able to get the green light from Cornell in time for construction to start on Appledore Island as soon as the spring weather had settled sufficiently to allow it.

THOSE TRUSTEES AGAIN

Things didn't quite work out as expected. The Cornell administration decided that enough time had passed and enough circumstances had changed materially since the Cornell Trustees had first looked at the Shoals project that the matter should be taken before them once again for a specific reapproval.

A large array of senior administrators, deans, provosts, directors, vice presidents, and the like assembled on March 19, 1971, to hear Dr. Kennedy and me present our case again in detail. They would decide, based on what we said, what to recommend to the Cornell Trustees who met next on April 19.

We hadn't received quite the a full $25,000 needed in contributions by March 19. Consequently, Jay and I decided to add in the value of our surplus property. With that, we were able to show capital assets of $263,000 consisting of cash, pledges, the SUNY contract, and surplus property.

The administrators were doubtful and waffled exquisitely. They requested further information, wanting particularly to know how solid the SUNY contract was and how much the contractor might hike his estimate as the time approached to write an actual contract with him. No decision was taken.

Immediately Dr. Kennedy went the rounds at SUNY. He firmed again what he already knew, that the marine interests at the faculty level in SUNY were solidly behind the project, as was Don Squires, director of the Marine Sciences Research Center at Stony Brook. It was equally true, on the other hand, as it always has been, that the State of New York is sometimes a slippery partner. When the going gets tough in the state's fiscal circumstances, as it was just then, already-committed budgets may be cut. The state always reserves the legal right to do that, and no state agency can sign a contract stating otherwise. The Shoals project would get its first $15,000 because that had been obligated in the approved budget of the Marine Sciences and Research Center, and was already available in its accounts. It would probably get the rest, too, so long as the state didn't cut it or take a percentage of it back after transferring it. So reported Dr. Kennedy.

I met with Dom Gratta in Portsmouth on March 30. We talked at length how to proceed and what it would now cost. Laighton House had been roofed and the Coast Guard building was now inhabitable, though at a primitive level; these were savings from the original estimate. From experience we had worked out less-expensive ways to meet some of the other needs. On the other hand, some of the buildings and utilities probably should be built larger or done better than we had thought at first, at greater expense. Inflation had to be considered as well; prices constantly were going up for the building materials Dominic would need. After quite a bit of pencil pushing, Dominic went from his original guesstimate of $299,000 (in 1968) to $303,000. Canny Keith Kennedy had already upped the original figure to $350,000, you may remember, before presenting it to the trustees the first time. We were still well within that figure, and Dr. Kennedy decided we could stay with it.

As the deans and others had requested, Jay Freer refigured the surplus situation, limiting what he counted in that figure to just those items of equipment we could show we would otherwise have had to purchase for construction. We were not to include items for teaching or furnishing laboratories or the like. This reduced the value of the surplus contribution considerably. Nevertheless, the overall total still came close to $250,000 and contributions were still arriving in good fashion. The administrators decided to recommend to the trustees that they approve the commencement of construction.

Dominic Gratta.

Then came a really unpleasant surprise. Someone in Cornell's administration realized that the project would have to be presented to the trustees' Buildings and Properties Committee for a recommendation before being taken to the full board. The presentation to the trustees' committee was to be made by Cornell's Division of Buildings and Properties. It, in turn, asked me for a copy of the building plans for the several proposed new buildings to accompany Dominic's estimate of their cost.

Of course no such plans existed —we had only space requirements expressed in terms of functions and square footage. Well then, what architect had we planned to employ for designing the buildings? None; we planned to do it ourselves. Immediate impasse.

Here's what I did. By telephoning around the planning office of the Division of Buildings and Properties I managed to invite one of its staff architects out to my home to talk about the Shoals project. My house was the best place for this because, having built it from plans and elevations I had drawn without benefit of architect, I could demonstrate some personal knowledge and abilities in the matter at hand.

We spread out my sketched floor plans on the dining room table, and we talked. We talked for two or three hours, or perhaps it was more that

I talked and he listened. At any event, the staff architect left my home sold on the Shoals Lab project. He would create a drawing of Appledore Island showing what the new and renovated buildings might look like in profile against the skyline. Perhaps that would serve to convince his department and the trustee's committee. He put his heart into that drawing and into presenting our position.

The Buildings and Properties Division recommended to the trustee's Buildings and Properties Committee that the project was worthy.

The trustees' committee met on the morning of April 19, the full board that same afternoon.

The board's Buildings and Properties Committee, however, had some doubting Thomases. There had been quite a go-around on whether to recommend the project to the full board or not. Eventually it compromised, recommending that the project be authorized to commence when $250,000 *in cash* was in hand. It would count none of the military surplus or pledges.

That put Dale Corson, President of Cornell, on the spot at the meeting of the board that afternoon. Two of the principal pledges had been made by separate anonymous donors, one of whom was a trustee. The president did not wish it to appear to either of the donors that the payment of their pledges was in question, and particularly not the payment of the funds pledged by the trustee who would be present for the discussion and vote. In presenting the matter to the board, he set forth the Buildings and Properties Committee's recommendation, but followed it immediately with a slightly different one of his own. He observed that one of the anonymous donors was present, and he (Corson), for one, had no doubt that the several pledges would be paid in full and on time. Dale Corson therefore recommended that the project be approved when $250,000 in cash *and pledges* was in hand. The trustees finally voted to approve the project contingent on a showing of $250,000 in cash and pledges, but not including the value of *any* of the military surplus already acquired.

I had no immediate way of learning what was going on during that day. Instead, I sat in my office in the Plant Science Building trying to act as though this were just another ordinary day in the life of a junior professor. Late in the morning the telephone rang. It was a long distance call from Florida. The connection was poor, but I soon gathered that Shoals newsletter reader Willard Kiggins had something to say. With him yelling at his end, and me at mine, he asked if I thought I could get word into the trustees' meeting. I said I could give it a good try if it were important enough.

"Well, I think the project ought to go forward, and it looks like you are still short several thousand dollars according to what you wrote in that last newsletter."

Surplus balsa rafts used to float the new Appledore dock.

"That's true," I shouted, "but maybe they will be willing to give us a green light even if we are a bit short."

"I want to be *sure!* You get word into that board meeting and tell them if they will pass it, I will give an additional $10,000—no! make it $20,000—for the project."

I thanked Mr. Kiggins profusely (at the top of my lungs) and told him I would find a way to interrupt the board meeting with this news as soon as he hung up, which he did thereupon. I called down to Day Hall and reached someone I thought could slip in the door of the board room with a message. This additional $20,000 should have just tipped the balance even if the military surplus hadn't, but it still would not have been quite enough if all pledges were excluded.

GO!

I learned later that the board had already gotten past the Shoals item on its agenda, with approval as noted above, before receiving the Kiggins news, but

New dock (with a plank to the land); the barge, Wrack, Hesperornis, *and Whaler tied alongside.*

the additional $20,000 enabled an unequivocal showing of the full $250,000 in cash and pledges in the weeks immediately following.

So "go" it was on April 27, 1971, when the Cornell treasurer added his official blessing. Prudent Mr. Peterson noted that we should restrict our actual spending in 1971 to cash on hand. We should not get into a deficit cash flow situation until we knew better just how well construction was actually going to go. We had no problem with that restriction; Dominic figured that the cash we had in hand, about $125,000, was about all he could spend in a summer anyway.

And "go" it went on April 29 when Dominic Gratta came to Ithaca to interview some 25 students who wanted to work for him on Appledore Island. He intended to hire five, but ended up being unable to resist the skills and entreaties of six (Barry Beitz, Karl Hohenstein, Mauricio Mangini, Bob Meadows, Phil Ritson, and Reinald Smith). The construction crew, consisting of these students, Dominic Gratta himself, and John, a qualified carpenter who worked for Dominic, now went about setting up operations on Appledore Island.

The construction crew was not the only operating force on Appledore Island in 1971. I also gathered a group of 12 student volunteers (Anne Barnard, Erica Dunn, Margaret Flowers, Alice Gates, Ron Harelstad, Howard Ludington, Steve O'Brien, Brian Rivest, Elizabeth Saltmarsh, Becky Scheckler, Stephen Scheckler, and Gary Vogel) who were ready to work in return for board and room.

As construction got underway in earnest, the first necessity was a dock. Dominic designed and built a float and brow (bridge). The float was buoyed originally by four balsa life rafts surfaced with fiberglass that had been obtained as military surplus. What a relief it was not to have to climb over the rocks or heave out and rig an anchor outhaul for each landing any more! The *Osprey* could come in right against the float. She began regular supply runs to the mainland for both food and construction materials.

The smaller of the two known island wells, on the shore below where Celia Thaxter's garden is now, was pumped down, cleaned out (including numerous muskrat skeletons), recapped, and sealed. Then it was allowed to fill, the water was chlorinated, and the well went into use. No more hauling drinking water from Star Island. We bucketed water out of the well at first; a pump came later.

After attending to the dock and well, the next immediate priority was to make the Coast Guard building livable and comfortable for all hands and to set up an office with some communications there. At first the windows were either covered with plywood or wide open. We could have our choice. Same for the doors. No running water or electricity was available. Sleeping privacy suffered from interior walls that consisted of naked studs, the plaster and lathing having been removed earlier by the 1968 volunteers.

Cornell's Division of Buildings and Properties wanted as much of the new work to be as fireproof as possible, a laudable objective. Without saying much to us, and nothing to Dominic, it ordered (with our money) and shipped to Portsmouth enough fireproofed quarter-inch interior plywood panels to clad all the interior walls of the Coast Guard building. The idea was excellent and Cornell got a very good deal on the plywood. But it caused a disaster. When it was delivered to the Ceres Street dock in Portsmouth some students and I went in to load it. The strapped bundles were broken open and the sheets carried onto the *Osprey* one by one. We thought they were mighty heavy for quarter-inch sheets. So did Dominic, who looked at them with a great frown when we got back to Appledore Island.

The method used for fireproofing plywood is to pressure saturate it with some kind of incombustible salt solution. This accounted for the added weight. It also meant that a circular saw lasted about two cuts before needing resharpening; same for handsaws. Pounding nails through those sheets was like trying to pound pins through telephone books. Finish nails bent double more often than not when we tried to nail the panels on the studs. The salts in the plywood attracted moisture and the walls sweated profusely in the damp marine air. Neither latex nor oil-based paints would dry properly nor stick to that plywood. Dominic's view of Cornell's "help" darkened, and I let the Division of Buildings and Properties know in no uncertain terms of the trouble it had caused in preempting ordering from our control. It didn't do it again.

A second-hand gas stove and refrigerator scrounged from somewhere now forgotten were installed in the Coast Guard building. Dominic often did the community cooking himself, though several of the students took turns as well. The plywood served to increase the general privacy, but proper baseboards to close the space at the bottom of the walls were not added until several years later. Fortunately, we all got along very well and the Coast Guard building became a real home for all of us working on Appledore Island.

One of the old cottages on Appledore Island belonging to the Star Island Corporation (the smallest, known to earlier inhabitants as the Rice Cottage), although one of the more ornate, had gone beyond the point of prudent repair in our judgment. The volunteer group set out to tear it down. It would provide some useful salvage that could be used to meet a last remaining real need of Appledore's new dwellers. The roof had already caved in. The rest of it came down fast with the help of a borrowed chain saw.

The Shoals Lab has never discriminated on the basis of sex (or knowingly in any way) in any of its activities. This was as true for the volunteer groups as it has been since, and the volunteer groups included female students from the beginning. Thus one of the earliest needs on Appledore Island was for the privacy of of functional male and female outhouses. Here's how we met that need almost instantly with the help of the Rice Cottage. The volunteers sawed solid ornately shingled sections of the walls of the demolished house into outhouse-sized pieces, dug two pits, and assembled the wall sections around them, leaving a small offset gap for the entrance. We then added a final pre-shingled piece to each for a slanting roof. The only real problem was the seat, more specifically the hole in the seat. Our tools were limited and the same could perhaps be said of our skills. The hole was created, finally, by chewing through a suitably heavy board with the tip of the chainsaw. A chainsawed outhouse hole must be experienced to be fully appreciated.

An early barge run brought the Ford tractor and mower back to Appledore Island for another season of work, but Dominic desperately wanted a backhoe and loader for digging foundations and moving materials.

Backhoes are expensive items, and none had appeared in the military surplus lists.

BREAKERS BAKER

Here's how we got ourselves a backhoe. By chance, on the inside back cover of the *Cornell Alumni News*, I had noticed an advertisement by a Long Island firm named "Expert Concrete Breakers." It was run by two brothers, Baker by name, both Cornell alumni. Their company dealt with concrete demolition and site work. Surely, they must have backhoes. Would they be willing to donate a used one to Cornell? A friendly letter came back saying they could not afford to donate a backhoe, but they had a used machine of the size we needed, manufactured by Case, that they could let the project have for a very reasonable price. The price they quoted was so reasonable, $2,200 delivered, that some among us doubted the usefulness of what we would be getting. But there was neither time nor budget to go to Long Island and have a look. Trusting to the beneficent nature and innate honesty of Cornell alumni, I wrote the brothers Baker to ship it to Portsmouth as quickly as possible.

Soon we heard that a backhoe addressed to Appledore had appeared on the Portsmouth State Port Authority dock. Then came the discovery that no one—paid students, volunteer students, Dominic, or I—had ever run a backhoe. No instruction book came with it. I went to town and looked the backhoe over very closely. Having grown up on a farm, I knew something about tractors. The controls seemed mostly understandable, though there were a few knobs, levers, and valves which were obscure as to function.

We decided that the best place to load the backhoe onto the barge was at the paved ramp behind the Kittery town dock at Frisbee's. Thus, the first problem was to get the backhoe across the Piscataqua River from Portsmouth, New Hampshire to Kittery, Maine, and then down to Kittery Point. Easy? Not on your life. The backhoe was unregistered. The Portsmouth police office was not very helpful. Temporary registration in New Hampshire was complicated, very expensive (especially in the context of a single five-mile trip), and probably not valid in the state of Maine. In Maine, the temporary registration situation was no better.

In the end, we took a chance. Rachel Gratta, Dominic's wife, followed closely behind the backhoe in her pickup truck with warning lights flashing as I drove it, naked of New Hampshire or Maine registration plates, across Memorial Bridge from New Hampshire into Maine.

The backhoe arrives at Appledore Island.

Most of the trip had to be made on main roads because there is no other way to get across the river. The Case started up immediately. It had gas enough for the trip, gearshift and clutch worked as expected, the buckets and legs went up when commanded, and off we went at the top speed available (about 18 miles per hour on the level). No problems at first. I pulled over whenever possible to let backed-up traffic pass.

There are a few small hills along the way, especially the rise on Memorial Bridge. For reasons I didn't understand then, the backhoe slowed down dramatically every time it was asked to climb a hill, even though the engine kept up to speed. It was just like having a slipping clutch. Some months later someone told me that one of those unknown levers was there for the purpose of changing the transmission from hydraulic drive (needed in scooping) to locked direct drive, and I should have used the latter on the open road. No matter; at the end of a half-hour's otherwise uneventful trip, the backhoe was proudly parked at the Kittery dock.

Would the barge that had floated the Ford tractor handsomely float the backhoe? That was the next question. Even though the weight of the backhoe was known (about five tons), the exact floatation of eight dented and somewhat compressed oil tanks is almost impossible to calculate accurately. Several of the best engineering and academic minds available on both Appledore Island and Star Island went to work with their calculators. The consensus was that the barge would just float the backhoe, but no one would bet on it.

The people of the Town of Kittery, at least the ones living near the town dock, take an interest in events like this. They turn out to watch. The barge had been settled at the bottom of the ramp at low tide. The backhoe went up the planks and onto the barge without the slightest hesitation. It seemed anxious to get to sea. Now came the long wait to see if the incoming tide would float the barge or rise over it.

Local fishermen always have opinions on matters like this. As near as we could tell from overheard conversations, they were about evenly divided on the question. They were less evenly divided about whether, if it floated, we could pull it to Appledore Island successfully. A clear majority was negative: what did those eggheads think they were doing! If it took as much time as transporting the Ford tractor, the barge trip out would require about three hours. Although the weather forecast was good, what coastal weather will actually do at sea in any three-hour period is always a question, and every trip a gamble.

As the water came closer and closer to the top of the barge, our depression deepened and the audience quieted. Finally, with only a few inches to spare, the barge floated. The relief was almost palpable. We put the backhoe's feet down, dropped the buckets to the deck fore and aft, and chocked the wheels. Towing lines were adjusted and the *Osprey* set to sea. The tow proceeded with pride out of Pepperrell Cove, past the several channel buoys and Whaleback Light, to the outer buoy, 2KR, or the "groaner" as it is known locally. We then headed on a straight course to Appledore Island, lengthened the tow line, and cast our die.

The tides work just right for a loaded tow going out. Leaving the mainland when the barge is floated on a half-risen tide means the tide will be high, just turning down, on arrival three hours later at Appledore Island. When the backhoe arrived there, the barge was transferred to *Hesperornis* power and taken directly against the shore at the small cobble beach that heads Babb's Cove. The ocean remained friendly for the entire trip, the barge went to shore just right, and the backhoe rolled off it onto the cobbles without incident.

The backhoe became almost like another human member of the crew. It went right to work and hardly a day passed without its showing new and unexpected talents. Besides the usual work for which a backhoe is intended, ours could serve as a mobile staging for working on structures overhead—we could stand in the raised bucket to paint the windows in the

Above: Old Joe.
Below: Changing Old Joe's tires by backhoe power.

Coast Guard building for example. It could easily lift and carry the Boston Whaler and the *Hesperornis* out of the water and across land for winter storage. It could (and often did) lift up Old Joe's (the dump truck) front end when a tire needed to be changed, saving the hassle and danger of an unstable jack. The Case backhoe served us well and faithfully on Appledore Island for several years until it finally expired and was replaced with a John Deere. But that is another story.

Old Joe was a noble Chevrolet dump truck belonging to Dominic Gratta. Joe came out to Appledore Island about the same time as the backhoe, on another barge run. Although Joe, venerable and well-used, looked like he was about ready to give up the ghost even before leaving the mainland, his straight six engine and heavy frame proved beyond defeat by either the topography or the marine atmosphere of Appledore Island. With a new front end and occasional mechanical attention over the years, Old Joe wore out several sets of tires on the rocks of Appledore Island, and remained faithful and functional right through 1985. This is a record matched only by the Ford tractor which remains functional even to the present, but it has been used less heavily.

CRIPPLED FLYER - II

The *Osprey*, however, began to show trouble early in 1971. All this barge hauling from the cleats at her stern, for which she was not designed, began to pull the transom out of her. The problem of the loosening transom was soon evident. Suddenly, the *Osprey* could no longer be used for towing, and would need major attention immediately, even if confined only to regular supply trips.

This development was no less than a first-class disaster now that Dominic and crew were hard at work on Appledore Island. The problem would be, we thought, finding the right second-hand boat, available for spot sale at a price we could afford. The fishermen's grapevine was one way of looking. Advertisements in the *Maine Coast Fisherman* were another. The fishermen couldn't help much; nothing suitable seemed to be available locally. The *Maine Coast Fisherman*, however, listed several attractive possibilities. Dominic checked them out when he was home the next weekend. He found a vessel at the small fishing village of Five Islands, Maine. Maine-bred Harry Lent, the Star Island Manager, and I immediately made an inspection trip.

A few years earlier, shrimp had appeared in Maine waters suddenly in abundance. Many lobstermen rerigged to go after them. Some even had boats built especially for this fishery, but which could be used as lobster boats during the shrimping off-season. The boat we went to look at was one of these. She had been built on a beach in Nova Scotia and was of a design typical for such vessels. They have to handle rugged waters year round down there, and a Nova Scotian hull, with a high stem and closely spaced bent ribbing, is a very good design for all-around work boats. This particular vessel was just two years old, was rigged with an excellent deck winch and pot hauler, was powered with a six-cylinder Chevrolet truck engine (like Old Joe's), and was in excellent general condition as near as we could tell without hauling her. No yacht, she looked as though she would stand well the knocks and stresses of heavy use. The asking price was $7,500. She was for sale only because the shrimp had disappeared as suddenly as they came. The two brothers who owned her couldn't keep her busy and they needed the money.

The real Down East accent is sometimes difficult to interpret, even for a native New Englander. The owners insisted, with obvious pride, repeatedly and emphatically, "She's evuhdoouhfaaah'snd!" About the third time that phrase crossed my ear I finally got it. Translated, it means the planks of the hull are nailed and clinched to the ribs with nonrusting bronze nails. This is a great advantage over the usual steel nails used by the Nova Scotian builders, because the need for periodic refastening (renailing) is almost eliminated. "Everdure" bronze fastening is expensive and makes a great selling point.

Those of us who had gone to see the boat on separate trips immediately got together on Appledore Island and compared notes. She looked very good to each of us and the price was reasonable. Best of all, we could have her on the spot.

Immediately another problem reared its head. I needed $7,500 from our $125,000. By legislation of the Cornell Trustees, when a construction project begins all funds to pay for it must be transferred into accounts administered by the Construction Office of the Division of Buildings and Properties and all payments made by it. Thus it now had possession of our entire fluid assets. Its approval was required before a check could be sent me from the funds I had raised. A check was necessary in order to have money-in-hand for dickering with fishermen. University paper promises do not work well in such situations. The situation was urgent enough to require telephoning.

During the initial construction years, telephone calls from Appledore Island were impossible, and pretty chancy by mobile telephone from Star Island. FCC regulations require firmly for some obscure reason that mobile stations be mobile. Star Island had obtained an official exception to that regulation and maintained an immobile mobile telephone that

Above: The Wrack *on her Appledore mooring.*
Below: The Wrack *at the dock.*

communicated with the mobile operator in Dover, New Hampshire. Those operators rarely understood that they were dealing with a fixed phone on an island at the perimeter of their effective reach. When transmissions were poor (often in those days), the operator would commonly interrupt the call and ask us to move a few hundred feet down the road and try again.

From the *Osprey*, which had a radiotelephone, calls were expensive and iffy, especially back to Ithaca. From either radiophone, the transmissions went over the public airways and your business was open to anyone who wanted to listen.

To make a dependable or private call, an islander had to go ashore and use a phone booth. The nearest public telephone to the Shoals is the booth at the edge of the road in the parking lot at Frisbee's General Store. Most of the intense island business with Ithaca over the next several years was conducted from that open booth, drowned out occasionally by passing trucks. Even so, it was better, much cheaper, and more private than using either of the radio links.

Thus it happened that I went ashore to ask for the transfer immediately of $7,500 to me personally for the purchase of a new boat to replace the *Osprey*. When I got through to the head of the construction department, who was already immensely skeptical of an ordinary professor's practicality, I told him I needed $7,500 of our funds to buy a supply boat. Would he telegraph that amount to a local bank? He was aghast. No way! If we really needed a new vessel, someone from his department would have to help us find and purchase a suitable one. I pleaded the urgency of the situation, with a construction crew not only at work but also requiring daily feeding. Contract hauling would have cost $100 per trip at that time. I pointed out that we had had more practical experience with boats than did anyone in his office. I urged that we had found an ideal boat at a good price. All this was to no avail. I got heated. What right did those administrators in Ithaca have to keep me from using "my" money? The head of the department got heated. Who did I think I was making absurd demands outside normal channels? I don't now remember which of us hung up on the other. Either way, no immediate money was coming from Ithaca.

CASH TALKS

How would I keep Dominic and his crew going? Here's how. Islanders are resourceful people. The word about this contretemps immediately got around at the Shoals, and help immediately appeared. Overnight, by passing the hat on Star and Appledore Islands, I obtained $6,000 and some change in

Above: Controls (before radar); including a surplus navy inclinometer.
Below: The indefatigable winch.

green cash. With a large wad of well-worn bills from $1 to $500 in hand, Harry Lent, Dave Pierson, and I departed for Five Islands, hoping this amount would be enough to obtain physical control of the vessel, if not outright purchase.

I wish I could do justice in print to the dialogue that ensued on the water at Five Islands. Our intense dickering was fortified by the visible presence of negotiable, anonymous cash, but only $6,000 of it. The fishermen were really hurting for money. Eventually we shook hands on $6,000 and the shrimper was ours. Harry Lent, Dave Pierson, and I went aboard, cast off, and headed out—but not to Appledore Island. Instead we went first in the opposite direction, down to Owls Head. Dave Pierson had independently purchased a lobster boat there, but her engine was not functional. He needed a tow back to Appledore Island; we were already able to begin repaying the help the islanders had given us. We picked up Dave's boat, used the stop at Owl's Head to provision and fuel our new Novi shrimper, and started off. The homeward journey took many hours, and we stood watches at the compass through the night. The next morning we hit dense fog and the navigating became more critical. It's always a little uncertain with an unfamiliar boat when you don't know just how water speed relates to engine speed or what the compass deviation may be. These problems are increased with a boat in tow. In those days a coastal fishing boat had neither loran nor radar. We did have a radio (but no directional antenna), and a good depth sounder (fish finder).

Fortunately, according to its loud foghorn, Boone Island was right where it was supposed to be, and we plotted the course from there to the Shoals with increased confidence. When course and time to the Shoals was nearly run out, we shut off the engine and listened for the White Island horn in the still-dense fog. Nothing. We started up again and ran five minutes more. Still no horn. Then another five minutes of sweating it out with the increasing possibility of running onto some part of Duck Island or Cedar Ledge or Anderson's Rock. Finally we heard the horn faintly ahead slightly to starboard. We kept a course well to port of the apparent horn direction, feeling our way over the bottom with the fish finder. When the horn sounded well to starboard we turned sharp right and soon saw the southwestern edge of Star Island rising from the fog. We had entered exactly into the passage between White and Star Islands, and now were back in very familiar waters.

So ended a successful and uneventful trip.

But the matter of getting the funds from Ithaca to repay the Shoals people who had emptied their pockets for us was not so easy. A day or two later I went ashore and telephoned Ithaca again to report that we had the new boat at Appledore Island and owed various people $6,000. I had no idea

Above: Wrack *beached for examination and repainting, Star Island.*
Below: Pride of ownership.

what the reaction would be. Fortunately, the director of the construction department had calmed down some in the interim. So had I. The urgent need for the vessel had gotten through to him, and he was concerned, then, only for our spending money wisely for a safe and sound vessel and for the availability of a suitable bill of sale that would satisfy the auditor. I had anticipated the latter and had gotten the sellers' signatures on the most official-looking bill of sale we could construct. The director of the construction department reluctantly agreed to the sale at $6,000 and he was prepared to initiate reimbursement. But then he tossed another blockbuster. He said that he had promised the university treasurer that the vessel would have a full marine inspection before purchase to ensure that she was sound and well found. That was now impossible because she was already purchased. But he felt he couldn't initiate reimbursement until a satisfactory survey had been made. The conversation heated up again. I told him that a survey required finding a qualified surveyor, getting time during the busy summer season on a marine railway to haul the boat, and taking her out of service for as long as needed for the inspection. That whole process would likely take several weeks at best and we needed to repay the Shoalers now. Besides, with supplies needed daily, it would be difficult to take the shrimper out of service for any length of time until the end of the construction season. He should remember that the people on Appledore Island needed food as well as construction materials daily.

The director thought about it a bit and then said, "Well, I can't break my word with the treasurer. I promised him the boat would be surveyed—but I didn't say who would do the survey." That was all the hint I needed. I thanked him and hung up. Here's what we did.

When I got back to Appledore Island and my typewriter, I wrote out an honest survey of the vessel, as well as I could without actually hauling her, and put into it all the technical marine terms I could think of plus more suggested by Dominic and other islanders who entered enthusiastically into the spirit of the situation. When the impressive, overbearingly nautical document was completed, I got Harry Lent and my brother (an MIT engineer who happened to be back out there then) to add their signatures to mine at the bottom. As expected, no one at Cornell could cope with the density of nautical terminology. A reimbursement check came to Appledore Island without further comment.

WRACK IS RIGHT

We named the new vessel the *Wrack*. Here's how that strange name came about. Ollie Hewitt and I had earlier sought a new name for the *Osprey*, to reflect his ornithological and my algal interests. The best we could come up with was *Wrack & Pinion,* but the etymological subtlety and oral appearance of that rather ruled it out. The word "wrack," however, was in my mind when we bought the new boat, and somehow everyone started calling her that. She was our first boat named to honor the botanical side of biology (wrack is usually defined as the floating seaweed that washes ashore on a beach). Anyway, that name found its way in due course onto insurance and registration papers and the vessel's radio license.

I then worried a bit how I could fix this unusual name in the minds of the general public—especially our donors—and wished to remove any hint of opprobrium it might otherwise carry. This resulted in the following essay published in the Lab's newsletter.

"The word is an old and honorable one. It was applied by the Irish to the seaweeds they gathered to spread on their fields as fertilizer, a process that has taken place for as long as folk memory goes back. A fascinating description of the economics and handling of wrack in the 16th century can be found in *Mourne Country; Landscape and Life in South Down* by E. Estyn Evans, who is director of the Institute of Irish Studies in Belfast (Dundalgen Press, 1967), which was brought to my attention by John Anderson (Professor Anderson reads omnivorously). Wrack supplied not only mineral nutrients but also moisture-holding capacity to the light potato soils where it was used. In fact, at one time it was so valuable that land within a mile of the shore with rights of access to the wrack beds was worth as much as 25 percent more than land farther inland.

"The beds themselves, sometimes called fucus farms (*fucus* is an ancient Latin word for seaweeds), were formed by bringing stones and boulders from the cultivated fields and placing them in rows about three feet apart on the sandy bay bottoms. Seaweeds would attach to these rocks and grow to maturity in one to three years. Three species were desired. The least valuable, growing nearest the shore, was knotted knob, sea whistle or whang wrack (*Ascophyllum nodosum*). Of second importance as manure was bladder, box, or black wrack (*Fucus vesiculosus*). Saw or lazy wrack (*Fucus serratus*) grew farthest from the shore, but this was the most valuable or right kind (as in right whale). Twelve loads of this right wrack equalled 18 loads of whang in manurial capacity.

"Wrack was cut and raked together by hand. In some areas it was brought ashore in special creels or racks and heaped in piles or ricks to drain before being hauled inland in carts to be spread on the fields. Harvest was controlled by watchmen to ensure that wrack rights were exercised only by those to whom they belonged, and harvest began on a predetermined day in late winter or early spring each year. Whole families were involved.

"Thus, at fucus farms, in annual rites, women left rick-rack to rake wrack into wrack racks, from right wrack rights first, then black wrack rights, finally whang wrack rights, and piled it on wrack ricks above the wrecks and rip-rap of the foreshore.

"Now," said I, "you should be able to remember the name of our new boat."

The name *Wrack* proved particularly helpful on the rare occasions that we had to radio ashore in distress. It was brief, unmistakable on the airwaves, and could not be confused with the cute, punny, or euphonious names often applied to pleasure yachts. It stood out from all the rest when spoken on the FCC's calling and emergency frequency, and it commanded immediate attention.

During the construction years the *Wrack* made two and often three trips a day to the mainland, and in occasional emergencies even four round trips between Appledore Island and the Ceres Street dock in Portsmouth or the Kittery town dock at Frisbee's. By October 1, 1971, the *Wrack* had made 59 trips to Portsmouth and back. At the commercial rate of $100 per trip, she had returned all but $100 of her $6,000 cost. She paid that last bit back on October 2—and kept right on going.

Daily *Wrack* trips were critical to progress through all the remaining years of construction on Appledore Island, and beyond. Trips went no matter what the weather. Many encountered stormy, rainy, or foggy conditions or the dark of night. Stormy seas could be troublesome, especially on the occasional unavoidable passage when the seas were running higher than the cabin top and we had to tack into the cresting waves to avoid the danger of rolling over. Even so, fog was the greater difficulty. Running back and forth between the mainland and the islands constantly, Ron Harelstad and I got quite good at finding our way through the fog by wristwatch and compass. The *Wrack* had neither radar nor loran at first, and the depth sounder (fish finder) worked only intermittantly; its recording paper was costly. Fortunately both ends of the course were marked by foghorns. We could easily put the *Wrack* within earshot of the horn at Whaleback Light off the Portsmouth Harbor entrance or the White Island Light at the Shoals by running time and course and then listening. Then, by ear, it was usually possible to find the important buoys, starting with the "groaner" off Whaleback or the bell at the mouth of Gosport Harbor that led safely to the dock. Getting there from those marker buoys involved some more course and distance work, and often some intuition about currents and wind and feeling around at dead low speed. Even so, we rarely got entirely lost for long, and always found our way to the dock eventually, neither hitting anything nor running aground.

Above: White Island Light possessing a foghorn with single blasts.
Below: Whaleback Light and a foghorn with double blasts.

Returning to the Shoals in a fog from other directions, such as York Harbor or Rye, took a little more effort. The trick was to get close enough to the islands to hear the resident birds, unseen in the fog. Then you had an aural picture (reinforced downwind by odor) of what was ahead. If you heard two foci of gull cries side by side ahead, two-parted Appledore Island was in front. Cormorants meant Duck Island or Square Rock. I doubt anyone could put it in exact words, but the feel of the water changes in the vicinity of the islands, and intuitive ideas of location often proved right on.

From the ship's log the second summer, I think it was, Ron and I calculated that the *Wrack* had by then travelled back and forth a distance equal to once around the world at the equator. She did it many more times before her sudden death on the rocks of Appledore Island in a severe line squall in 1982.

The *Wrack* required continuous care and attention. Local people helped Ron and me to learn how to do things right, and by ourselves whenever possible. We soon knew all the tidal eddies in the Piscataqua River and how to use them to make time against river flow. We learned how to listen for surf on the rocks east of Whaleback Light in a fog and figure out how far off course we were. We learned which beaches at the Shoals could be used safely for careening and what tides were necessary for success. Our principal tutor was Captain Ned McIntosh, then skipper of UNH's *Jere Chase,* who would share his immense practical knowledge of boats and local waters with us freely and nudge us into doing things right in his quiet but effective way. Shoals fisherman Norm Foye also took us under his wing. His knowledge of tides, currents, and storm effects at the Isles of Shoals was extremely useful in constructing and positioning moorings, docks, and the like, and he knew what best to do with our vessels and gear in severe storms. Merchant Marine Captain Ted Brown, retired and living in Kittery, even showed me the complicated ranges he had worked out to allow a boat the size of the *Wrack* to pass east of Whaleback into the river safely at any tide, but I never dared that hazardous course without Ted aboard.

The Chevrolet truck engine that the *Wrack* had when she came from Five Islands eventually wore out and was replaced with a Ford diesel (safer). The fuel tank was also replaced with one that would not rust. Dominic rigged a steel boom on her stub mast for loading and unloading heavy deck items with the winch. The exhaust pipe and muffler were replaced and rerouted to advantage. The steering was rebuilt with a better linkage from wheel to rudder. Ron completely rewired the *Wrack* over the years, some circuits more than once. We took her out of the water once a year for bottom painting and general repair, the first time (to spare the budget the cost of hauling) by careening her on the beach at Star Island.

Above: Square Rock; so named, it is said, by the fishermen because in all aspects, vertical and horizontal, it is rounded. Below: Cormorants nesting on Duck Island.

The bones of the Wrack, *1982.*

The original idea had been to move heavy items by barge. Each one-way passage of the barge took three hours as opposed to one hour in the *Wrack*, and towing was a more complicated operation than simple boat passage. Soon we found ways to carry nearly everything except vehicles directly aboard the *Wrack*, which, if the load was carefully balanced, would actually float almost as much weight as would the barge.

Heavy framing lumber—even shoved forward into the cabin as far as it would go—was longer than the *Wrack's* deck and protruded aft over the transom. We carried a lot of it that way. After a while the transom itself began to show signs of sagging. Dominic stiffened it with more timber. Somehow a rib got cracked. Ron Harelstad sistered it. No matter how hard and indecently we used her, or how heavy or poorly balanced the loads, the magnificent *Wrack* stood up to her work and carried through. She soon seemed like a human member of the work crew, always ready to do her share of the work and more, asking little attention in return.

Black-backed gulls with their deep, scratchy, nasal calls reminded Dominic of a Frenchman (Maurice Chevalier, perhaps). To me, the jaunty, saucy *Wrack*, with her red-striped black hull and a lilt to her ways, seemed the more French. I would not have been in the least surprised to see her approaching, wearing a beret on her cabin top.

Considering her beginnings, the record should show that the *Wrack* was one of the best bargains Cornell ever got.

TRUST A CONTRACTOR? NO WAY!

The Gratta Construction Company consisted in 1971 of Dominic, the foreman; his wife, Rachel, who was in charge of accounts and supplies; and one carpenter, John by name. Tall and lean of frame, long hair in the modern vogue, slightly graying, Dominic was in his late fifties when the project began. He was entirely vigorous of muscle and brain and well experienced in his trade. Despite the ethnic connotations of his name, Dominic had been born and brought up just south of Boston and his thinking patterns were those of an old-time New Englander. He had, in fact, moved to southern Maine partly to escape the corruption and politics that were unavoidable doing business as a contractor around Boston at that time. For Dominic Gratta, a simple understanding followed by a handshake established an unbreakable contract. He expected the other partner in the handshake to respond the same.

Things had happened too fast for the administrative offices at Cornell. After work was well under way, someone in Ithaca realized no contract had been written or signed. Cornell brought out its big guns in the Division of Buildings and Properties. Cornell *only* contracted by a bid process, it said. No exceptions! Here there was no bid and no competition. Then, if there was no bid, Cornell *required* a fixed-figure agreement, it said. Dominic responded quite honestly that if he had to submit a fixed figure for a contract, he would have to add perhaps as much as one hundred percent of the base figure to cover the very real contingencies of the construction site and all that went with it.

Dominic proposed instead that Cornell trust him and that the best deal for the Shoals Lab would be construction on a cost-plus basis. His original guesstimate had been figured on that basis. He would charge (and account fully) for his actual costs of labor and materials, would add ten percent for design and supervision services, and ten percent for profit.

The Division of Buildings and Properties had great difficulty with the concept that a contractor need not be held at arm's length as an adversary. But now it really had no other option. Any realistic contractor, if asked for a firm figure, would have had to protect himself against all possible difficulties of wind, sea, and uncertain delivery of materials, to say nothing

Above: Dominic Gratta Below: Rachel Gratta with John Anderson.

of meeting the housing and dining requirements of the workmen on an uninhabited island with no electricity, no plumbed water supply or sewer facilities, no communications, no vessel (except the small boats), and no properly habitable housing. Cost-plus it had to be. And mutual trust was absolutely necessary. Cornell finally yielded on these points but still required a detailed, signed contract. The university's legal people wrote such a document, added the usual several pages of "boiler-plate" language that they used on all building contracts, and sent it to me to get Dominic's signature.

Dominic read through the contract document with an increasing frown until he got to the place in the boiler-plate pages where the contractor was required to provide parking for all his employees within so many hundred feet of the construction site. Dominic took one look at that and finally exploded!

"What kind of people has Cornell got in that buildings and properties department? I'm not signing anything as stupid as that!"

"But," I said, "you've already started work and I don't think I can get Cornell to pay you unless they have a signed paper."

"You know what you want; I know what you want. If you'll trust me to build what you want on a least-cost basis, I'll trust you to get the money out of Cornell. Shake?"

"Shake."

And so it was. I'm not sure to the present day whether Cornell ever got a signed contract from Dominic; I doubt it. To the best of my memory, one never went through me.

THE BOOTSTRAP PHASE

He pulled himself up with his own bootstrap. That is sometimes said of a person who starts with almost nothing and builds it into a success. It could, in a way, be said about the Shoals project, only in this case the bootstrap itself had to be built first. Dominic was sure we could get enough done to move the summer program from Star to Appledore Island by August 1, 1972. On August 1, 1971, looking back at what had been accomplished up to then, I was not so sure. Building the bootstrap had taken longer than he or I thought it would.

We had had to build docks, buy the boat, move the vehicles, make the Coast Guard building minimally adequate for housing and dining, build privies and roads, spray poison ivy, clean out the shore well, and establish a means of communications with Rachel Gratta on the mainland. Then we had had to bring to Appledore Island cement, sand, gravel, a cement mixer, concrete blocks, lumber, roofing, plumbing, electrical materials, gasoline, diesel fuel, propane gas, and miscellaneous hardware and spare parts to keep us dependably in motion—a seemingly endless array of needs. Then and only then we could begin to build.

At the beginning of construction, in April of 1971, the word of the day was "Maybe they've got one over on Star. I'll check the next time someone goes over in the Whaler." By midsummer the word was "I'll put it on the list. You should have it (from Portsmouth) tomorrow or the next day if Rachel can find one." By late summer the word was "I think there's some of that on the island somewhere. Try looking in the gas shack."

The first radio link was by means of CB (Civilian Broadcast) vacuum tube sets (even then an outdated technology), which we obtained for almost nothing from enthusiast Lenny Reed, the Star Island chef. One set was installed in the Coast Guard building with an antenna competing with the gulls for the roof, the other in Rachel Gratta's home overlooking the water at York Harbor. Good antennas were installed at both locations. Transmission was over open water the whole way. It should have worked well, but the distance was just a little too far. Incoming signals at either end were often no stronger than the background noise on the CB frequencies. Vacuum tube sets with electrical contacts and mechanical rheostats had a way of becoming temperamental in the marine atmosphere. Each set had to have a separate crystal for each frequency it used, and the sockets for crystals were limited in number. We had only three or four channels to choose among in those old sets. The mobile radiotelephone on Star Island (expensive), the *Wrack* radio, or the telephone booth ashore were the only alternatives to the CB at first.

The nightly communications exercise, Appledore Island to York Harbor, to arrange deliveries of supplies and materials became the major entertainment most evenings in the Coast Guard building, where we all lived. It was almost as good as listening in on party-line telephones. Dominic and Rachel had to have both sets on and turned up at the right time and set on the same channel. It's very tempting to turn down an everlastingly noisy set after it has assaulted the ears for awhile. Transmissions were made after the end of the work day and after Dominic had time to figure the next day's needs. Dominic originated most calls, usually between 10 and 11 p.m. Sometimes it took 15 minutes or more of calling to get through.

"Appledore to York Harbor, come back; Appledore to York Harbor, come back."

Eventually Rachel's voice would materialize out of Dominic's set, clearly or barely discernable depending on conditions, and the ordering would begin.

"I need 30 galvanized carriage bolts with nuts and two washers each right away for the float. They should be at least three-quarters by eight inches. Over."

"What do you need them for now? I thought the float was finished weeks ago. Over."

"It was, but one of the corners has been loosening where the mooring chain is attached, and I've got to reinforce it before it tears apart. Over."

"Oh. OK, I'll try and get them at Peavey's tomorrow, unless you can wait until I go to Portland again."

"When will that be?" Silence... Finally,

"Dominic, you didn't wait until I finished transmitting. I didn't hear what you said. Over."

"I said, *when are you going to Portland?* Over."

"Oh, probably not until the middle of next week. I can't go all the way up there just to save some money on bolts, but I've got to go after that 25 gallons of engine oil you need."

"Get them at Peavey's and bring them to the dock around three tomorrow." Silence again... Finally,

"Dominic, you didn't wait again. I only heard something about the dock at three. Over."

"I said, *get the bolts at Peavey's and bring them to the dock at three.* Jack and Ron will be in then. I need 30 bags of cement and another load of groceries. We're nearly out of milk, too, and John (the carpenter) wants another case of beer. Over." Silence.

Eventually, "Appledore to York Harbor; Appledore to York Harbor. Did you hear that?"

Rachel's voice, recognizable but unintelligible.

"Appledore to York. I can tell you're on the air, but I can't hear you. Turn up your squelch a little."

Dominic with set volume full up; Rachel, barely audible, "I got what you said about the cement and groceries and something about a case of beer. Over."

"We need milk too. *Milk.* MILK."

Rachel, suddenly stronger, "I got all that."

Dominic: "Why did you send out 10 mil plastic? I wanted 20 mil. Over."

"The salesman said 10 mil was right for the job and it costs a lot less."

"I don't care what the salesman said. He doesn't know what it's like out here. I want 20 mil. Don't listen to those damn salesmen; I know what I want. I'll have to send it back in and you get it changed. Can you meet the morning run at eleven? Over."

"Well, I was planning to make a run to Lowell tomorrow morning after the windows."

"The windows can wait another day. I need the plastic out here as soon as possible. I can't finish pouring cement until you send it. Over."

"Dominic, you started talking again before I was through. I didn't hear all you said, but I get the idea. Skip the windows and get the plastic. Why does John need another case of beer already?"

And so it went for a half hour or thereabouts each evening.

These exchanges, it turned out, provided entertainment beyond the Coast Guard building. Anyone with a CB set could listen in, and it was evident from time to time that many did. Rachel discovered inadvertently that her end of the broadcasts came in on the neighbor's television set and were preferred to the regular programming.

Communications were frustrating. Another frustration was waiting at the dock for Rachel to deliver an urgent item, such as the plastic. Expected at eleven, she might not show up until noon or after, always with a good excuse. Sometimes she just hadn't heard Dom's instructions clearly enough over the radio. In any event, this usually disrupted the day's careful plans, set the schedule off, and might mean that the second or third trip would not get back to Appledore Island until well after supper. That threw the kitchen off.

THE MAINLAND TAKES A PEEK

Despite the frustrations and setbacks, things got done and the momentum began to spread. Word about the Appledore Island project was getting about on the mainland. We were visited in midsummer by reporters from the local newspapers. They were uniformly impressed with what they saw.

Louisa Woodman wrote the following editorial in the *Portsmouth Herald* (August 7, 1971).

The Young on Appledore

So often newspapers are blamed for writing all the "bad" about young adults, ignoring the good things these people do like the plague.

This is true, in some measure, the same way it's true that newspapers don't run regular stories about motorists driving safely from Portsmouth to Kittery, or Exeter to Hampton. Every day there are news stories about motorists who haven't made these and other trips without event, for this is what makes "news."

It's the same with young people; where they're "good" they seldom make news, but when they're "bad," it's almost always newsworthy.

Right now, though, there's a small group of young adults working on Appledore Island, not raising cain or practicing free love, not freaking out on any of society's many and varied substitutes for an infant thumb.

These youngsters on Appledore are all that's good about the United States, clean cut, temperate, hard working, and dedicated.

Don't get me wrong, older and more conservative readers. The boys aren't all sporting crew cuts, smooth cheeks, and white T-shirts.

The girls don't have on pale-pastel full-skirted dresses, modestly at just-above-knee length.

These people working on Appledore look like any other group of American young. There are all manner of hair styles and lengths, and clothes are, for the most part, a bit grubby and tacky.

That's to be expected, when you're working in a place where a bath comes in pails of 45 degree water, and plumbing is his and hers outhouses.

But if only a few of the constant critics of the younger generation could meet and visit with these people, their faith in the future would be restored.

If you could hear a bearded youth, surprisingly clean, expound on the joys of taking pails of cold-cold water into the bushes, away from everyone, and stripping for a real, old-fashioned sponge bath;

If you could hear two or three of them, together discussing the health status of a pair of baby sea gulls at the same time they're surrounded by thousands of the sometimes pesky birds;

If you could see them pitch into the work, not having to be pushed but performing willingly and happily;

And if you could see their pride in accomplishment, for a project which will end up being not a public monument, but a simple oceanside laboratory and study area;

Then you'd take heart.

These young people are America, the land of the free. America, land of opportunity and achievement.

They are our future, they and millions like them.

Fine, fine people, a credit to themselves and looking towards the future without the oft seen jaundiced eye.

It was a pleasure to meet them, see their work, and to go away a bit more sure that when their time comes the country will be in good hands.

The young on Appledore are the rule, not the exception. Thank God.

A bit fulsome, perhaps, but Louisa Woodman caught the flavor of what was happening that summer.

PAUCITY OF VELOCITY

After some weeks Dominic and Rachel Gratta had used up all their spare cash in purchasing materials for the project. They needed to be paid. Their first bill caused intense disarray in Ithaca and opened new territory at Cornell as it went through the labyrinthine administrative paths from receipt to the issuance of a check.

The actual process of getting Gratta Construction paid turned out to be rather more complex than Dominic or I had envisaged. Cornell University was initially unaware of two dominating factors in the life of Gratta Construction. The first was that Gratta Construction considered Cornell as a bank in which it could leave funds until needed, even for years, with no worry. The second was that Rachel Gratta hated to figure and write bills. She would much rather have been running around from Portland to Boston in her white Ford pickup truck collecting necessary supplies. The net effect of this was that Gratta Construction got around to billing only when Dominic and Rachel were at the extreme bottom limit of their financial resources. They even went so far more than once as to mortgage their personal vehicles (a Cadillac sedan and the Ford pickup) when they got really short of cash. When a bill from Rachel finally came, it was always meticulous in detail, accurately figured, well presented—and she inevitably needed the money yesterday!

Cornell had great difficulty relating to this kind of billing. In the first place, the bills were always behind the pace of construction; some of them were more than two years late toward the end of the really active phase. Second, getting a construction check out of Cornell yesterday was impossible. Getting it in two weeks was a miracle. Getting is in four to six weeks was realistic. Getting it in two months was only a bit slow.

The construction season on Appledore Island is only four to five months long. Dominic and Rachel believed in paying their own bills on time, a general Yankee principle, and always to take advantage of any cash discounts that might be available thereby. Under those conditions, when Gratta Construction ran out of money the consequences were immediate and serious.

When I received a detailed bill for tens of thousands of dollars hand-delivered by Dominic, it was always accompanied by an eloquent oral presentation of the dire consequences to the Gratta financial condition and thus to the project, if it were not paid immediately. I always checked the bills carefully against my on-the-spot participation in the construction activities, and always I was able to certify to Cornell that the bill was, of my own knowledge, accurate, and urged that it be expedited by all possible means. Then followed a chain of events with a bit of Gilbert and Sullivan flavor.

As stated earlier, trustee legislation required that all construction bills owed by any part of Cornell University must be paid through the accounts of the Division of Buildings and Properties. All construction funds raised by the Shoals project had therefore been transferred reluctantly into those accounts. The head of construction in that Division had not personally approved, did not approve, and it seemed never would approve doing anything on a cost-plus basis, despite what the university had decided to the contrary. Neither did he believe that I or any other professor, unworldly by definition, could know enough about construction to certify the accuracy of such a bill. He *always* balked at approving Dominic's bills for payment. The net effect was that weeks passed and no check came to Appledore Island. Instead there were urgent trips ashore to telephone Jay Freer at Cornell.

"Where is it? Dominic's desperate."

"It's not out of Construction yet."

"What's holding it up?"

"It's not approved."

"Damn."

Obviously, the matter had to be taken up Cornell's chain of command for an overriding decision. At the time this was to Vice President (for Planning) Tom Mackesey's office. Tom, who once penned "Academe abounds with curiosity, precocity, pomposity, and verbosity. The problem is: paucity of velocity," was not lacking in imagination, nor was he unfamiliar with the realities of construction in New England. He had risen to the vice presidency of the university from the ranks of the Department of Architecture. His very first professional job after graduation had been, it turned out, to do a land-use survey for the Town of Rye, New Hampshire. He remembered the Shoals. At first he generally approved payment of Rachel's bills, countersigned by me, without hesitation and told the construction department to pay them.

The delayed billing created another, more serious, problem for Tom Mackesey, however. Cornell, naturally, liked to know where it stood in its debt obligations at least annually. The question arose periodically as Cornell balanced its official books: How much does Cornell owe Dominic Gratta now? When this need was communicated from the vice president's or treasurer's office back to the Shoals office, we redoubled our efforts to get timely bills out of Rachel Gratta. Our personal pleas were reinforced by formal letters to the Grattas from various offices at Cornell. As each year's accounting period drew to a close, the volley of communications from Ithaca and the vigor of their presentation increased. Finally there would be telephoned demands from Cornell to Rachel that she get those bills in.

Rachel was entirely immune to blandishments of this sort. She billed when Gratta Construction was ready (meaning out of cash) and not before. She always had a pretty good supply of excuses, too. On one occasion, Vice President Tom Mackesey himself called her to plead for a bill. He later told me she answered, "Oh, Mr. Mackesey, I can't work on a bill just now. Dominic has been cutting bricks in my office, and the adding machine is just full of brick dust." Tom was totally defeated, a rare event.

Once, Tom Mackesey actually went all the way out to Appledore Island from Cornell to speed up the billing. Dominic, Rachel, Tom, and I retired to the derelict room with sagging floor, which is now part of the spiffy library in Laighton House. Tom pleaded with the Grattas to speed up their billing. As near as we could tell, they were more than $100,000 behind just then. Rachel looked hurt. Tom hastily added that her bills were lovely when they came—Cornell didn't have any trouble with the kind of bill, only the fact that it was months late. Perhaps Rachel need not account for every box of screws separately. Cornell didn't really need all that detail.

"But that wouldn't be right", said Rachel.

Could Rachel hire someone part-time to help her?

"Oh, but I can't be sure anyone else will do it correctly for you. That wouldn't be right."

Finally in desperation, after about a half hour of fervent pleading, and figuratively on his knees, Tom Mackesey begged, "Please, please, please! Just put all your receipts in a shoebox and send it to Ithaca. We'll be more than happy to do the figuring."

"Oh, Mr. Mackesey, Cornell shouldn't have to do my job for me. That wouldn't be *right!*"

Tom left Appledore Island no better off for billing than he came, but he did see the island and its construction challenge first-hand, the latter clearly overshadowing even the difficulties of paperwork. And he understood better why neither Dominic nor I could move the billing process forward any faster.

Jay Freer and I maintained some idea of how construction expenses were running and how much we were in debt to the Grattas by keeping track of man-days of work on the island. We multiplied that by a figure for average cost of construction per man-day that we had developed from experience as the project progressed. Although this is like positioning a boat by dead reckoning after many days' voyage without sextant readings, it usually put us in the right neighborhood when the bills finally came and ensured that we could honestly say we had not violated Cornell's line of credit balance when asked, even though there were no hard figures in evidence.

Despite all this effort, billing for materials actually got progressively slower during the three years of major construction. When Dominic finally left Appledore Island for good, Cornell owed him an amount in six figures. Some of that, even now, has not been billed and never will be. It has become instead a significant contribution by the Grattas to the Shoals project, joining Old Joe (the dump truck) and other important equipment purchased by Dominic personally but left on Appledore Island without charge at the end of construction. Together with foregone interest on unpaid balances owed them, Jay and I once figured that the Grattas had personally contributed at least the cost of one of the dormitories to the project. But Dominic wouldn't let us put the Gratta name on it when we asked to do so.

I cannot leave this billing topic, however, without just a bit more comment. I believe the late billing for materials was mostly because Rachel didn't like to do it. Using Cornell like a bank, on the other hand, was mostly because Dominic didn't like to pay heavy state and federal tax bills on profit. He preferred to keep his profits unbilled until he could pass them through as business expenses on purchases of materials needed next. I came to these conclusions not from anything said directly, but rather from a number of comments in passing and observations over the years.

THE ANONYMOUS GENTLEMAN

In midsummer 1971, when things were busiest, a strange, totally unexpected event took place. I write carefully, even after these many years, in case what follows might still prove embarrassing to anyone.

Dominic and crew usually worked a five-day week. They went ashore for the weekend to do their laundry and otherwise recover from the intensity of nonstop activity on the island. Normally, I remained on Appledore Island seven days a week.

For some forgotten reason, I had gone ashore briefly one weekend and was returning to Appledore Island on the ferry. The *Viking* was generally crowded on weekends with tourists (daytrippers, as they are called at the Shoals). The reactions of first-time visitors to the Shoals are sometimes interesting to overhear, but I usually wanted a quiet ride and sought out a peaceful corner somewhere on deck to be alone with my thoughts.

Those were the days, remember, of the early '70s when a small number of politically active students were protesting, striking, disrupting, demanding, occupying buildings, and otherwise promoting confrontation on campuses across the country and seeking attention from the news media over a variety of difficult societal issues. They were regularly making headlines in the public press. That kind of thing was farthest from my mind summers at the Shoals where a more typical group of students were working their guts out, though getting no headlines (beyond Portsmouth) for it.

An undesired interruption in my quiet thoughts occurred when a member of the *Viking* crew sought me out that Sunday morning accompanied by a mature couple asking questions about Appledore Island. He introduced me to them as a professor who could answer their questions about the island. Immediately their questions shifted from Appledore to a stinging denunciation of college students in general. At Cornell a group of armed Black students had taken over the student union building and held it for some days, attracting national attention. How could I explain that? I didn't try to. Instead I told them not about protesting students whom they knew through headlines, but about the silent majority of students and what a few of them were doing at that moment on Appledore Island. The gentleman, particularly, was incensed about the activist students and not prepared to believe there was any other kind. The discussion became loud, then heated. I finally said, "Come over to Appledore and see some real college students for yourself if you don't believe me." Much to my surprise, they did.

The gentleman and his wife landed on Star Island and accompanied me across Gosport Harbor in the Whaler. On arriving I had to attend to some urgency or other and left them on their own. All this time I had no idea who these visitors might be. They did not offer to introduce themselves by name or occupation at any time. When it came time for them to go back to Star Island to catch the afternoon *Viking* run to Portsmouth, I found them waiting at the Appledore dock as earlier instructed, and I took them back across the harbor. Now the questions were entirely different, having to do with the purpose of the construction, the program it would serve, and where the funding was coming from. The anonymous gentleman wanted particularly to know how much federal funding was involved. His quizzing was neither friendly nor unfriendly, but still intense. I told him we had no direct federal funding of any kind, only access to state and federal surplus. He was aghast. How could such a worthy project fail to attract federal support?

As the couple climbed aboard the *Viking* at departure, the gentleman finally introduced himself. He was, it turned out, the regional director for all of New England for a major federal agency. He said I would be hearing from him.

Subdued, I searched my memory and my soul that evening for what damage I might have done in our heated exchanges. I even lay awake a night or two—something almost unknown at the end of a long and wearying day on Appledore Island—wondering what might happen.

The answer was not long in coming. I began to receive copies of letters over our visitor's signature to the heads of a number of other federal agencies asking them to look into the project on Appledore Island with a view to seeing if it would qualify for support under any of their programs. He had determined, somewhat ashamedly I think, that his own agency was not able, under its operating regulations, to support us in any way. If any other federal agency could help us, he proposed to them that he might be able to find a way to help that other agency from his own programs in return. Most of the agencies to which he wrote had no programs under which we qualified, and copies of their replies to that effect began coming to me. Our friendly federal director learned in some detail what had been evident to us already from our own look at the Washington scene some time earlier: the federal government was not interested in educational efforts such as ours.

Eventually one federal agency surfaced that proved able to help. It was The New England Regional Commission, whose mandate was to spend designated funds in a way that would improve the business prospects of New England as a region. Helping to open historic Appledore Island to visitation by the public and furthering marine instruction and research were both eminently regional and deemed reasonably supportable as help to the tourism business and fisheries industry, it turned out. Mr. Richard Johnson, codirector of the commission, soon came out to Appledore Island and asked us to submit a request for funding along lines he would suggest. We needed a boat of greater capacity than the Whaler for getting groups of people back and forth from the ferry at Star Island without tying up the ever-busy *Wrack*. After an exchange of paperwork suggested (almost written) by the New England Regional Commission, it awarded us a handsome grant to pay half the cost of construction of our next new vessel, the *Scomber*.

Sometimes it pays to speak one's mind to an anonymous gentleman, even if he turns out to be a fed.

Over the years we have probably been lucky not to have qualified for direct federal support. The boiler plate regulations that go with successful grants from the usual federal agencies are as unrealistic or constricting in our circumstances as was the Cornell boiler plate that angered Dominic Gratta, and far more extensive. Dominic would perhaps have revolted if some federal auditor showed up on Appledore Island to enforce that kind of mainland foolishness. Figuratively, hanging on to an island beachhead by the skin of our teeth in those days, none of us were emotionally prepared to accept any kind of heavy-handed federal regulation. I, too, would have revolted if my work day had been seriously eroded in having to organize and write the nine detailed applications out of ten (or so) that are routinely turned down by granting agencies. An immense amount of useless effort and futile paper goes into such things. I am not constitutionally suited for useless effort. Neither is Dominic Gratta. We got along better, Dominic and I, without federal help, and so did the project.

In fact, as a unit of Cornell University, we were already governed by a whole host of federal rules and regulations applicable to businesses generally, and more that encumbered specifically those receiving federal funds as did Cornell. It was Cornell's responsibility to see that we followed the rules. For the most part we were blissfully unaware of them, and only occasionally did Cornell think to check on us, a small fraction of its far-flung operations. Once in a while it did happen. That summer, for example, somewhere along the line in Ithaca someone noticed that Gratta Construction was not supporting its bills for labor with time slips. I received a vigorously worded memorandum demanding time slips. In responding to Cornell I noted simply that Appledore Island had no clocks (this was before quartz accuracy), and that if we did get some electric clocks, the only thing they would tell us was the speed of our generator. Apparently this situation was beyond Cornell's powers of correction; I heard no more about time slips.

We did, in fact, have a battery-driven pendulum clock in the kitchen in later years that kept moderately accurate time. It governed meal preparation, and meals, in turn, governed most other construction activities. All personal watches were set by it. The kitchen clock was, however, sometimes spastic. When anyone noted we were fifteen minutes or so off mainland time he would push the hands around with a broom stick to the approximate correct position. Sometimes the chef, wanting to hurry things up or slow them down, would quietly adjust the hands accordingly to his particular needs of the moment. The fundamental reality on Appledore Island always was getting done what needed to be done, not watching or punching spastic time clocks.

Elsewhere, on the legal front, offices of Cornell and the Star Island Corporation had gotten together sufficiently for the drawing of a proper lease. The following terms, among others, were mutually agreed: The duration of the lease was to be 25 years, renewable for another 25 years along similar lines. Cornell was to own any new buildings built on Appledore Island, but they would revert to the Star Island Corporation if we failed to use them regularly. The Star Island Corporation would retain title to all the old buildings it already owned, even after improvement by Cornell, owing Cornell nothing for that improvement. The corporation granted Cornell full rights and privileges of the owner in the use of the property, except that we must submit the plans and siting of each new building for the corporation's prior review. Understandably, it wished to protect the visual character of the Appledore skyline as seen from the conference center porch on Star Island. We must also pay all real property taxes assessed the Star Island Corporation by the Town of Kittery or the State of Maine, and abide by whatever terms they struck with the ferry for service. The agreed rent for some 80 acres of land and all the buildings on it was nominal, $1,000 per year, pegged to a national inflation index.

When Cornell muttered under its breath about paying taxes as a tax-exempt institution, I pointed out that they were really very small (then about $375) and that by paying them we could present ourselves to the Kittery Town Offices as resident taxpayers. That might make a very considerable difference in our ability to use the town dock, get help from the police, find free parking for our personal vehicles, influence zoning decisions, and the like. It would even qualify us for a resident lobster license—no small matter! Operating in a Maine town is much easier as an insider than as a foreigner. Cornell actually agreed with this view and didn't insist on filing papers to resist the tax.

THE GRASS LAB

The construction phase (as opposed to the bootstrap phase) began with the proposed utility building (now the Grass Foundation Laboratory).

In mid-1971, with a dock built; living quarters in good progress; the *Wrack* on dependable supply duty; and a muscular backhoe, tractor, and dump truck roaming the island on call, Dominic could turn his attention to starting a new building. The choice of which building to erect first was easy. We needed island wide power and water systems as soon as we could have them. To house them the utility building would be built first.

As with all the new buildings on Appledore Island from then through construction of the third dormitory, no proper architect was ever involved; they were too expensive. I had a good idea of fitting floor plans to function, and Dominic needed no help in working out constructional details when given floor plans and some crude elevation sketches. Thus, for the proposed utility building, I drew a floor plan showing what amounted to two buildings separated by a long expanse of roof. One end of this composite structure was to be built of concrete blocks (fireproof) to house generators and pumps. The other was a small, winterized, two-story building with a laboratory downstairs and living quarters above. Between, roofed over and walled in, was a large barnlike expanse intended for equipment repair and winter storage. That space would also serve to isolate the noise of the generators and pumps from the activities of the inhabited end of the building. The interior of the front part was to provide winterized housing upstairs for the engineer who kept the generator running and a small laboratory for teaching or research downstairs, usable year round.

Dominic began thinking of how best to build such a building, what the weathering surface should be for low maintenance, how to keep construction costs as low as possible, and the like. He had to face the problem of pouring concrete footings and floors. What would we use for aggregate? None of the salty, water-rounded gravel on Appledore's shores was suitable. Would the small well provide enough fresh water? What kind of roof material would best survive the gulls? What kind of trusses would work best to span the central area? Should they be ready-built ashore, or should we build them on the island. How would they be hoisted into place?

Here's what we did. Just as Dominic interacted with me on the floor plan, I commented on building materials and appearance, and we worked things out until we were both satisfied. We found this mutual interaction in the design and construction of buildings worked well, integrating my knowledge of needs and uses with Dominic's of building materials and techniques. One or two decades of experience with the new buildings since then has shown, I think, that they fit their functions and circumstances better than most buildings on the home campus do. Dominic and I are proud of them and would probably not change very much if we were to build them again.

Siting the new buildings sometimes elicited much argument. Not so for the utility building. Remember the old military tank embedded in an artificial hillside? Why not use it as the basis of the island freshwater system? The question of its basic soundness was asked in 1970 and answered through the efforts of the volunteer students that summer. The smallest of them, Lucy Palmer, was just barely able to squeeze through the oval port hole on the visible end of the tank. Would she go inside? Bravely, yes. She took a flashlight, a hammer, and tape measure and wriggled through the narrow hole. She found no holes or punk-sounding areas, but she said there was flaking rust and an accumulation of sediment on the bottom. We passed a scraper, broom, dust pan, brush, and face mask to her. Lucy gave the tank a good cleaning. Still no obvious problems appeared, and Lucy, not having eaten anything in the meantime, got back out.

Dominic approached the question of the serviceability of the military tank from the outside by digging away the dirt from one side of it with the backhoe. Then he obtained a new porthole door from somewhere, added an air gauge to one of the pipe openings, closing off the others, and slowly pressurized the tank with the small air compressor. The pressure held, the military tank was judged sound, and it is still sound as I write.

Lucy Palmer ready to come out.

Dominic began pegging out the foundation of the utility building directly in front of the tank, incorporating its face into the back wall of the building. He erected corner boards and the demarking strings around the perimeter as is common construction practice.

The utility building required concrete foundations and floors. This forced Dominic to consider how we were going to pour concrete on the island. No ready-mix truck will back to the site after a telephone call from Appledore Island. We needed sharp gravel, fresh water, and cement, as well as a way to mix them. The last was easiest. We borrowed the Star Island cement mixer and brought it across for the first simple jobs. Later Dominic bought a somewhat larger diesel-powered mixer, which we brought out from the mainland.

Cement comes in bags, heavy but readily handled. These Rachel Gratta ordered delivered to the dock, and we brought them out on the *Wrack* as they arrived. Dominic ranged the island looking for suitable gravel. The beaches are composed almost exclusively of a coarse gravel (very little sand), but the stones are all water rounded and salty, not suitable for good concrete. I suppose we could have sifted some passible gravel out of the

The dock at Ceres Street in Portsmouth.

glacial till in the valley, but that would have been not only a daunting but a defacing undertaking. In the end, Dominic decided that we would have to transport concrete aggregate out from the mainland.

Here's how we did it. During the initial construction season we took all building supplies over the fragile dock the Star Island Corporation leased from the Colonial Dames at Ceres Street in Portsmouth. Like most such docks it had a wooden deck at street level extending like a finger into the river on pilings of dubious age and condition. A brow (light wooden bridge) led from that dock to a float that would go underwater if more than a dozen people stood on it at one time. We generally loaded directly off the edge of the dock rather than using the float, passing materials directly from dock level down into the boat.

The gravel was transported to Appledore Island in 55-gallon steel drums from which the tops had been removed. These occupied most of the deck of the *Wrack*. The first year the gravel was delivered by dump truck to the Ceres Street parking lot next to the dock. It had to be moved from the pile there to the barrels on the boat. We tried to load only at high tide when the tops of the barrels on deck were only slightly lower than the level of the

Initially, gravel and other heavy loads were tranferred to the barge at Appledore and run onto the beach at the head of Babb's Cove where the backhoe could unload them. Later we built a high-tide dock at the head of the cove that the Wrack *could reach directly by backing in against it (shown above).*

dock. The gravel was shovelled from the pile into a wheelbarrow and then walked down a plank laid from the dock to the rim of each barrel in turn, into which it was tipped. This required quite a bit of dexterity because the boat was undulating on the water and before the first wheelbarrow load went into each barrel the barrel itself was unstable. However, the barrels were packed pretty tightly together on deck. They couldn't really tip over completely. We lost a full wheelbarrow load once or twice, but never the person manning it.

At Appledore Island the *Wrack* was docked alongside the barge at the island dock and the barrels were transferred from boat to barge using the donkey winch on the boat. When two or three boatloads of gravel were on the barge, it was pushed to the head of Babb's Cove on the next high tide and the barrels picked up by the backhoe, chained one by one to the scoop, and deposited in a stockpile above high tide. It took three *Wrack* trips to move one truckload of gravel.

Later, when we were moving building supplies across the Kittery town dock at Frisbee's (which meant a significantly shorter boat trip for us), we improved on the walk-the-plank method. Rachel learned that the Portsmouth concrete company she had been using to supply gravel couldn't deliver it to Frisbee's because its dump trucks were not licensed to operate in Maine. That led to the further discovery that its ready-mix cement trucks were licensed in Maine and could legally carry gravel to Kittery. Why not try chuting gravel directly from the ready-mix truck into our barrels on the *Wrack*'s deck at Frisbees? It worked very well for the first boatload of barrels. No more shovelling or wheelbarrows or planks to teeter down. But it still took three *Wrack* trips to move one truckload of gravel, and we still had to shovel the barrels full for the second and third trips because the ready-mix truck could not hang around for the three hours or so required for each *Wrack* round trip. Another advantage of this new arrangement, however, was that the ready-mix truck could chute the pile of gravel for the next two trips precisely at dock's edge, close enough to the boat that we could shovel it directly into the barrels without wheelbarrow or plank. Now all that our shovelers needed was a good aim. Kittery residents got used to seeing gravel coming out of a ready-mix cement truck at their town dock.

Back on Appledore Island the time had come, with the string lines in place, for digging a trench for the utility building foundations. There had been considerable prior discussion about foundations. The granite bedrock shows through nearly everywhere over most of Appledore Island, except in the waist of the island where the utility building is located. How far below the surface was the solid rock there? What was the soil like? The general thought at first, before we began digging, was that the soil was probably shallow.

It wasn't. The first foundation trench for the utility building went four feet down in dry gravelly glacial till without finding a solid bottom. The problem was not adequate depth for a good footing, but rather where that first four-foot-deep ditch had been dug.

By default, I had become the principal backhoe operator for the first summer. Dominic told me to start digging for the foundation as he had marked it out, and go down four feet if I could—simple, clear instructions, understandable even by a college professor. But he didn't tell me which side of the string I was supposed to dig on. I started on the footings for the front wall of the building. On the theory that if I dug inside the rectangle of string I would have to destroy it getting the backhoe out at the end, I assumed the logical relationship was to leave the string intact on the inside of the ditch by digging the ditch on the outside. I dug that front-wall ditch on the outside of the string.

Above: Footings. Below: Backhoe and gin pole hoist the trusses constructed on the island into place.

Above: Nearly finished building;
Below: ... with hand-carved sign.

Dominic came back to see how things were going when I had just about finished digging the footing ditch down to four feet the full length of the front wall. He let me know immediately and forcefully that I had done it wrong. Logic had nothing to do with it. The string was supposed to be on the outside of the ditch! The ditch was thus about two feet farther forward than the building was supposed to extend. I offered to fill it in and dig the ditch over. Dominic thought about it and decided it would be easier, given the instability of the gravel till, to use the ditch I had dug and just make the building two feet longer than planned. We would simply extend the front two-story part of the building by two feet.

And so it was. The downstairs of the utility building is two feet larger than originally drawn. What about the upstairs overhang? Supply Officer Rachel Gratta could get the 2x10-inch joists for that floor only in four foot increments. Dominic decided, when they had arrived on the island, that it would be a criminal waste to cut two feet off the end of each one. I agreed that the upstairs could be two feet larger than the downstairs, and we had ourselves a building with a two-foot overhang. Now every time I visit the island I am reminded pleasantly of that serendipitous mistake in ditch digging by a building that has a lot more character than it would have had if built as drawn.

SINKING BACKHOES AND HANGING JEEPS

After the battle to purchase the *Wrack,* our continuing troubles getting checks out of Cornell to pay Dominic's bills, and the disastrous plywood episode, one can understand that our operations were viewed with some concern in many offices at Cornell. We were subjected to repeated on-site examination in 1971 and later. Those examinations were conducted by a number of people from a variety of departments, including construction, safety, insurance, the vice president's office, and after students were on the island, even the president, Dale Corson, himself. Of these, it was visitations by the head of the construction department that were the most worrisome at first.

When the top officials came to see Appledore Island, we generally had to make a special run in with the *Wrack* to bring them out, to conserve their time. I remember two such visits particularly well. Once in the early days I arrived at the Appledore float accompanied by such a visitor only to watch a shocking tableau on shore. Dominic had just finished picking barrels of gravel off the barge at the head of Babb's Cove with the backhoe. The barge was being backed out of the cove under tow by the Whaler. Seeing us

Dominic on the backhoe (actually the second one, a John Deere).

arrive, Dominic stopped the backhoe at the top of the steep beach, put the bucket down, left the backhoe in gear, killed the engine, and started walking up the hill toward us. Just a few seconds later he heard, as did we, a loud shout from the person operating the Whaler. The backhoe had started rolling slowly down the beach, bucket skidding ahead, aimed for the water. Dominic turned and started running after it, hair streaming in the wind. He wasn't quite quick enough. The backhoe gathered speed and plowed majestically into the ocean up past its belly, Dominic gesticulating wildly behind it at water's edge, hurling imprecations. I directed the visitor's attention elsewhere as best I could.

Dominic learned firsthand on that occasion that putting vehicles with hydraulic drives into gear was not sufficient to hold them in place. We also learned that even a diesel engine (without spark plugs and attendant electrical complications) nevertheless required a large effort to overcome the effects of immersion in salt water. By the time our visitor left Appledore Island some hours later, the backhoe had been dredged out of the ocean (using the tractor and jeep in tandem), flushed with large amounts of fresh water, dried, and reignited successfully. Our distinguished visitor saw a problem arise, but he also saw that we could deal effectively and rapidly with problems of this sort.

Visitors from the construction department were not prepared to believe that a work force of students with people like Dominic and me in charge could possibly be doing well. Their heads were, I think, already composing blistering memoranda long before they reached the island to be put on paper as soon as they returned home. In fact, not once was any honest visitor from Cornell ever able to meet my challenge (always given) to show me that they could do in Ithaca the same amount of work of similar quality for a lesser figure or with a better safety record than ours. Never once during the construction years did anyone from Cornell challenge our cost-effectiveness or construction detail. Some people, in fact, became enthusiastic supporters of the Appledore project, even if we did occasionally let a backhoe slip into the drink.

Keeping brake lines from rusting through is impossible on Appledore Island. Sooner or later the brakes fail and everyone who drives vehicles on Star or Appledore Island has to know what to do when it happens. What you do is aim the vehicle for the nearest soft landing (if there is one) and prepare to bail out if necessary.

On one occasion, I brought a Cornell construction department visitor over from Star Island, where he had arrived by ferry unexpectedly. I landed with him in the Whaler at Appledore Island to find the jeep perched over the edge of Babb's Cove to the left of the dock, its front wheels dangling in the air as seen from below where we were. The jeep's brakes had failed as it was coming down the road from Laighton House. It had rounded the corner on route successfully but could not handle the T intersection with the shore road. There it had gone straight ahead, bouncing over the granite ledges. All hands bailed out and the jeep stopped providentially just before the final plunge, when its rear differential got hung up on a high point in the rock ledge. Using this fine unexpected demonstration, I instantly pointed out to our visitor the special need for safety on an offshore island, and how well we were actually prepared to deal with the occasional accident to preserve human life and health at all times. He took all he saw in stride.

Perhaps some of these stories began circulating at Cornell. In any event, Cornell's Safety Department began to take an interest in us. Its head at that time was Eugene Dymek; he soon called me down to his office.

Having worked with the volunteers on Appledore Island, and having seen the precautions against fire taken on Star Island, I had developed some strong ideas of the best way to deal with safety on offshore islands. It requires an approach somewhat different from that on the Cornell home campus.

The jeep, freshly painted with rust resistant surplus lacquer.

At the university the uniformed safety inspector goes around campus cutting plugs off extension cords with a pair of scissors, writing up reports on corridors where furniture or cabinets have been placed temporarily, and the like. I could imagine the havoc a person so minded could create on Appledore Island. Campus procedures would probably reduce actual safety on our island. I had to be sure Mr. Dymek didn't send that sort of person out.

We hit it off right away. I talked about the ways in which an offshore island is dangerous, and the fact that anyone who sets foot on one is immediately aware of the dangers: no fire department, no professional medical resources, no police, no health inspectors, no paved paths, buildings in derelict condition, slippery rocks, unstable boats, lethally cold surrounding waters, and so on. The key to safe operation is to think safety at all times and use common sense. Island people, each and every one, are naturally given to thinking safety when their life and well-being is so clearly and immediately depend on it. Consistent safe thinking is vastly more important than any number of fire detectors, cut extension cords, or the like. I pointed out that since the first class and the first volunteers had studied and worked on the islands, there had been not one really serious accident among us islanders.

None. I intended to keep it that way by impressing on everyone at all times the importance of safe thinking and acting. Dominic Gratta felt exactly the same way about safety as did I.

Eugene Dymek decided to see for himself. He came out to Appledore Island in late August, charging the costs of the trip to our budget. He liked what he saw, made a few useful suggestions, and volunteered that although someone from Cornell should check us over annually for our own protection and benefit, he would send someone who was capable of realizing our special circumstances and able to make genuinely useful recommendations. No extension cord cutters. So it has been.

All conferences on Star Island are presented with what its senior resident, Fred McGill, calls the fire-and-water-and-firewater speech soon after the conferees arrive. The speech warns, among other things, of the absence of fire hydrants for fire fighting and the real danger of a muddled head at any time on the islands. I developed a modification of that speech for use on Appledore Island with incoming groups, and current director J. B. Heiser continues the practice. We believe the speech is more important in our circumstances than any number of alarms, fire extinguishers, exit signs, or severed plugs, and results have proved the effectiveness of this policy on both islands over a great many years of freedom from major preventable accidents. To date, there have been no serious accidents in the water or on the shoreside rocks of Appledore Island. The common accidents are the sprained thumb on the volleyball court (such as it is), the sprained ankle on the porch steps, the foreign object in eye, and the inevitable cases of poison ivy before the students learn to recognize it.

RUNNING WATER OR BLASTING AIR

At the same time all this was happening, Dominic was still at work making the Coast Guard building increasingly more livable.

Despite the plywood difficulties, we moved some partitions and repositioned some doors to make better use of the government-designed space, and with daily saw-sharpening and extra finish nails (galvanized, as were all nails Dominic used on Appledore Island, even if he had to have them galvanized specially), the fireproof plywood was applied to the naked studs of the walls. Even now, almost a quarter century later, Shoals people are still fighting the flaking paint on those peeling fireproof plywood walls in the Coast Guard building.

Here's how the window problem was solved quickly and effectively, for all the old buildings. Rachel Gratta ordered combination aluminum

The volley ball court got heavy use. It doubled in early years as a helicopter landing pad. The privately owned Winkley House, now collapsed, stands on the hill.

storm windows and screens from a supplier she knew well, making sure that the frames and screening were of a grade of aluminum capable of withstanding corrosion in the marine environment. These went on quickly, fastened to the face boards of the window openings, and soon the building was closed in properly once again. Doors, both exterior and interior, appeared more slowly, because hanging each properly takes time and skill. Plumbing began to appear, too. The original sewer system at the Coast Guard building, discharging into a septic tank in the back yard, required only a little work with a plumber's snake to make it operational again. Dominic installed a toilet, shower, and washstands in each of the two original bathrooms and a sink in the room we were using as a kitchen. He connected those fixtures to the old sewer system and to hot and cold water supply lines. Now the problem was how to get water into this elegant system before the main island water system was built.

Here's how that one was solved. A 250-gallon galvanized hot-water tank, scrounged from Star Island, was mounted on one of the military rust-proof magnesium bomb trailers. It could be towed from the Coast Guard

The mobile water tank returning from the shore well.

building down the back trail to the seaside well behind the Ford tractor or the jeep and filled with water by a small gasoline pump that we had obtained. Then the tank was dragged back up the hill to the Coast Guard building and connected to the building plumbing. The final problem was to pressurize the system and force tank water into the building's pipes.

The building's new electrical system had been evolving even faster than the windows and plumbing. Everyone wanted to get away from candlelight evenings and burned-out flashlights, romantic though the former might seem to the reader. We first tried using the portable generator, which had been bought to power hand tools. It was hard to start, noisy, profligate of gasoline, and undependable. It was not built for continuous service, either. The next generator we tried was a five-kilowatt gasoline machine obtained from military surplus. Wiring (up to code, more or less) began to appear in the Coast Guard building and ceiling lights, worked by wall switches, began to light on demand when the generator was running. Wonderful!

Then Dominic bought an ordinary small air compressor and installed an air fitting on the top of the water supply tank. The compressor had an automatic pressure-regulated switch. When the generator was running, the compressor would come on automatically and pump air into the tank periodically to maintain pressure. This provided adequate pressure to push the water into the house. Dominic also installed a new bottled-gas water heater. The sense of pride and achievement as hot water first flowed in the arteries of the building after a quarter century, and as a ceiling light went on when a wall switch was flicked, are difficult for a mainlander to imagine. Outhouses were no longer needed and cleanliness was again possible at the end of each work day without resorting to buckets of cold water or the poison ivy thickets. Human life became almost civilized amid the gulls and cormorants.

But it still wasn't city living. That first five-kilowatt generator was a trouble-maker. Like most military surplus, it had not been used much but had sat around in various places for a good many years before we got it. Crud had collected in tanks and fuel lines. Brushes and electrical connections, already poor, worsened in our marine air. Keeping gasoline clean and water-free was difficult under our conditions of transportation and supply. Whenever it rained (not infrequently) things went from tenuous to obstinate. Condenser points and spark plugs fouled or pitted. Starter batteries died when cranking was excessive and, without the generator, there was no way on Appledore Island to recharge them. Even when the generator was running, output voltage climbed and fell erratically and cycles-per-second varied wildly. Altogether, many people spent many frustrating hours feeding, caring for, disassembling, repairing, handcranking, and swearing at that generator. Each time it was down inhabitants of the Coast Guard building went back to candles and the outhouses for as long as necessary to get it functioning again.

By the end of the summer of 1971 we had a surplus 15-kilowatt generator up and running. With its diesel engine it was considerably more dependable than the 5-kilowatt gasoline beast, but there were still the occasional interruptions when all power ceased, which brought down also the water and radio systems when the generator couldn't be restarted immediately.

Another frustration occurred when the water tank ran dry while someone was in the shower, all soaped up. In this case there was no doubt as to what was wrong. The water stopped flowing suddenly, without warning of any sort, and a blast of air came out of the shower head. It took about an hour to detach the water tank from the house, lug it down to the well, pump it full, haul it back up the hill, reattach it to the house, and repressurize it with the little compressor (providing that wasn't preempted to pump up a flat tire). People soon learned to check the water level in the tank by thumping it before starting a shower.

Above: 5-kilowatt generator.
Below: 15-kilowatt generator; Anthony Gratta in front.

Two other facts of life help to round out this early picture. There wasn't much to do in the evenings except sit and talk or read. Toward summer's end quiet talks were often interrupted by the scuttling of large rats in the basement of our home, the Coast Guard building, and sometimes in the upstairs rooms, too. When this first happened it led to the discovery that the island had a resident population of rats that lived well and reproduced rapidly when the gulls were there by taking advantage of the gulls' high mortality rate during the breeding season. When the gulls left, beginning in August, the rats began looking for other sources of sustenance and started appearing inside the buildings. It was not comfortable living in the same building with foraging rats, so we began a rat-eradication project. A case of rodenticide was ordered over the CB connection with the mainland. In the meantime, one of the fellows used his free evening time creatively to fashion a grid of electrified wires about two inches apart, with grounded wires running between them. He placed this across an obvious rat runway in the basement and plugged it in. We sat upstairs waiting. Soon a rat ventured across the grid. The rat died—so did the generator. The short circuit caused by a rat bridging hot to ground was more than the generator could handle; the engine just dragged down and stalled.

The rodenticide worked better.

DRUNKEN GULLS?

Another unusual feature of nocturnal life in the Coast Guard building was the presence of gulls in large numbers on the roof. Real gulls are nothing like the Jonathan Livingston Seagull of literary fame. Except in free flight, gulls are really pretty clumsy. They are smart as thieves, but dumb in social context (from a human view, at least). They contend vigorously, day and night, for a spot on the ridge pole of every building at the Shoals that had one. The gulls were never entirely asleep or quiet at night. We had to learn to live with the squeaks, shrieks, calls, and mewing. What I never could quite get used to was the sound of a ridgetop gull that fell asleep and lost its balance in the middle of the night. They tumble, scrabbling frantically, cawing, clawing, and flapping, down the wooden shingles, slippery with gull droppings and night moisture, all the way from the ridge to the gutter and on over the edge. Those of us with upstairs bedrooms could expect one or two such events to awaken us nightly.

By the end of the first construction season, the utility building was entirely framed in and closed; the Coast Guard building was reasonably comfortable; an efficient supply route from the mainland was established;

Above: Jonathan Livingston Seagull.
Below: Veteran Appledore gull.

November, 1971.

docks, floats, and roads were created for moving materials on the island; and some work had been done on the other derelict buildings, much of it by volunteers. We were on schedule and within budget as nearly as anyone could tell as Appledore Island, radiant with the russet glory of poison ivy in autumn, was closed for the winter and the *Wrack* finally went ashore for the last time in November with more than a trace of snow in the air.

Tallying our efforts for the annual meeting, we found we had accomplished a lot that first summer. We had brought to Appledore Island a dump truck, a backhoe, a jeep, a tractor, three generators, six magnesium bomb trailers, one cement mixer, five tons of cement in bags, 25 yards of sand and gravel, innumerable concrete blocks, much hardware, lumber, roofing materials, electrical and plumbing supplies, mattresses, blankets, beds, chairs, dressers, gasoline, diesel oil, lubricating oils, propane cylinders, and all our food.

We had installed interior walls, windows, doors, hot and cold water systems, wiring, a gas stove, refrigerator, and communications radios in the Coast Guard building, which had also received an unplanned new roof over the back half of the building when a leak over the stove had sufficiently

New roof on the Coast Guard building Dominic's way (top down).

irritated chef Dominic Gratta. Dominic also made over the tower room for his personal quarters. He said he could tell how hard the wind was blowing without getting out of bed by how much the tower shook, and plan the day's work accordingly. We had bought a new boat, the *Wrack*, and put her in service. We had built or rebuilt more than a half mile of roadway to first-class condition (defined in island terms as passable to all vehicles).

We had designed, sited, and closed in the Grass Foundation Laboratory, built a fireproof generator/pump room there of concrete block, moved in a 60-kilowatt generator, and made functional the military water tank there.

We had agreed on tentative plans and construction details for the new commons building, located a suitable site, cleared it, and built an access road to it.

We had removed plaster from Laighton House and installed windows in it, removed plaster and done some cleanup in the Operations Building (later Hewitt Hall), and reroofed the gas shack storage shed. We had cleaned and activated the smaller well and pumped down the larger well for five days without being able to get to its bottom. We would have to get a bigger pump and try again next summer.

Broad Cove beach.

As near as we could tell, without some key bills from Gratta Construction, about $101,000 had been spent to accomplish all the above. Nearly $25,000 was still left in our accounts, with which Dominic could accumulate materials during winter to speed forward the next summer's construction.

The Shoals Program annual meeting convened on December 1. This summary information was presented. It had now become necessary to keep construction costs separate from those of the teaching program. This presented some difficulty because, not wishing the burden of keeping picky records, we had to guess a bit about such things as how much boat time was used for the one purpose and for the other. Jay Freer showed an excellent ability to use common sense in these matters.

The most pressing question for those assembled at the annual meeting was whether to gamble that we would be ready to present a full month's program on Appledore Island for 40 people by August 1, 1972. Flyer copy had to go to press immediately after the meeting. After much vigorous discussion those assembled decided not to gamble. The 1972 teaching program would be presented at Star Island and in Durham in June as in the past. If some short-course possibility presented itself seeking to use the

Appledore facilities late in the summer, it could perhaps serve as a shakedown experience for our new facilities.

Irwin Novak's Ph.D. thesis, entitled *The Origin, Distribution, and Transport of Gravel on Broad Cove Beach, Appledore Island, Maine,* appeared in the island library and served to prove that not all academic activity on Appledore Island was the teaching of undergraduates. Besides that geological research, other graduate students were at work. Erica Dunn of the University of Michigan was working on cormorant heat relations, and Frederick "Ric" Martini was investigating the physiology of shark's blood. Both students subsequently earned doctoral degrees from their work at Appledore Island, and several more theses have appeared since. These graduate investigations reactivated the distinguished record of thesis production on Appledore Island begun under Professor C. Floyd Jackson a quarter century earlier.

The Summer Program budget, running about $25,000 per season, had had a positive balance of nearly $500 after all bills for 1971 were paid.

All in all, we appeared to be on target, on time, and within budget for both construction and teaching programs as 1971 came to a close. The future looked rosy indeed, wouldn't you think?

It was not to be so!

Chapter Nine

THE UNOFFICIAL OPENING
1972

CONSTRUCTION CRISIS

Where was the cash for 1972's summer construction to come from? In the projections it would have been fully met by capitalizing the SUNY contract for $15,000 per year for ten years. The SUNY budget for 1971 had been unblocked in time for the Marine Sciences Research Center at SUNY Stony Brook to make its second annual payment before the year closed. I had naively assumed that would settle the capitalization question. It did not. The State of New York began crying poorer than ever for its 1972 budget. Cornell's administration decided not to run the implied risk. Instead of capitalizing the SUNY contract and allowing us to borrow against it, Cornell asked us, right after the December annual meeting, to do the best we could to find $125,000 in new cash before April. This was a tall order, indeed.

The Shoals Lab Newsletter of January 14, 1972, raised the cry: "Construction on Appledore Will Stop—Is Stopped—Unless the Trustees Authorize Further Spending for Summer 1972 at Their March Meeting. We propose to do everything we can to place the tustees in such a position that they can authorize further spending when they meet. We have to do this without suggesting that our earlier support from any quarter has failed, for it has not, or that construction has not gone reasonably so far, for it has."

The newsletter then went on to announce the formation of the august Society of Vicarious Shoalers. "Charter membership will consist of all donors to date plus all who designate a contribution or pledge to the Shoals before February 15 (the date on which the March trustees' agenda closes). History will accord to these persons the honor of bringing the Shoals Marine Laboratory into being."

Cornell's Development Office discouragingly said I shouldn't expect very much from a simple unedited appeal in a typewritten, multilithed nonprofessional newsletter that lacked glossy spreads or color. Who would read it?

Apparently our entire mailing list read it, and many responded on the spot. When the Cornell administrators who had to recommend our future to the trustees met on February 15, I was able to tell them that $63,000 had been received, and contributions were still coming in strongly. Treasurer A. H. Peterson, Vice President for Planning Thomas Mackesey, and Vice Provost W. Keith Kennedy placed an item on the agenda of the trustees' March meeting recommending that Cornell advance to the Shoals project as much as $125,000, as needed, for the 1972 construction season. By March 15 when the trustees met, contributions (cash and pledges) had grown to just shy of $90,000 and were still coming in. The trustees had no trouble agreeing with the Shoals recommendation this time. We were advanced a credit line of $125,000 by Cornell University, at interest of course if we used any of it. Those Vicarious Shoalers were great!

Another less-public crisis appeared after the 1971 annual meeting. Martin Sampson, director of the Summer School, somewhat regretfully decided that our growing academic program which was about to occupy its own facilities had reached a size and complexity that no longer fit comfortably within the strictures under which the Summer School operated. The accounting confusion that discomforted us discomforted him, too. What he actually said was, "You're getting too big for us. It's time you found a better home." That action didn't come from any hidden negativity on his part; he and Mrs. Sampson continued to be generous and faithful Vicarious Shoalers.

No department or college at Cornell had volunteered to accept the challenge of administering the Shoals project earlier. None appeared ready to do so now. What should we do to provide a new home for our teaching accounts and a route for our course credits to reach the Registrar for transcript purposes?

Jay Freer and I thought about this problem for some time, weighing theoretical alternatives carefully. Here's what we did.

Years earlier the Summer School had set up a separate account in the endowed business office through which it handled our academic receipts and disbursements. What was to prevent us from taking over that account in our own name? Apparently nothing. With the quiet blessing of Marge Van Ness, who was in charge of accounts in the Summer School, we did so. She also told the Registrar's Office that it would be getting the Shoals summer program course grades directly from us in the future. We didn't ask permission of anyone else, but just began operating independently with that Summer School endowed account now reregistered in the name of the Shoals Marine Laboratory. Where did that name "Shoals Marine Laboratory" come from? So far as I know, no faculty group or college committee formally reviewed it. No administrative office at Cornell or the University of New Hampshire approved it. We just began using it when we needed a name to identify that new entity on Appledore Island.

The name was not assumed without some thought, however. The matter of naming was discussed extensively among Shoals faculty members and others. No paramount donor had surfaced whom we might logically honor in naming the laboratory. More important, we needed a name with obvious character, something a person would remember, something that would say "nautical" to any mind, and something that would reflect our island spirit.

"Shoals" is a strong word, perhaps a bit mordant from its connection with rocks and wrecks. The "shoals" of the Isles of Shoals, historians say, is not of that kind. It refers instead to the dense schools of fish around the islands in the sixteenth century. Of itself it strengthens the "marine" in our title, and it has a certain insouciance, a certain iconoclasm, well-suited to an island venture, and perhaps just a touch of black humor appropriate to an uncharted venture in undergraduate education.

An unappointed director, an unapproved name, subsumed accounts; the full import of these honestly motivated ways of getting around obstructive offices and red tape at Cornell dawned on Jay and me only slowly. By simply doing what needed doing when it needed it, we now had unconsciously achieved the creation within Cornell of a semiautonomous unit with an unofficial name and an undesignated director who was utilizing very real accounts and substantial authority, to which he had no officially sanctioned claim.

Officially Jay and I had been empowered by Cornell's administration to spend money through an account in the university's construction department requiring that department's approval. The faculties at Cornell and the University of New Hampshire had authorized us to present *Introduction to Marine Science* for credit. Finally, the Cornell trustees had authorized an intrauniversity loan of up to $125,000 to our account managed by the construction department.

Beyond the authority of those few approved functions, the non-director of the unrecognized Shoals Lab, with consultation from his colleagues, actually was able to do many additional important things. He could and did appoint faculty members and teaching assistants in the name of Cornell and determined their responsibilities and honoraria. He could set and publish an academic schedule, purchase teaching supplies and equipment, cause checks to be issued, accept students into courses, determine the tuition and fees (and also board and room) they paid, issue bills, and deposit checks directly into Shoals accounts. He could place grades on Cornell and University of New Hampshire transcripts through the Registrars of those institutions. He could offer programs for alumni of both universities in their names, and solicit contributions from their alumni for deposit in Shoals Lab's accounts. So long as we ran no accounts significantly or repeatedly into the red, or bothered the auditor, no one seemed to notice what was going on.

When you stop to think about it, as writing this book has forced me to do, these are really the powers of a college and its dean (or the Summer School and its director). For those powers to be exercised, without supervision, by a then-junior faculty member was a bit unusual, even though the funds involved were relatively small in the Cornell scheme of things. The flip side for me was that I never got paid a cent extra for those duties and responsibilities. They weren't in my formal job description. Officially, Cornell never knew I was doing them.

MR. PETERSON

While the academic accounts of the Shoals Lab went into relative obscurity when they moved into our own hands, the top Cornell administrators kept the costs of the Shoals construction project fully in mind at all times. After all, the trustees themselves were watching those expenditures. Every time Rachel Gratta failed to submit a bill on time, or submitted one that would not meet the approval of the Construction Department (always), Vice President Tom Mackesey got bothered.

As the vice president became more urgently concerned with other matters in the next few years and as the billing delay and the size of Rachel's bills increased, he felt increasingly inadequate to the situation and began bucking the Gratta bills the next level up, namely to the controller and treasurer of the university. During the years under review that person was Arthur H. Peterson, known informally but nonetheless respectfully as Pete among his colleagues and with somewhat fearful formal respect as Mr. Peterson (although he possessed a doctorate) at all other levels of Cornell.

He had worked his way to the top of Cornell's administrative ladder from a start as professor of agricultural economics in the College of Agriculture. Mr. Peterson knew his business, and with long years of administrative experience in that state-supported college before he moved up, he understood just how New York State actually worked better than did many in Albany. The president and provost regularly sought his opinion if money or the handling of money was involved, and rarely disagreed with his conclusions.

"He opened and closed the university daily." In just seven words author Helen Peterson said a lot about her husband, his importance to Cornell's business, and, not least, his faithfulness to his own drummer. Arthur Peterson created many legends. He was the stuff from which lore derives. Part of his "stuff" was an unassuming, quiet, self-effacing nature. He refused to countenance a retirement party, sold his house, and left Ithaca almost the day after he retired. He wished to leave no shadow for those (and they were several) who had to assume the roles of Arthur Peterson, the administrator and the man. The daily management of that complex fiscal hybrid that is Cornell University, which should have been dead at birth and is demonstrably unworkable in theory, is made to work and work well by a few people at the top, like Arthur Peterson, who possess imagination and good will.

Mr. Peterson was initially concerned about the university's exposure in the line of credit it had extended to the Shoals Lab. He was concerned also to know that the money actually spent on Appledore Island was honestly and productively spent. When Tom Mackesey withdrew from our chain of command, a series of regular and emergency command reviews of the Shoals Lab situation commenced in Mr. Peterson's office. Throughout his career at Cornell, Mr. Peterson arrived at his office by 6:00 a.m. daily, often well before, and stayed until the dinner hour. He worked every week day of every year, never took a leave of absence for any reason, and was out sick only eight days in over 37 years. He never came to his office in attire other than a black suit, white shirt, and black tie (at least I never saw him wearing anything else). Mr. Peterson was a man of inscrutable demeanor, and few but pithy, not to say pointed, words. He had an uncanny ability to put his finger on soft places in columns of figures, and weak positions in reasoning. He always read all documents fully before a meeting in which they would be discussed. He kept his appointments on time and terminated them within scheduled limits. Those characteristics gave Mr. Peterson a certain reputation throughout the management levels of the university.

Fortunately, Jay Freer was a sound accountant, and I knew that the dollars spent on Appledore Island were buying more than they would have if spent through regular administrative channels at Cornell. I am sure Jay remembers as well as I our first visit to Mr. Peterson's office. We had prepared as for a doctoral exam, but we didn't know just what to expect, having been awed by Mr. Peterson's reputation. We were admitted to the inner office exactly at the appointed hour.

The first meeting was much like later ones. Negligible preliminaries. Mr. Peterson expressed his concerns succinctly. "How much more has to be done to get the salt water system functional and what will it cost? How does Dominic Gratta cover his costs given his delayed billing? Is he creating any particular liability for Cornell by acting that way? Why didn't you purchase that on state contract?" At the end he usually asked us how the project was going in our opinion. We always thought it was going reasonably well, and said so.

On the other hand, it was impossible to judge how things were going during any particular visit to Mr. Peterson's office. His expression was always entirely unreadable. At the end of such a visit he usually said something like "You are fully extended; be careful." Once, when I asked for approval of something a little beyond the usual, he said—and I remember each word with crystal clarity to the present day—"John, your neck is so far out now a little more won't make any difference."

Invariably Mr. Peterson concluded that we were honest, that we were presenting the situation as it really was, that any other department of the university probably would not have done better, and that our academic goals were worthy. We never left his office comforted, but never in trouble either. When troubles did arise with other Cornell offices, his help, freely given, took care of all problems while arousing little enmity toward the Shoals Lab. If Mr. Peterson said to do it, it was as good as done.

After only a few Gratta billings had gotten stuck in the construction department, and after Tom Mackesey had departed the Shoals scene, Mr. Peterson got tired of being bothered with having to approve each of those bills separately. They were, after all, pretty small pickings among the vastly greater numbers he dealt with daily. In typical Peterson fashion he sent a letter to the head of the Construction Department which said, word for word as closely as I remember, "I know you don't like this kind of billing, but henceforth when John Kingsbury countersigns one of those Gratta bills, you pay it."

Our command review appearances in Mr. Peterson's office occurred at least yearly and sometimes more frequently when there were major problems or changes in the picture. On the theory that a person ought to see something of our island reality before he could properly appreciate construction accomplishments at the far end of ten miles of open water, I

Mr. Peterson finally visits Appledore Island. Willard Kiggins at left, Gilbert Kiggins at right.

took a few photos with me on the first visit. Mr. Peterson looked at them with interest and seemed to appreciate them. On the strength of that, I brought a handful of color slides and a projector with me on the second visit. Mr. Peterson would not look at the slides until after the grilling phase, but then he invited me to project them on his wall. This pattern continued for all following meetings. I soon began adding a personal invitation for Mr. Peterson to come out to Appledore Island and see things for himself firsthand. He wouldn't. I kept at him to come out. Finally, after a particularly vigorous invitation (we were getting to know each other better), he said, "John, I have seen too many people at Cornell I know to have good judgment go out there and come back with their judgment impaired. I'm not going to take that risk until I no longer have any responsibility for the project."

And so it was. A few months after Mr. Peterson had officially announced his retirement, but before he left Ithaca, Arthur and Helen Peterson journeyed to Appledore Island for the dedication of Kiggins Commons and the Grass Foundation Lab, and they had a great visit. Those on the island who bet that he would appear in black suit and tie won, but we soon got the coat off him and the tie discarded. We even got a glass into his hand.

The Shoals Lab owes a great deal to the faith the indomitable Arthur Peterson had in our project and the authority he exercised on campus in its behalf during the construction years immediately prior to his retirement.

With effective signatory control over Shoals project funds in the construction department accounts, I now had a power that even deans do not have. In consequence, my ability to meet my handshake agreement with Dominic Gratta was now greatly enhanced.

The Shoals Lab's newsletters of 1971 and 1972 chronicled the fiscal crises that beset the early construction years. A large number of people responded with contributions or pledges or in other ways. I've already mentioned Superscrounge Dr. Peter Beck. Another unusual form of help was initiated through the interest of Robert Zottoli. He found out about us through his son, Robert Zottoli, Jr., who was a teacher of invertebrate zoology in Massachusetts who had been involved in our Summer Program. At Robert, Jr.'s urging Robert, Sr. came out to Appledore Island and was sold on what he saw happening, both in the teaching and in the construction. He hit it off particularly well with Dominic Gratta, perhaps because they both had grown up in the same area of Massachusetts. It turned out that Robert Zottoli was a trustee of the Grass Foundation. He prevailed upon Albert Grass and his daughter-in-law Mary Grass to come out. They, too, became enthusiastic about what they saw happening. Albert Grass was the creator of the Grass Foundation, Mary its secretary. Unfortunately, the tax-exempt purposes of the Grass Foundation, to further research in neurobiology, did not mesh with the construction of a field station for undergraduate instruction in marine sciences.

In setting up the Grass Foundation, Albert and Ellen Grass had the eleemosynary idea to "pay" the trustees by giving them the opportunity to make significant donations to charities of their own choice rather than claiming remuneration for themselves. Bob Zottoli began giving his annual trustee's fee to the Shoals Lab. So did Al Grass himself.

To our surprise (and his, too, I think), we discovered yet another connection between the Grass Foundation and the Shoals Lab: Dr. Robert Morison, the first director of Cornell's Division of Biological Sciences, was also a long-standing trustee of the Grass Foundation. Since his first trip to see Appledore Island in the Star Island garbage scow, Bob Morison had never returned. Thus he found himself in the rather awkward position of learning more about what was happening at the new Shoals Lab at Grass Foundation trustee meetings than he did in Ithaca—he never came to our annual meetings. Bob Morison soon began contributing his Grass

Foundation trustee's fee to the Shoals Lab, too. Those three annual donations, continuing for several years, added up to a handsome amount. I asked Al Grass if he would be willing to let us recognize them in the name of the utility building. He seemed tickled with the idea, and we did it. The original sign identifying the Grass Lab was something I carved myself.

Another unusual source of funds also surfaced in 1971. Roger Duncan, author of *A Cruising Guide to the New England Coast,* arrived at the Shoals one day in his photogenic Friendship sloop, *Eastward.* He was scouting around in preparation for a new edition of this classic among yachtsman's guides. After seeing what was going on, he spontaneously announced he would contribute a portion of the royalties from the new edition of the guide to the Shoals project. And so he did.

Also rising to our fiscal needs were alumni of Professor C. Floyd Jackson's Zoological Laboratory of the University of New Hampshire on Appledore Island. The Barnacles, as they called themselves, constituted a group of ready-made successful foster alumni for a marine station yet to open. The Appledore Island magic had worked on them in the 1930s, and they were grateful. Olive Brock was a prime catalyst in bringing them back together. A particularly nice discovery was that Professor Jackson's son Herb, who ran the lab's vessel the *Shankhassick* (actually Professor Jackson's personal boat) among other youthful duties at the UNH Lab, had just retired from federal employment as chief biologist at The Robert A. Taft Sanitary Engineering Center, Cincinnati, Ohio, and had returned to the family home in Durham, New Hampshire. Herb Jackson, with Ph.D. from Cornell, was invited to lecture at the Shoals. He immediately became a strong link between the Barnacles and the new Shoals Lab.

ONE HUNDRED TWENTY-FIVE TONS CLOSER TO OPENING!

Following the decision not to push our luck by trying to present the summer program on Appledore Island in 1972, we went ahead with a flyer announcing it instead for Star Island as before. Again the calendar cooperated, and the 1972 Summer Program in Marine Science had three weeks on Star followed by one in Durham. On Star Island the availability of the brand new Rutledge Marine Lab in the Brookfield Building allowed us to increase our enrollment from 30 to 40 (we actually took 41), and efforts at Cornell and UNH bore fruit when faculty of both institutions approved increasing the credits for successful completion of the Shoals course from four to five. The Dyson Fund was added to the list of those supplying grants for scholarships.

Ron Harelstad (left) with Jim and Martha Palmer (1975).

Once again, things went well both fiscally and in terms of student achievement. Not once had the Summer Program stumbled in the seven times it had been presented since 1966.

Dominic started construction as early in 1972 as the weather allowed. The *Wrack* was reactivated from winter storage, and Ron Harelstad, earlier a volunteer, became her principal skipper. Ron had taken courses in welding and diesel engines during the winter months (at his own expense) to make himself more useful on the island. Construction was slowed near the beginning of the season by particularly heavy spring storms that damaged the dock and float. Dominic rebuilt both with significantly heavier timbers and replaced the balsa rafts under the float with specially fabricated heavy steel tanks. It would now support more than one hundred people without sinking.

We needed better moorings for the *Wrack* and the Whaler, and we also needed to replace the chain that held the dock float in place. Perhaps the Baldt Anchor and Chain Corporation, through which we had received the Dyson scholarship, could use some good tax write-offs of the kind that would result from donating items appropriate to our needs. It could and did,

Steel beams scrounged from the Marshall House used in Kiggins Commons.

thereby greatly relieving our construction budget. Large anchors and heavy chain are very expensive items.

The Appledore Island scroungers also were hard at work on shore as the spring advanced. Superscrounge Dr. Peter Beck liberated an institutional dishwasher being discarded by the Portsmouth Hospital, and Dominic laid hands on an institutional stove from the Emerson House, then being torn down in York Harbor. He also salvaged several steel beams from the Marshall House of York Harbor, which was also being demolished. All three of those items later showed up in the structure or the furnishings of Kiggins Commons.

I say, "showed up" a little too loosely. They didn't simply materialize on Appledore Island from thin air. Altogether the Shoals staff toted by *Wrack* and by barge some 125 tons of building materials from Kittery to Appledore Island for just the Kiggins Commons building. These materials moved across the Kittery town dock behind Frisbee's, where operations had shifted in 1972 from the original staging area at the Ceres Street dock in Portsmouth to shorten the boat runs significantly and eliminate the necessity of handling the barge in the difficult currents of the Piscataqua River.

The summer of 1972 saw some memorable barge trips, including one on which the steel beams from the Marshall House were brought out, and another, particularly, that delivered to Appledore Island at one time all of the large laminated arch beams now visible in the dining room of Kiggins Commons. The barge was barely afloat with those beams aboard, and waves washed across their extended ends as the tow bucked the choppy seas the day they came out.

One of the heavier storms of the 1972 spring season was Tropical Storm Agnes. After the storm had passed, someone noted a strange shape floating past Appledore Island headed for Gosport Harbor. Just on the chance it might be something useful, we got in the Whaler and took a closer look. It turned out to be a one-hole outhouse in nearly new condition, carefully crafted, fully assembled with a hinged door and proper crescent, and hardly dented by the storm. We never knew its source on the mainland, but, exercising rights of salvage of abandoned marine property, we dragged it out of the water, dug a hole with the backhoe, and established our find in some heavy bushes next to the picnic area near the Grass Lab for the convenience of the visiting public, which was beginning to show up on Appledore Island on weekends even back then. In honor of its source, we named our unexpected new building "Gift-from-the-Sea."

SCOMBER BLOWS UP

Gull of Bristol, the company that was building our next vessel, the *Scomber*, had promised delivery for April 1972. It was not to happen. Here's what did happen. *Scomber* was being built under Coast Guard supervision for special licensing for passengers-for-hire service. This meant that certain features had to meet higher standards than the standard model. Mr. Currie of Gull of Bristol was having trouble with his suppliers in obtaining some necessities such as monel metal fuel tanks. Meanwhile, I had scheduled a dedication ceremony for early May to give Mr. Chester Wiggin and Mr. Richard Johnson of the New England Regional Commission a chance to see what their federal funds had helped purchase. They worked the dedication into their busy schedules so they would be in York Harbor for the ceremony. We chose York Harbor for its gently sloping ramp which would make launching easier than at the steeply sloping ramp in Kittery. Reporters and others were also alerted, and plans were made final.

Then things began to go wrong. Mr. Currie called to say that the *Scomber* wouldn't be quite ready at the appointed time. I responded that I couldn't easily undo all the complicated scheduling involved. Cooperatively,

Above: Scomber *about to dock. Below:* Scomber *with dedication plaque.*

Above: Dedication of Surrogate Scomber *as shown in newspapers.*
Below: Same, as it really happened.

he said that he could send a surrogate boat up to York Harbor to stand in for the genuine *Scomber*. I wrote the New England Commission to that effect, and they agreed to the dedication of a surrogate. At the last minute Mr. Currie couldn't come because of severe illness in his family. He sent an employee with the rather large surrogate boat on a rather small trailer, towed by a rather aged station wagon. But it arrived in time. Because when we got there the launching ramp at York Harbor was still blocked by winter boat storage, which we hadn't foreseen, the whole entourage snaked off to Kittery. We launched surrogate *Scomber* at the Kittery ramp behind Frisbee's after all.

Actually, because of further complications, we didn't really launch her. There was no winch on the trailer by which to retrieve the vessel, and surrogate *Scomber* had no engine. Thus, there could be neither a demonstration ride or even a full launching. What actually happened was that surrogate *Scomber* was backed down the steep ramp at Kittery until she was mostly in the water. At that point we realized that we were not aboard, and because we couldn't move the boat to the dock we could get aboard now only by climbing down along the trailer hitch and over the bow. Thus it occurred that our distinguished guests (who were very good sports about all this) had to climb down the slippery trailer tongue and upend themselves on their bellies over the high freeboard of the *Scomber's* bow to board her. They did. Once dignity proper to a dedication had been reestablished there were some words about what the real *Scomber* would be like and we looked at the dedication plaque. Then we upended back out of the boat; she was retrieved from the water never having left the trailer and departed for Massachusetts.

The local reporters were good to us. They published pictures that made the boat look as though launched.

But that was not the end of the story. A few weeks later the real *Scomber* blew up. Not just *Scomber*, but the whole Gull of Bristol factory. *Scomber* was literally within a few hours of completion when this happened. We went through the season without *Scomber*, though we had planned otherwise. Mr. Currie, however, did rebuild his factory, produced another *Scomber*, achieved Coast Guard approval of her, and eventually delivered the real *Scomber* to Maine the next spring.

In all previous cases we possessed our boats before we selected names. This time the name came first. We chose *Scomber*, the scientific name of the mackerel. Not only did the boat prove initially unlucky, but the name itself soon presented an unexpected problem. At that time it seems a senior administrator in the State Business Office at Cornell was named Stuart Comber. He often used only his first initial in signing his name. Soon our boat began to get confused in Cornell's paperwork with S. Comber, to the difficulty of both parties.

Other matters went better than did the *Scomber*. To the delight and relief of everyone, a check was received from the Marine Sciences Research Center at Stony Brook constituting SUNY's third annual contribution to our effort. The James B. Palmer family also gave us to understand that we would have resources to build on Appledore Island a teaching laboratory in a new building similar to Star Island's Rutledge Laboratory, which had impressed them, and we should begin planning for it now.

THE UNION OCCUPATION

Things were now moving forward rapidly as spring 1972 turned into summer. A request had come from Dr. Carl George at Union College to bring a group of students to Appledore Island in late summer. He planned to spend a week with them at the Marine Biological Laboratory in Woods Hole, and wanted them also to see some of the more rugged coast further Down East. In his opinion, Appledore Island would be an ideal place. His calendar required that the Union students come to Appledore Island for a week *before* going to Woods Hole.

Dominic was positive that enough construction would be done by late summer to accommodate the Union class. I told them they were welcome to come but should be prepared to rough it a bit. Dominic went to work with the particular aims of finishing the interior of the Grass Foundation Lab to provide bench space for 15 students by midsummer and to fix up what we then called the Operations Building (now Hewitt) with at least a tight roof and closable windows so the Union students would have dry housing. He had to give thought, also, to facilities for feeding an additional 17 people. No problem, so he said! But things weren't so simple. Here's what actually happened.

Opening a teaching laboratory is something like having a large number of distinguished guests to dinner—there's a host of last-minute details some expected, some unexpected, all important. On an island the problems are magnified. We all did our best to get ready for the Union students, but inevitably some loose ends remained. We did install smoke and heat detectors in the Operations Building and attach fire escapes (ladders to the upper windows on each end of the building) in time for Cornell's Safety Division inspector to certify the building safe for 15 students to sleep in. But the Operations Building roof wasn't quite finished when Tropical Storm Carrie hit just after the students had settled in. Carrie blew off the roofing paper where the shingles were not yet laid, drenching the front rooms upstairs and down and forcing the relocation of several students into beds

Students in an early class from Stockton University at work in a corner of the Grass Foundation Laboratory.

usually occupied by our own construction crew in the Coast Guard building. Fortunately, those beds were then vacant because the storm hit on a weekend when most of the construction crew was ashore.

We were also having problems with the 15-kilowatt generator, which meant that for most of the time the Union class was at the island we could not operate the newly installed electric steam table and the refrigerator simultaneously. The former lost out, and meals became even a greater challenge than feeding 30 people from institutional-sized pots on a three-burner, home-style gas stove supplemented by a plumber's furnace would already have been. Heroic efforts on the part of the cook (Louise Kingsbury), the cook's assistant (Ric Martini), and the food supplier (Rachel Gratta) prevented this situation from becoming the disaster that it might have been.

With those forced inhospitalities fresh in mind, we were particularly gratified to receive Carl George's letter after the Union class had left us for Woods Hole and home:

"It gives me great pleasure to inform you that we, the Union College marine biology course, had a superb and most productive learning experience at Appledore Island. On the basis of this, I would very much like to endorse your program and urge that it be supported as actively as possible—and immediately. As it presently stands, the best learning experience in marine biology now available in the northeastern United States is at your laboratory. The Marine Biological Laboratory at Woods Hole, though a superb facility, is well removed from the environment where the organisms are found. A disarticulation of the experience results and too much time is spent traveling to good study sites. Another problem is that there are too many sources of distraction. The other laboratories besides the MBL suffer this latter problem especially. Furthermore recent developments are turning once suitable collecting places into impoverished and unpleasant experiences.

"Another fine thing about Appledore is its rustic character. This generates a distinctive and memorable comradeship which in turn induces good exchange—and learning 'thrill.' This may be an awkward way of expressing the point, but it was our observation that the circumstances led to a very rewarding mutual stimulation. . . .Still another feature of Appledore is the opportunity to interact with the lobstermen and fishermen. I think this was grand and conducive to real perspective in terms of such concepts as marine pollution, the interfaces between economics and biology, politics and ecology-biology, the values of knowing such things as how a lobsterman thinks about the interactions of urchins, seals, seaweeds—and lobsters."

Exactly. Union forsook the MBL the next year and spent its whole time on Appledore Island.

ANNUAL MEETING

Looking back on it, as we did at the Shoals Lab annual meeting in early winter, the summer of 1972 checked out well. The teaching program on Star, newly expanded from 30 to 40 students, was again excellent and its budget of about $25,000 stayed in the black by a few hundred dollars. The Grass Laboratory was finished (all but the concrete floor of the central bay, which came some years later) and two generators (one 50-kilowatt, one 60-kilowatt) were installed there and made operational. Kiggins Commons was fully framed and closed in, and the beginnings of island wide fresh-water, salt-water, electrical, and sewage systems were in place. Union College students had come and gone and a class had been taught most successfully on Appledore Island once again after a hiatus of more than three decades since the last students of Professor Jackson's Zoological Laboratory were there. Those present at that meeting, assured by Dominic Gratta's strong recommendation, voted to open the new Appledore Island facilities on

August 1, 1973, for a four-week class of 40 students. We would not change our successful course materially, or increase its length or the number of students, but we would move the program to the latter part of the season and to a different island. Doing this would mean uniting the separate Star and Durham parts of the course into one, presenting the united course in new and untested facilities, and providing housing and dining services for faculty, staff, and students in the midst of an active construction season. This was challenge enough for one year. Here's how we did it.

Professor Anderson improves the hour and the roadway behind Laighton by swinging a magnet to remove bent nails that had been disabling Old Joe nearly daily.

Happiness is a big Laminaria.

Chapter Ten

THE OFFICIAL OPENING
1973

DOMINIC GRATTA

In January the annual financial crisis arose once again. We had spent essentially all the construction cash received during the 1972 season and needed to have the $125,000 debt authorization renewed for 1973. Without it we would be in a pickle. If Dominic couldn't work for lack of funds, he couldn't get Kiggins Commons done, and without dining facilities we couldn't take a class on August 1. Nor could we go back to Star Island in the middle of its season. The program would have to be cancelled. The pressure was really on.

In reviewing construction funding early in the year before taking our case to Mr. Peterson, Cornell's treasurer, Jay Freer and I figured that although we had good balances in all our accounts because of Dom's delayed billing practices, we were probably actually about $56,000 in debt. Unfortunately, Mr. Peterson would be interested not so much in the accounts but in the actual position. Like a miracle, just a few days after this somewhat gloomy picture, a check for $50,000 arrived unexpectedly from the Doherty Foundation. It was sent to ameliorate the apparent fiscal crisis of the previous year, but was just as applicable to the new one. With it, the construction accounts were in balance, or nearly so. All we had to show Mr. Peterson now was that our prospects for continuing to raise some $125,000 a year were still good. He was convinced, and the trustees continued their $125,000 debt authorization (at five percent interest, a high figure for those times). Dominic now could continue with his work crew of 10 or 12 students.

Incidentally, I don't know what would have happened if Cornell ever told Dominic to stop. I doubt he would have done so. He never worried about whether he was going to get paid, at least not until he was really destitute. His attitude always was "Cornell will come through when I need it, and I'm not going to worry about that end of it at all. I'm too busy building. Anyway, we've got to get Appledore ready for the students, whatever Cornell does, don't we?"

Dominic's personal attitude toward students was interesting. He watched the island magic happening in students lives each summer, first on Star Island, later on Appledore, and he got quite wrapped up in it himself. Perhaps from lack of a similar opportunity in his own youth he appreciated more than most people (even some Cornell administrators) exactly what we were able to accomplish with a class and each individual in it. In any event, Dominic participated fully in island life, engaging students in conversations at meals, listening to their concerns and personal problems, and imparting his own brand of practical wisdom into the educational stream of student experience. Not only did Dominic fill the role of the senior father figure on Appledore Island, but for several of the construction years his son, Anthony, then of high-school age, began to learn the construction business as part of Dominic's crew. That sharpened Dominic's perceptions of the special problems of adolescence.

When a class had just left, and the vacuum of its absence was acute, Dominic would always offer the comment, "I think they really enjoyed the course, every one of them." He continued to do this over the years, even after repeated observations on my part that the real aim of a quality educational course was not exactly enjoyment. A good course meant, rather, hard work and intense application. If, at the same time, it turned out to be enjoyable, fine. But that was not the faculty's measure of success with a class. Never mind, it remained Dominic's measure, and he always found our courses successful by his measure.

No one gave more of himself to the Appledore dream than did Dominic. The financial part of his reward was, I am sure, a much smaller motivator than the joy of seeing and participating in what happened to students out at the Shoals.

Fortunately, the Society of Vicarious Shoalers remained faithful, and I never had to try and stop Dominic. It became a truism that, without effort greater than telling our story to those who would listen, cash continued to come in for construction about as fast as we needed it to spend.

Wendy Zomparelli.

Starting up a kitchen and dormitory business was clearly going to add considerably more paper pushing to our office functions, already stretched very thin. Up to now the Shoals courses and construction projects had been managed by a junior professor unrelieved of any of his normal campus load or obligations, and a half-time Jay Freer. It just wasn't enough. Sneaking costs such as photocopying, postal, and stationery through the office of the Section of Genetics, Development, and Physiology was becoming increasingly difficult as these needs increased. We would have to live honestly henceforward and put them on our own accounts. Jay and I decided that all this absolutely dictated the hiring of a full-time office person to hold things together better than we could alone.

Thus came Wendy Zomparelli into the picture. Wendy had recently graduated from Cornell with an English major and Phi Beta Kappa honors. Intuitively we both felt Wendy had the ability, sparkle, character, devotion, enthusiasm, and iconoclasm necessary to true island people, and we hired her (on Shoals funds, not Cornell's or UNH's). We were right, as that first year proved amply. Wendy immediately became as indispensable as the island chef who, as anyone knows, is the most indispensable person on Appledore Island. But Wendy was indispensable year round.

LOBSTERS, LINES, AND THE SUPREME COURT

The business of construction on Appledore Island, by now as nearly routine as such an effort can be, was livened in the spring of 1973 by a sudden lobster war in our midst. It seems that a Maine warden nabbed a New Hampshire lobsterman, took him to a Maine court, and had him fined for fishing in Maine waters illegally. The line between the State of New Hampshire and the State of Maine runs down the Piscataqua River and then out to the Isles of Shoals where it divides Gosport Harbor and the islands about equally. As then shown on marine charts, the legal line ran somewhat southwest of a straight run from the river mouth to the islands. The working fishermen on both sides of the line did not have sufficient time, motivation, or navigational equipment to determine exactly how that imaginary line in the water ran. Instead, they used the practical straight line, determined by eye, from Whaleback Light on shore to White Island Light at the Shoals. This line is even roughly determinable in a fog by a person with a careful ear; both lights sound fog horn signals when visibility is impaired.

This practical situation, which kept lobstermen on both sides of the state line reasonably happy, didn't suit Maine's idea of legality, however, and its heavy-handed solution did not sit well with Governor Meldrim Thomson of New Hampshire. He immediately entered the fray and escalated it into headline news. Governor Thomson stated that the correct line between Maine and New Hampshire would henceforth run due east, parallel to New Hampshire's southern boundary with Massachusetts. This would put all the Isles of Shoals well within New Hampshire territory, and a good deal of additional lobster bottom as well. Instead of converging near shore, the effect of New Hampshire's new lines as described by the governor would be to open New Hampshire's sea territory all the way out to the two-hundred mile fishery zone limit then being established.

It turned out that the line between New Hampshire and Maine was initially established in 1622 in the charter of the Plymouth Company as follows: ". . .to crosse over Lande from Piscataway Harbor (Portsmouth) through Newichewanocke River (Salmon River) and also the North halfe of the Isles of Sholes. . ." This designation had been refined, but changed little, in resolutions of 1737 and 1829. Governor Thomson had initiated the first major change in three-and-a-half centuries.

We soon learned that the court of initial resort when states dispute their boundaries is the U.S. Supreme Court. Obviously, it is the court of last resort as well.

This almost farcical situation did, in due course of judicial time and effort, indeed result in a ruling from the Supreme Court that defined the line ever more closely but changed it little from the general description of 1622. The principal effect was to lay it out in straight segments that would be easier for fishermen and fish wardens to locate in a practical way. Maine actually gained some good lobster grounds at the expense of New Hampshire when all this had run its course.

While the Supreme Court had the matter under advisement, I wondered mildly whether our Maine licenses and permits would suddenly become void. But we continued to act as though we were in Maine, and in Maine the Supreme Court eventually left us.

WHAT DOESN'T GO IN CAN'T COME OUT

One of the Maine licenses that had to be won (the word is used advisedly) about then was a permit to dump treated sewage into the ocean. Maine law required generally that sewage was to be treated and the effluent discharged into a leaching bed. This law envisaged that fresh water would be used in creating the sewage. Appledore toilets, on the contrary, were to be flushed with seawater to conserve the island's limited freshwater, and soil for a leaching bed of the size needed on the island was nearly non-existent. Further, it made no sense to put a brackish effluent (saline toilet water mixed with fresh kitchen and shower water) into a limited amount of soil that also had to provide our drinking water. Would the State of Maine be broadminded enough to deal satisfactorily with this reality?

For some years I had served as a biological consultant for the Onondaga Lake cleanup project at Syracuse, New York, which student Philip Sze had made the subject of his doctoral thesis. The primary contractors were O'Brien and Gere, a respected firm of what are now called environmental engineers. With that relationship, Phil and I sought advice and design drawings from O'Brien and Gere. They developed a proposal that we handle Appledore Island sewage as follows. It would be collected in a large digesting tank, where sediments would drop to the bottom and anaerobic digestion would take place ("primary treatment" in the language of the sanitary engineer). From there it would be pumped with air into another large holding tank. Finally, it would be introduced at a carefully controlled rate into one end of a newly invented device called a biodisk. This consisted of a cylinder cut in half lengthwise and laid on its side to constitute a trough, with an axle running its length. Mounted on the axle were numerous closely spaced corrugated wheel-like fiberglass discs that rotated slowly in the cylindrical trough. The plan was that the sewage would enter the upper end of the trough at a controlled rate, and pass slowly down its

The biodisks.

length as the turning disks rotated through it. Digesting microorganisms would soon establish themselves richly on the corrugated surfaces of the disks and the sewage would receive final and thorough aerobic digestion (secondary and partial tertiary treatment) through the action of these populations of microorganisms. It would then be suitable for discharge back into the ocean with all organics fully digested and oxygen demand satisfied.

I travelled to Augusta, Maine, to present this plan to state officials. Starting at the bottom, with a proposal at the cutting edge of sewage technology, I was bucked upward through the regulatory layers until eventually I reached the chief sewage licensing officer. He reviewed my plans and arguments and after some further discussion seemed ready to issue us a permit to do as proposed. Suddenly a real problem arose.

"I don't see a chlorination chamber in your outfall line."

"We don't propose to chlorinate the effluent. I have read several recent scientific papers that show chlorinated effluent is seriously harmful to marine organisms at the point of discharge."

"State law requires chlorination."

"Why does state law require chlorination?"

"To kill any pathogenic organisms in the effluent and protect the public health."

"Where are pathogenic organisms going to come from in the effluent?"

"Why from the human population producing it, of course."

"What pathogenic organisms will be produced by a small number of college students whose health is among the most carefully monitored of any class of citizens in this country? If we don't put pathogenic organisms into the system, they can't come out of it, can they? Besides, seawater itself is lethal to most intestinal pathogens."

The official was on the horns of a dilemma. My arguments were sound (this was before much was known about marine viruses), and he would be pretty picky to insist on the letter of a law that appeared unreasonable in the particular circumstances. Clearly, with the biodisks we were on the cutting edge of investigating how to treat saltwater sewage responsibly, a problem that his office would undoubtedly face more seriously in the future as sewage systems for offshore islands were required to upgrade. It was to the state's benefit to cooperate.

In the end the state official undertook a typically Maine-type conversation which, while admitting nothing and staying within the letter of the law, let me understand clearly that if we didn't bring up the matter of chlorination when his inspectors made the periodic island inspections required of them, neither would they. I departed his office with the necessary discharge license in hand and took it to Kittery for endorsement, which precipitated the interactions with the town assessor and the building inspector that were described at the beginning of this book. So the situation continued for many years. The inspectors came regularly but never mentioned chlorination, nor did we.

Unfortunately, the two biodisks never worked out well. It took too long to establish a functioning population of digesting microorganisms on them at the start of the season, and they were too sensitive to biological upset when someone spilled a bottle of concentrated cleaning solution down the kitchen drain or the like. But they made a good argument for the licensers and soon resulted in a Ph.D. thesis for Shoals student Nancy Kinner, now a professor at UNH, which started her on that professional career.

Even when the biodisks failed us, our sewage was not a significant biological or health problem. The outfall area was monitered in the annual class transect study of intertidal organisms and showed no enrichment or depauperation of species compared with the rest of the island. Coliform bacteria, indicators of sewage contamination, were undetectable more than a few feet from the discharge end of the pipe when we made those tests. The real problem was the odor of biodisks with a digestive upset.

INVITE WHICH GOVERNOR?

The University of New Hampshire administration was becoming increasingly aware of happenings at the Shoals and their possible utility in the politics of that state. In May I received a letter from Vice Provost Robert N. Faiman. The following is excerpted (somewhat paraphrased for brevity) from my response to it.

"I was pleased to provide information on the history of the boundary line between the states, that it was useful to you in responding to a request for information from the governor's office, and that it was well received there.

"You suggested inviting the governor to official opening ceremonies in August. Frankly, the idea of opening ceremonies had not crossed my mind, much less the inviting of distinguished guests. Right now we know we will have 40 students arriving on August 1, together with faculty, staff, and the construction workers already here. Right now, also, we have no kitchen, no dining room, no laboratory, no fresh water system, no salt water system, no sewerage system, and only about two-thirds the number of dormitory rooms we need. Just opening is occupying me fully.

"When the first class appeared at Louis Agassiz's new marine laboratory on Penikese Island in Buzzards Bay exactly one hundred years ago this summer, carpenters were still working on the building to house them. Yet the event proved worthy of ceremony and public record, which it received amply, for it is to that event that the Marine Biological Laboratory at Woods Hole traces its origins. (The distinguished Dr. Agassiz stalled the entering class on the dock by lecturing to them there for more than an hour after they got off the boat while frantic finishing was going on.)

"Perhaps personal notice by the governor of the State of New Hampshire and other state officials might prove equally salutary for the Shoals Lab, providing of course some of the unfinished things get done by the time of an official dedication and current entropy yields to appropriate order. I am willing to consider an appropriate ceremonial occasion for August 18 or 19. But there is another problem.

"Although the governor is trying to annex all the Isles of Shoals into New Hampshire, Appledore remains in Maine in the eyes of the rest of the world. If we were to have dedicatory ceremonies, would not failure to invite Maine's Governor Curtis and state officials (to say nothing of Kittery officials) be a major faux pas? And considering another source of funds that has meant much to us, what about the proprieties of a similar invitation to New York officialdom?

"Fortunately, except for help in building the R/V *Scomber,* the Shoals Lab has had no federal support so we have no obligations in that direction. We did have a dedication for the *Scomber,* but still-vivid memories of that event lead me to wonder whether we ought attempt another. Perhaps it would be better to let the Shoals Laboratory simply slip quietly into being, trusting to its work to earn it whatever recognition it may come to merit."

Fortunately, as will become clear, we had no opening ceremonies.

I do still have some sharp memories indeed of that first class arriving on Appledore Island eighteen years ago, but memories fade with time. Perhaps the best way to convey the reality of those hectic weeks is to abstract from a description penned for the Shoals Lab newsletter soon after that first class had left Appledore.

IT WAS THE BEST OF TIMES; IT WAS THE WORST OF TIMES

"It was the best of times, it was the worst of times." That bit of Dickens has been running through my head as I report to you, faithful reader, how the summer went. Never again will our facilities be as unready for occupancy as they were on August 1, 1973. Yet never in the eight-year history of the program have we had, in my opinion, a better academic experience. Ask any of the faculty or students.

"Prior to opening, the largest human population fed and housed on Appledore Island had not exceeded 30. On August 1, the expected population was suddenly to increase to about 80 (42 students, some dozen faculty, ten staff, and about 15 construction workers). We expected that Dominic Gratta would not get done all he had promised to accomplish by August 1 so we had fall-back positions for many but not all systems. Dominic had, in fact, moved forward on almost all fronts, with the consequence that many necessary facilities were *almost* ready—but not actually functioning. It is an awesome responsibility to find oneself (even with help) faced with the realities of housing, feeding, and taking care of the medical and academic needs of a population of eighty on a remote island. A small difficulty multiplied by eighty has a way of becoming a large difficulty.

"And we had a lot of just plain bad luck. The Whaler was out of service—our gamble that we could get one more season out of the outboard engine proved a mistake. The *Scomber* was temporarily out of service, the result of a belligerent encounter with a wooden lobster pot buoy that bent the skeg and blade. The backhoe was out of service—the oil heat exchanger in the radiator had begun exchanging hydraulic oil directly with the radiator water instead of just the heat. Without the backhoe, moving 55-gallon drums of fuel oil for the generators was particularly cumbersome. The radio in the

Wrack was transmitting only intermittently, giving forth silence more often than signals when information transfer was most urgently needed. Both generators were giving us problems. It was rare that all of our complicated machinery was functional at the same time, but it was equally rare to have this much out of service at once—at the worst possible time of the summer.

"On August 1, despite Dominic's promises, the kitchen was not ready. Briefly, there was no stove, no oven, no dishwasher, no water, no walk-in refrigerator, and no sewage system in the new Kiggins Commons. The long-ordered dining room tables came just the day before the class did; the chairs, equally long-ordered, didn't appear until after the class had left. The island population sat at table in the dining room (on unfinished subflooring) on staging planks laid across milk crates. The washrooms were not ready. We had only four functional toilets on the island, none near where most of the people lived. Because the Kiggins Commons kitchen was not ready, the temporary kitchen in the Coast Guard building had not been disassembled; hence we did not have all the faculty housing we had counted on and assigned. Some bedrooms in the Operations Building (Hewitt Hall) still lacked doors, but we borrowed drapes from Star Island to cover this contingency. A few rooms lacked glass in the windows from a small error in dynamiting a few days before the class arrived.

The newsletter account quoted here failed to describe the housing situation fully. Knowing well in advance that by themselves the beds we could crowd into the rooms in the Operations Building were fewer than the 42 needed, we had scanned the surplus lists assiduously and been rewarded by obtaining two 12-person military tents. One of these had been erected on a platform that Dominic built in the waist of Appledore Island near the foundation of the old Appledore House hotel. Before the class arrived I worried about the potential consequences of having two distinctly different kinds of housing for the students. Students react negatively to either coercion or arbitrary decisions. How could I get anyone voluntarily to choose to live in the tent when bedrooms with doors and windows were available?

Actually it was easy. Before asking the new students to choose, I described the alternatives in some detail, emphasizing the advantages of a brand new tent and noting the holes in walls, ceilings, and even some floors in the Operations Building. In the end, the problem turned out to be getting enough students to choose Operations over the tent after my sales pitch.

Experience soon showed that the tent had two major disadvantages: active muskrats under the floorboards at night, and little red biting ants at all times. The latter were controlled on the beds (more or less) by placing the bed legs in cans of water.

The first tent.

Returning to the newsletter description: "The projected seawater system for the laboratory sea tables and for flushing toilets was still rudimentary. Since we didn't actually have toilets to flush, we didn't miss it for that purpose, nor did we miss the absence of an island sewage system, for the same reason. The existing four toilets in the Coast Guard building and Grass Foundation Lab were on independent septic systems. We also had the outhouse, Gift-from-the-Sea, which remained faithfully functional throughout

"But when the institutional stove from the Marshall House salvage was placed in the Kiggins Commons kitchen soon after the class arrived, and water appeared in the fixtures there nearly simultaneously, and sinks were installed for washing dishes, the missing sewage system became more of a problem. What goes in has to come out—more or less immediately. More on that later.

"Laighton House sported new doors and a new laboratory bench (finished about two days before the class arrived) capable of seating 42 students. That marked the first time in our history when each student could have his own laboratory station throughout the entire program, and it

Building Kiggins Commons: The laminated beams were barged out to the islands, carried to the site by the backhoe, fastened into galvanized shoes on the subflooring in the dining room, and erected by means of scaffolding and a block-and-tackle.

The galvanized shoes were tied down by means of steel rods through the cement blocks below, cemented into holes in the granite rock beneath. This basic technique was used on all new buildings to prevent roofs from lifting in storm winds. Below: The finished building (before the porch was enlarged).

represented a great advance. Electric fixtures had been installed so that all microscope lights worked, but some of the wiring, though safe, was temporary. The library contained some 350 books, spacious work tables, and the only armchair on the entire island. We had routed out and found most of the stored scientific gear that had been shuffled from corner to corner during various phases of construction. We had also worked out adequate provision for "running" seawater for the sea table—the students were to run down to the shore with jerry cans as sea water was needed.

"Heat and smoke detectors had been placed in sleeping areas, fire extinguishers checked, fire ladders reexamined, and the inspector from Cornell's Safety Division gave us the green light.

"But other things beyond our control were happening on the mainland. Diesel oil was nationally in short supply. (This was 1973, the summer of the oil crisis and of long lines at filling stations.) One of our two suppliers was out for a full week, the other for several days just before August 1, and we could see the definite possibility of having no oil, and hence no electricity, on opening. No electricity means, among other things, no water except what can be hand pumped, and no refrigeration. But oil started flowing again just before the class came.

"August 1 was a difficult day. The main generator (60-kilowatt Old Oscar) refused to start that morning (he was regularly shut down at night to save fuel). He started as soon as a stuck fuel solenoid was diagnosed and freed. Then the early morning radio reported a cyclonic disturbance developing unexpectedly off Nantucket, and storm signals had been hoisted. Therefore the ferry wouldn't bring the students out at the expected time. Perhaps they could be brought out later in the day. Rain, fog. *Wrack's* radio wouldn't work right. The CB radio was impossible with storm static. Luggage going awry on shore. Students scattered throughout Portsmouth. But they finally arrived, all 42, with most of their luggage, just before sundown. The valiant kitchen crew fed them from the "temporary" three-burner stove in the Coast Guard building. And the dishes got washed. And the students found the Operations Building or the tent in the dark. And they got reconnected with their luggage—most of it.

"That was Wednesday. Thursday morning, Old Oscar started with a will. Breakfast appeared. So did more fog and rain. The academic day started well, but the kitchen became more of a disaster area. At that time we had exactly two refrigerators, one vintage GE cast off from Star Island (remember the kind with the compressor out in the open on top?), and one small institutional machine scrounged from somewhere. At best, food supply on an island is a considerable problem, especially when you have no prior experience of how much people are going to eat, and snacks are not available

Above: Gill-netter Diane Holley *at dock.*
Below: The daily menu was chalked on a bit of blackboard.

in a store around the corner. Add to the problem of already-inadequate refrigerator space the fact that the institutional refrigerator (the larger of the two) quit on Thursday. This meant that meat had to be bought hand to mouth, for it could not be stored. The week of August 1 was the week of greatest stress nationally, all summer, in the meat-supply situation, which was then tenuous because of the oil shortage. Our supplier told us not to count on his being able to get us much of anything in the meat line, much less on any particular time schedule. What to do? Nightmare: eighty hungry mouths opening like young gulls' to be fed.

"The obvious thing to do was to live off the sea. I am proud to say that our fishermen friends responded superbly to our crisis. In the next few weeks they supplied us with many hundred pounds of mackerel, dabs, sole, cod, squid, an occasional haddock, lobsters, clams, and some more-exotic species. Not only did we get these fresh off the draggers, purse seiners, gill-netters, and right out of the lobster cars, but in nearly all cases the fishermen refused to take our money in payment. In effect, these boats and their crews made contributions worth several hundred dollars to our program. We were pleased to invite them to join us at table, and several did. This extended the marine biology conversation down to a very practical, one could almost say salty, level.

"Consider the difficulties enumerated above. Then consider that I heard not one complaint from students or faculty about food throughout the four weeks of the course. Consider further that left-overs were completely utilized (nothing was thrown out), no gastrointestinal problems occurred during the month, and menus were not repeated once. Food costs were kept within budget. We owe this remarkable achievement to the heroic efforts of our first kitchen crew: Stu Feigenbaum, our head chef, who bore the responsibility for food ordering and meal preparation and was a student in Cornell's hotel school; Rob Morris, a graduate student in food science at Cornell who cooked gourmet meals for the construction crew prior to the class arrival and who stayed on to help with the initial kitchen crisis; and Carolyn Arnold, a nutrition major in the Cornell College of Human Ecology who was our assistant chef.

"Another miracle was achieved by our housekeeper and registered nurse, Marcy Sheehan, in keeping the four bathrooms and general areas immaculately clean despite the intensity of use, and who coped with the problems of changing bed linen once in a while even though there were not enough sheets to satisfy the beds and the laundry simultaneously. She also skillfully dealt with lacerations, sprains, and poison ivy, which seemed to cause more trouble than usual this year.

Chef Stu Feigenbaum in his new functional kitchen in Kiggins Commons.

"We owe thanks to the several students who did chores in the kitchen or housekeeping departments in return for a small remission in charges we were able to afford, and to the many more students who pitched in for free when they saw something needing doing. Thanks also to Ron Harelstad for holding his end of the operations (boats, waterfront safety, and machinery) together under considerable difficulty. And to Jay Freer and Wendy Zomparelli for keeping office and other things together both on Appledore Island and at Cornell in my often disorganized wake. And to Dominic Gratta for being Dom, and to the faculty who put up with much, and to the assistants who put up with more.

"But enough of that. We survived and prospered. With time, facilities appeared and systems became increasingly functional. The main well tested safe. The partial sewage system accepted effluent. Boats and machinery got repaired and went back into duty. The walk-in cooler got cold. The mainland field trip went like clockwork. Volleyball games were as spirited as the questions after lectures. One student was heard to remark, subtly, that succeeding classes would never have it as good because conditions would be better."

In almost two decades since writing the above, I have thought repeatedly about the philosophical truth that stands behind it. We must take care that island life never abstracts itself so far from the fundamentals that islanders lose sight of them, for in that relationship is one of the largest lessons we can teach or students can learn on our small refuge from the mainland. Consider the following event: One sunny day, purse seiner Norm Brackett found a school of mackerel inside Gosport Harbor and deployed his sein boat and its net to round them up. I gathered a Whaler-load of students and we went into the harbor for a close look at this kind of fishing. When the fish were all aboard, I asked Norm if I could buy enough for the class for supper. He scooped up a crate-full of mackerel for us but refused payment. The mackerel went immediately into the kitchen where the students cleaned them for the chef. I then got a plankton net and we went back to the spot where the fish were caught to take a water sample. Returning to the laboratory with that, the students examined under the microscope the planktonic organisms on which the mackerel had been feeding. At day's end, the students ate the mackerel. An experience like this demonstrates vividly what a food chain is all about, and those students will remember that lesson in fundamentals the rest of their lives.

What was the "small dynamiting error" that left the south side of the Operations Building with missing glass? In order to get the main sewage line down the hill more or less at a constant slope, Dominic had to blast a channel through an intervening ledge of island granite bedrock. He drilled

*Above: Norm Brackett aboard his seine boat; the purse boat beyond.
Below: Dynamiting.*

the holes, six as I remember. He then stuck a fused stick of dynamite in each, tamped them down with some mud, gathered the wires, and attached them to the firing box. He cleared the area of people and stroked the plunger down. All six sticks fired—straight up out of the holes as from rifle bores and into the air. The rock was unmoved. Dominic muttered, "That's hard rock."

Dominic tried again, this time with two sticks per hole, tamped down well with mud tamped tightly on top to fill the holes. He covered the area with a few old horsehair mattresses. Again the dynamite shot to the skies taking some mattress contents with it.

"Damn! I'll get it this time," said Dominic. Third try: again he put two sticks down each well-worn hole, tamped them intensely, and then filled each hole to the top with "Por-rok," a quick-setting cement. At his request while the cement was setting, we rounded up all the remaining old horsehair mattresses that had originally been scrounged from Star Island when we first set up housekeeping on Appledore Island; they now were superseded in use by better ones salvaged from Cornell dormitories. Dominic piled a score of horsehair mattresses several deep over the entire blasting site. He erected a small sandbag redoubt behind which to crouch as he shoved the plunger home, and cleared the entire area of people. He particularly made sure everyone was out of Operations and Kiggins, just in case.

This time it worked! Rock and mattresses went sky high. A few of the windows on the near side of Operations also fractured. Windows are easily reglazed, but for the rest of the summer, and for some years after, we found ourselves picking horsehair out of the wild cherry bushes along the paths throughout the center of Appledore Island.

Now the sewage pipe could be installed. Dominic would not have called this situation a dynamiting error as I have done. It was, in his mind, an achievement well worth a few windows and mattresses.

MRS. JEFFERSON PATTERSON

The need for a good set of mainland clothes on Appledore Island had been indelibly impressed on me in an earlier year, but I was still scarcely prepared for a letter that came during the height of our construction season in 1973. A formal note appeared in the mail from Mrs. Jefferson Patterson, whom I knew not at all. I soon learned from Rachel Gratta (who knows all such things) that Mrs. Patterson was a Goodrich (of the rubber company) and that Mr. Patterson had retired some years earlier from the U.S. State Department, where his career had included several major ambassadorial appointments. The Pattersons owned a magnificent estate just inshore on the York River at York Harbor, Maine. Mrs. Patterson had invited me there to an evening gathering that would commence with cocktails in the White Garden. Duty (and curiosity) propelled me to accept. Two things stood firmly in the way. First, the matter of clothes. Second, the matter of getting there. Here's what I did.

From the beginning the Shoals project had needed several small vehicles on Appledore Island. The least expensive vehicles we could obtain were Chevrolet carryalls, always dull green, that belonged to the College of Agriculture at Cornell. These became available when they were sufficiently rusted through or otherwise no longer capable of passing the New York State vehicle examination. They had high wheelbases and a very low "crawler" gear, and were eminently suited to the rigors of Appledore Island, where they rarely got out of first gear. We could obtain them for $50 each and had moved one to Appledore early on. We bought a second almost immediately. Vehicle examinations in Maine differed significantly at that time from the New York examinations. Our second $50 carryall passed the Maine inspection when it got there, and it became the project's shore vehicle. It would go out to Appledore Island when it could no longer pass the Maine inspection.

The dented, rusted, and sunburned carryall on shore was the only vehicle available for me to drive to the Patterson's at the time the invitation came. But in no way could I arrive among the Lincolns and Cadillacs in that derelict. Moreover, based on recent experience, the chances were that I would have to do some fiddling with battery connections and the distributor before it would start after sitting in Frisbee's parking lot for a week or so. That kind of activity didn't bode well for clothes otherwise suitable for hobnobbing with the ambassadorial crowd.

Just assembling reasonable attire for the evening was a formidable challenge. Time was too brief to get ashore and rent tie and tails, if they were required, and I had no idea whether they were. The island crew sympathized with my concerns, but urged me strongly to do what I could to go. The islanders pledged their full support.

I placed a radiotelephone call to Mrs. Patterson from the island. The conversation was, of course, broadcast up and down the New England coast. Anyone with a marine radio could listen in, and many made it a practice to do so when they had nothing better to do. I knew that, but I don't think Mrs. Patterson ever realized it. Eventually the connection through the marine operator was made.

"I have your kind invitation and am extremely flattered to have been invited, but I really don't think I can accept. Over."

"Oh dear, I was counting on you. There will be several others here whom you ought to meet."

"You know, out here at the Shoals it is pretty difficult to dress properly for such an occasion. Over."

"But it won't be formal, particularly if that is difficult for you."

"I'm afraid sports clothes is the highest level attainable out here right now. Over."

"Oh. But you could wear a blazer and a tie?"

"Yes, I think I could manage that. Over."

"Splendid. I'll expect you around 7:00. We are gathering in the White Garden.

"Would it be all right if I came in by boat to your estate? Over."

"I don't think anyone has ever done that, but I don't see why not. We have a dock on the river not far above the second bridge. Just tie up at the dock and walk up across the lawn. The White Garden will be on your left as you approach."

So it was settled and the die was cast for better or worse. The entire island—construction crew, staff, volunteers—rallied to the cause. A brand new white shirt that fit appeared. So did some shoe polish and a travel iron to put a proper crease in my pants (if it didn't kill the generator). Among his collection Ron Harelstad found a tie sufficiently subdued to go with the rest of the outfit.

But another problem immediately arose. I had planned to go in with the *Wrack*, which would keep me reasonably dry and presentable. Dominic Gratta, who lives in York Harbor, said, "You can't use the *Wrack* for that. The bridges are too close to the water and the *Wrack* won't go under either of them, even at low tide. You'll have to take the *Scomber*."

The *Scomber* is an open launch. I left Appledore Island plenty early just in case I had figured course or current wrong. There was a moderate chop. Otherwise the weather was clear and finding my way to the entrance of York Harbor was no problem at all. The chop was a bit of a problem because it set up spray that blew back across the boat and threatened to wet down my hard-won sartorial excellence. To prevent that, I donned the bright yellow oilskins I had brought along. Although the strong currents of the York River were against the boat I followed the buoys around the two right-angle turns and arrived in the harbor at the river mouth nearly at low tide. This gave plenty of clearance for the *Scomber* under both upriver bridges. Eventually, at about dusk, I recognized the immense house from the rear that I had only glimpsed before from the front while driving along Route 1 to York. It loomed at the crest of a vast spreading green lawn, like the approach to an antebellum southern plantation. I had removed the oilskins on entering the harbor. After locating the small dock, I tied the *Scomber* to it, stepped ashore, and began to climb up to the house.

Not exactly sure just what the White Garden was, I proceeded slowly, listening for the sound of cocktails. That was soon audible, and I passed through a hedge into a garden in which all the blooms were white. There assembled were the guests who had already arrived. My own arrival was moderately dramatic, as some had watched me cross the lawn, and I found no conversational vacuum in the ensuing hours.

After cocktails we assembled in an immense Victorian dining room around a long manorial table with Mrs. Patterson at one end and the ambassador at the other. Each place setting displayed an impressive array of carefully placed silverware, china, and crystal in varying sizes and shapes. I followed my neighbor, who seemed to know, in choosing which utensil to use for each event. The dinner advanced through seven courses, with wines and toasts to match. Fortunately, no toast was expected of me, and I did recognize the finger bowl for what it was when that stage arrived. Altogether, it was a delightful evening for me and apparently adequate from Mrs. Patterson's point of view, for it was the first of several I spent at that magnificent estate by her invitation in following years.

Getting back to Appledore Island that night was another matter. The tide had risen and the Patterson dock itself was slightly under water when I left the house in complete darkness. I had a flashlight with me in the boat, but not at the dinner. The darkness was both an advantage and a disadvantage. I walked right into the water, polished shoes and all, before I saw it, but nobody saw me do it. Soggy-footed, I attained the boat, found the flashlight, started the engine, turned on the running lights, cast off, and started down the river with the current.

The York River is not meant for serious boating and is neither lit nor buoyed well. At night in a rapid current finding one's way out is a lot more difficult than coming upriver against the current in daylight. The first problem was staying in deep water. I didn't worry much about that because at high tide, the water was deep enough nearly everywhere. The second was spotting the bridges, and then getting under them. The upriver bridge was so close to the water surface at high tide that I could get through only by climbing back and forth in the boat, depressing first the bow and then the stern to clear it girder by girder. It must have been just after dead high tide of a spring series. Finally I glided into the harbor and looked for the buoyed passage that would take me round the sharp turns and safely out to sea. Everything was fine until part way out I hit a fog bank and solid obscurity. I could have maintained a course by compass easily enough, but the current was racing in the outer harbor and the area is peppered with lobster pot buoys. These were totally invisible in the combination of dark and fog.

Above: First class on Star Island, 1966.
Below: First class on Appledore Island, 1973 (front steps of Laighton House).

Discretion seemed called for, and despite my strong desire back to get back to the island, out of my good clothes, and into my own bed, I turned around, went back into York Harbor and tied up at the town dock.

The night was immensely cold with the fog and a penetrating breeze across the water. I took off my wet shoes, put on my oilskins again for warmth, curled up in some of the life preservers forward under the canvas dodger, piled more of them on top, and went to sleep. It seemed only moments later that I was awakened by a barking dog that objected to the presence of the boat at the town dock, followed immediately by the first of the several early-rising lobstermen who put out from moorings in that vicinity. It was still hardly light, but the fog had lifted. I roused my aching bones, beat a little life into my extremities, started the engine, and headed out. This time I made it uneventfully.

These few vignettes do not fully cover the reality of 1973, but they may give the reader a general picture of what life on Appledore Island was like then. Our major objective had been to house and instruct a class with the usual level of success. We achieved, in fact, excellent results. The numerous problems of island life receded into perspective in the context of that paramount reality.

The students who lived in the ramshackle Operations Building rose to the occasion by naming it after one of their instructors, Professor Hewitt. They erected an illuminated sign reading "Hewitt Hall" over the front door. That informal name has stuck to this day.

Those who attended the autumn annual meeting back in Ithaca learned that the 1973 teaching budget had remained in the black despite the earlier fiscal unknowns attendant on joining the Durham faculty with the Shoals faculty and those arising from the new dining and housing operations. Actually, the move to Appledore Island made it easier to keep the teaching budget in the black because we now had total freedom, within reason, to allocate as we wished the costs of shared facilities to construction or to teaching accounts. Who could tell exactly how much of the kitchen costs ought to be met by students and how much by the construction budget, or of the operating costs of the *Wrack*, which brought the food out while also carrying construction supplies, or of the office that attended to both functions? SUNY had come through with its annual $15,000 for the fourth time. Wabash College had joined Union in bringing a small class to our facilities at the end of the season, again both successfully.

Construction spending had been heavy. As near as Jay could tell, we ended the summer owing Dominic some $145,000 in unpresented bills. In consequence, despite what we owed some of our accounts had substantial balances, and none was in the red. Kiggins Commons was operating, though

The new roadway was continued from Kiggins Commons to the Coast Guard Building. Old steam radiators from the latter and other debris provided much-needed fill for climbing the steep ledge between.

still largely unfinished inside. Most of the major island utility systems were working successfully, though jury-rigged in some details that would have to be corrected. We had banked the substantial gift from the Palmers toward the construction of the new teaching laboratory until Dominic was ready to start on that project. Those present at the annual meeting were well pleased with all this, given the potential for disaster that existed at the beginning of the year, and they enthusiastically voted to offer *Introduction to Marine Science* twice in 1974, once at the beginning of the summer and again at the end, thereby doubling the number of students we would teach in 1974.

Little did those academic people gathered in Ithaca know that a potential disaster of a far greater magnitude than anything to date would strike the Shoals without warning just as 1973 ended.

Chapter Eleven

ARISTOTLE SOCRATES ONASSIS
1973-1974

BOMBSHELL

In November 1973, just after the Shoals annual meeting, Mr. Aristotle Socrates Onassis announced to the world that, as soon as it could be done, he would create in Durham, New Hampshire, the largest oil refinery ever built at one time anywhere in the world and would supply it from a supertanker terminal to be constructed at the Isles of Shoals.

Perhaps the squabble over the location of the state line and the long lines at gasoline filling stations in the summer of 1973 should have been premonitions. For the insular and innocent people of the Shoals, they weren't. The Onassis announcement hit without warning so far as we were concerned and with the force of an avalanche. It brought planning for further construction on Appledore Island instantly to a halt and endangered the summer program already announced for 1974. Overnight, fighting the Onassis proposal became the paramount order of business for the Shoals Lab, and for me it took precedence over all other activity except the obligatory meeting of classes in Ithaca.

Again, I resort to the immediacy of language composed during and just after the refinery battle to capture and convey the immense reality of what happened. The following is largely excerpted from *Oil and Water, The New Hampshire Story*, published by the Shoals Marine Laboratory in 1975.

OVERVIEW

Aristotle Socrates Onassis (doing business as Olympic Refineries) had quietly obtained firm purchase options on nearly one-fourth of the town of Durham, New Hampshire, from September through November 1973. On November 27 from Governor Meldrim Thomson's office in Concord, Olympic spokesmen announced their intention to build in Durham the largest oil refinery ever started from scratch anywhere in the world. They said their refinery would receive crude oil from supertankers at a deepwater terminal just offshore, and most of the refined oil would be taken away by smaller tankers. Furious activity, pro and con, immediately commandeered the full attention of the seacoast residents and the occasional attention of the rest of the country for the next several months.

Vignettes of embattled Victorian sisters in a colonial family homestead astride the route of the proposed pipeline jostled with images of realtors bearing gifts. Homespun (and then emotional) accents defending home rule responded to wooing (and then emotional) accents from Georgia, Texas, and farther afield. Local names elbowed Olympic's group, U.S. Energy Czar Simon, and King Faisal for attention on newspaper displays. Rough hands of a fisherman clenched in protest contrasted with smooth hands shaking hands in Olympic's hospitality suite. Mr. Onassis's opinion—"Its a free world, I do what I like"—was faced down by the New Hampshire state motto displayed on every license plate, "Live free or die." These are rich images indeed. Each one in its own way is a measure of what happened.

In the end, Olympic presented its detailed plans to the people of the town of Durham at two much-postponed public meetings held on February 27 and March 3, 1974. On March 6, the townspeople voted nine to one against siting a refinery in Durham. The state legislature, meeting simultaneously, voted a day later not to override Durham's decision. To have reached such a firm conclusion of such regional—even national—importance, in so short a time by so ancient a method, warrants a close look. The speed with which this proposal surfaced, the emotion on both sides, the vigor of attack and defense, the depth of public involvement, the weight of money and political ambition, and the overwhelming magnitude of the proposal made the swiftness and decisiveness of this outcome truly remarkable.

If nothing else, Olympic's efforts accomplished two things normally very difficult to achieve in New England. They got the townspeople out to town meeting in unprecedented numbers, and they brought forth a vote as nearly unanimous as ever happens. That the vote was contrary to Olympic's wishes detracts in no way from the magnitude of this accomplishment.

A tiny Olympic tanker of the kind serving Portsmouth in 1974.

Here is a case study in which the issues were clearly drawn and sharply in focus. The true conclusions to be drawn from such a study, however, are not exactly those that appeared in the national press at the time.

The Shoals Marine Laboratory was involved from the beginning, whether we wished it to be or not, by Olympic's plan to build a deepwater terminal next to Appledore's shores. I would not see the Appledore dream sunk without a fight, and a good fight we Shoalers had!

GENERAL BACKGROUND

The coastline is finite. Population is not. Human demands for energy and other consumable resources increase even faster than does the population. Mankind must exercise wisdom to resolve the inevitable conflicts. Wisdom develops from understanding. The biological and geological complexity of the coastal zone and continental shelf are poorly understood. Much greater knowledge of these areas is urgently needed before genuinely wise social and economic decisions can be made. Political and regulatory mechanisms can stand some improvement, too, before knowledge is applied to human betterment with full effectiveness.

New England needed large amounts of oil when Onassis appeared on the scene, and the entire region had no refinery. All oil was imported. A major New England refinery would reduce the dependence of this part of the country on other regions and on the vagaries of federal policy for its energy needs.

Supertankers can't get into American ports. Except in Maine, ports generally have depths of 50 feet or less. Supertankers require up to one hundred feet. Given the clear economic advantages of moving oil in large volumes, the question is not will there be supertankers, but where will they land? Any location capable of taking them near land is an obvious target for development as a supertanker terminal.

We of the Shoals Lab are in the education business. To us it seems self-evident that knowledge of the coastal zone and continental shelf will develop from research into their complexities. Research is a peculiarly human endeavor. The quality of work depends largely on the abilities of those who do it and also on pure luck. Those of my generation who are currently wearing the term "oceanographer" or "marine biologist" are almost always retreaded somethings else, for when we went to graduate school oceanography and marine biology were not recognized graduate fields except in a very few forward-looking institutions. Now those specializations exist. Most marine stations concentrate on research at the graduate level. Certainly the need for information generated at these stations is enormous; but we should not neglect the undergraduates, for they are the seeds from which the rest grows. The Shoals Marine Laboratory was conceived on, has developed from, and remains committed to the idea of providing the best possible field and academic experience in marine sciences for undergraduates. Nationally, the Shoals Lab is one of very few institutions dedicated to this objective.

A primary, perhaps overriding justification for building such a facility on a difficult offshore island was its freedom from coastal pollution. Unfortunately, no oil company can yet guarantee absence of pollution at points of oil transfer. The technology does not yet exist to permit such a guarantee and oil companies have not developed methods to eliminate the possibility of human error in handling oil. Some forms of oil are devastating to marine life, even in very low concentrations.

Special irony existed, then, in Olympic's proposal to build an oil refinery at Durham Point with a pipeline to a supertanker terminal at the Shoals. Possibly nowhere else in the world could such a proposal threaten the work of two important marine facilities (the Shoals Lab and the University of New Hampshire's Jackson Estuarine Laboratory on Adams Point). From our vantage, American energy needs and the sheer weight of ready investment capital in 1973-4 seemed to talk so loudly against a background of ignorance, and the emotion of concerned response was so great, that the quieter voice of wisdom was likely to be swamped entirely.

With the Shoals Lab just barely born and with construction and other birth pains still paramount, we did not wish to become involved in an emotional response to terminal proposals. We did not wish to challenge the necessity of additional refinery capacity for New England or the need for additional unloading facilities for the United States. We did not have the expertise to know what the real needs were. On the other hand, we did believe firmly that the growing Shoals Marine Laboratory represented a distinct asset to New Hampshire and New England, an asset that had the potential for development into one of national significance. We were and still are prepared to defend the thesis that better-informed people will make better judgments as decisions involving the coastal zone become increasingly pressing and complex. Our primary mission is to educate both directly in the classroom and indirectly as our students become active in their own careers and interact with decision makers. A single oil spill at the Shoals could put us permanently out of business.

SPECIFICS

At a press conference in Concord, New Hampshire, on November 27, 1973, Governor Meldrim Thomson reiterated his opinion that New Hampshire needed both a nuclear generator and an oil refinery. He reminded voters that he had been actively seeking to attract a refinery to the state for some time. He was pleased to announce plans of Olympic Refineries to locate in New Hampshire. Mr. Peter Booras, who had served as Republican state finance chairman and who had run unsuccessfully for U.S. senator in the previous national election, then made the formal announcement: Olympic had obtained firm purchase options on several thousand acres in the sparsely settled Durham Point area and was prepared to invest $600 million immediately to create a four-hundred-thousand barrel-per-day refinery. Light crude oil from Saudi Arabia would be brought to a monobuoy in the vicinity of the Isles of Shoals, one of the best protected unloading spots on the East Coast according to Mr. Booras, and thence to the refinery by pipeline. According to the press release, the project was not to stop with the refinery alone. Additional quantities of crude were to be received for transshipment to other East Coast destinations in smaller vessels. The refinery would also attract petrochemical plants that would supply New

England markets with many additional products. Generous employment figures were estimated for construction and operation of the refinery.

Immediately much that had been in the uneasy background in the seacoast area surfaced and made sense. The feelings of the old New England families for the land that has nurtured them for ten generations or more are special, intense, and mostly private. Acres may be sold if the price is right and the reasons are sound, but the price is not talked about in public in case an assessor or a competitor is listening. Since September three firms of realtors had been seeking options on land in Rye, Portsmouth, and Durham. In Durham Point, they stated that a New Hampshire gentleman wanted the land for a hunting preserve or for conservation purposes (the story varied some). By early November, enough activity had taken place that highly charged rumors were afield. Astutely, the Durham selectmen queried Governor Thomson to learn if the land acquisition had any relation to his previously announced intention to bring refineries and major nuclear generators to New Hampshire. The governor did not respond then but later said, "I'm sorry that I was not at liberty to give you that answer before public announcement. I had been asked by the Olympic Group to treat their plans in confidence and I felt it to be in the best interest of the state to do exactly that." The selectmen were not pleased.

The option prices were right and they went up as word got around. By November 27, the day of the public announcement, some 3,500 acres of Durham—more than 20 percent of the town—had been optioned at a total purchase price just shy of $6 million. In Portsmouth, about seven hundred acres, or nearly eight percent of the land area of the city (not counting Pease Air Force Base), had been optioned (as later made public) for pipelines and truck terminals. A large swath had also been cut by options across Rye to the shore at Concord Point.

The intensity of Governor Thomson's earlier reaction in the "lobster war" over the offshore location of the state boundary with Maine suddenly made sense, too, in light of pipelines, oil terminals, and possible offshore drilling.

At the time of Olympic's press release, Governor Thomson announced that he was assigning a top aide, Frederick Goode, full time on the refinery matter for the following six months. Mr. Goode's instructions were to expedite all state and local reviews and actions that might be necessary to establish the Olympic refinery in New Hampshire. Public statements were made to the effect that the refinery could be built and operating by 1976. Just before the November announcement, Governor Thomson requested of UNH's President Bonner that the university conduct a three-month study of the effects of a refinery on the state. Apparently recognizing that there might be local resistance to a refinery in Durham, the governor specified that the study was to address itself to the general question and not to the specifics of any particular proposal. This, of course, hamstrung the study, for its authors had to speak to assumptions, not facts. President Bonner sought assurances that the results of such a study would be presented to the public without undue pressure for changes or imposition of biases from the governor's office in the final report.

Although the University of New Hampshire was probably the only institution in the state capable of producing such a report in three months, and although hundreds of professional man-hours would be required to accomplish such a task, the governor offered no funds to the university to do it, then or later. The 48 people involved worked many extra hours—hours robbed from other important duties and from family life—in getting out a good report in the allotted time. The Olympic consultants eventually worked long, difficult hours amassing information, but in their case the reward was of a different kind, magnitude, and potential.

THE LOCAL SITUATION WHEN THE PROPOSAL WAS MADE

New Hampshire is an unusual state. It has no broad-base tax (no sales tax, no income tax), and keeping the state that way is a major, emotional issue in any election. It is also an implied issue in any state act that will cost money or produce revenue. Tax pressure on real estate is high. State government in New Hampshire, apart from the executive office, centers in an unusually large House of Representatives (four hundred members paid $100 per annum in 1973) "balanced" by a Senate of only 24 members. The population center of the state is inland along the Merrimack Valley and is associated with the industrialized cities of Nashua, Manchester, and Concord, the state capital. The seacoast is approximately 18 miles long and mostly residential. The tourist industry predominates along the coast in summer. Portsmouth represents the only year-round focus of population density. In 1973 that city was dependent largely on the presence of Pease Air Force Base and the Portsmouth Naval Shipyard, which actually is in Maine. Perhaps because its major interest is inland, New Hampshire had erected coastal zone protection by 1973 that was minimal compared to the statutes and regulation of other coastal New England states.

The role of the county in governance is minor in New Hampshire. Town governments are strong, but their strength comes from state authority and can be withdrawn (in theory, anyway). On the books are a lot of laws giving New Hampshire state agencies wide authority in regulatory matters. Frequently, however, the authority of the agency is greater than its ability to use the authority effectively. State agencies are often severely hampered by insufficient support and inadequate staffing for investigation or enforcement. I suppose this can be expected in a state with opinions on taxation as strong as those found in New Hampshire. Failure of the state to fund the UNH study is a good example of the way this manifests itself. Other states would have paid for it.

Most New Hampshire towns are small enough to be governed effectively by open town meeting. Town meetings are convened at least annually to discuss (and argue over) a warrant containing as many articles as necessary to conduct the town's business and take its opinions. Articles may be petitioned into the annual warrant by citizens rather easily. All citizens of a town may speak and vote at a town meeting within the rules laid down by the moderator. In a stable community, one can predict with considerable accuracy who will rise to say what about what, and to what effect. Some vocal opinions are often discounted ahead of time. Daily operating decisions during the year are made by elected selectmen, often with some sociological justification called the town fathers.

Durham was, at the time described, a residential community of about five thousand people governed by simple town meeting. Its major employer is the University of New Hampshire which had approximately ten thousand students then. A small number of them, usually married graduate students, had established legal residence in Durham and were able to vote at town meeting. The population of Durham is only moderately stable, as faculty come and go. The instability and dominance of town decisions by people who work at the university (the "newcomers") are resented by many of the older families who see their taxes going up inexorably and their right to free use of their land diminished by zoning and planning voted by the newcomers.

Rye is a coastal community with a population expanded in summer by owners of cottages and tourists. It shrinks considerably in winter when town meetings are held. Local citizens are generally not as busy in the winter as they are in summer and have more time to talk.

Portsmouth is organized politically as a city with a mayor and city council in charge of most daily decisions. It suffers the economic ups and downs of any community dependent on the waxing and waning of military installations. At the time of this narrative, Portsmouth was enjoying a period of relative stability, with unemployment below the national and state averages.

Another potent factor in the state scene at that time was Mr. Loeb's *Manchester Union Leader*. It had the largest circulation of any newspaper in the state and maintained that position by an astute combination of excellent local reporting and shrill, emotional editorial positions that aimed pretty low. The paper was reflexively against taxes, welfare, and usually UNH. It supported Governor Thomson vigorously—he was Mr. Loeb's candidate—and gave full backing to Olympic at all stages of the refinery issue. All the other New Hampshire papers in the seacoast area were editorially at the opposite pole. The *Portsmouth Herald* spoke almost as emotionally against the refinery as Mr. Loeb spoke for it in the heat of campaign. A new weekly was born in Newmarket just before the refinery issue broke. Named after the first newspaper in America, *Publick Occurrences* needed some controversial issue to launch its career, and it got one that it used well. The *New York Times,* the *York County Coast Star,* the *New Hampshire Times,* and the Concord paper also put reporters into the fray. Some of the Boston papers took occasional shots at the situation.

On the state scene, earlier actions of the legislature had confused the issues of locating, taxing, and regulating a refinery. In order to speed state permit procedures for utilities (a commendable purpose in my opinion), and in response to the proposal for a nuclear generator at Seabrook, New Hampshire, a single State Site Evaluation Commission had been established. Certain recent changes in state taxing laws were also pertinent to the refinery question. The net effect was to create much initial uncertainty how these and earlier laws affected refineries and oil terminals. Is a refinery a public utility? Does it come under the site evaluation law? Are pipelines and their terminals a public utility? Does whether they are privately or publicly owned make a difference in how they are located, taxed, or regulated? Does the power of eminent domain apply to any or all of this? Are refinery tanks taxable as real property or not taxable as machinery? What role might the New Hampshire Port Authority take? Could a terminal next to the Shoals be state owned and operated? If so, would that take it out of local jurisdiction and give it the power of eminent domain? Different authorities gave different opinions on these crucial questions when they could be made to give any opinion at all.

The federal picture also was unclear. No deepwater port then existed in the United States. How federal, state, and international authority related to deepwater ports had not been worked out in practice. The Corps of Engineers had just produced a massive study (five-and-a-half inches thick) of deepwater ports, their possibilities and implications. Permits and requirements were not at all clear, either, for a refinery or for a deepwater port. These issues never did resolve themselves in relation to Olympic's proposal because Olympic never submitted a formal permit application to anyone. Olympic's repeated promise that all environmental safeguards would be employed and all state and federal standards would be met were somewhat hollow, with no further resolution of these questions.

Both Maine and Massachusetts soon had visions of massive oil spills originating at the Shoals and coming onto recreational beaches and clamming flats from Portland to Cape Cod. A lot of thought took place in official circles in both states as to what they might do to protect their shores from the effects of unilateral action by New Hampshire.

WHAT WAS ACTUALLY PROPOSED

Olympic's planned refinery was soon known to be a major installation by everyone who read newspapers, heard radio, or watched television. At four hundred thousand barrels a day, it would have been the largest new refinery ever built in the United States. By itself, it would have met New Hampshire's total petroleum needs several times over. Its output would have been approximately equal to the output of all the refineries in New Jersey at that time, and it could have met 25 percent of total New England demand for petroleum products. It would have been built on a modular plan. The land initially optioned and pipelines proposed could have supported major expansion beyond those already massive figures if the company wished. Details of the terminal were not initially available except that Olympic proposed to receive oil in supertankers that would discharge at a monobuoy (or possibly a fixed dock) "in the lee" of the Shoals. It was possible to extrapolate quite a lot of information from these few facts by adding the known characteristics of supertankers, monobuoys, fixed terminals, and the needs of a plant operating at four-hundred-thousand barrel-a-day capacity. Such extrapolations in the Laboratory newsletter proved to be reasonably accurate as the details of the terminal slowly became public.

The enormity of the docking operation gradually worked into the public mind. It became clear that each supertanker would physically be as large as or larger than two of the three islands of the New Hampshire Shoals and would loom higher on the horizon as seen from the mainland than any of the islands themselves. These tankers and their support vessels would occupy much ocean previously devoted to lobstering, fishing, recreation, and marine study, to the detriment and possibly the total exclusion of fishermen, party boats, and the Shoals Lab. They also brought the real threat of a major oil spill.

WHO PROPOSED IT?

At the November press meeting in the governor's office, few details were given concerning Olympic Refineries itself. It was described as a major international corporation backed by Aristotle Onassis and represented in the United Sates by Constantine Gratsos. Reporters calling Olympic's New York telephone number found they had reached the offices of Olympia Airways, also owned by Mr. Onassis. It turned out that Olympic Refineries was established in Monaco, had not yet built or operated any refineries anywhere, but had made an unsuccessful proposal for one in Greece and had options for one in Nova Scotia. How Olympic Refineries related in organization to Mr. Onassis's shipping interests was not clear, and how it or its tankers might be held accountable for damage was even less clear. Some remembered that the Canadian government had found it impossible to recover more than a fraction of the cost of cleaning up after the grounding of the *Olympic Arrow* off the coast of Nova Scotia in 1970 (that was disputed by Olympic) and that the company nominally owning the vessel was dissolved two days after the grounding. Apparently each of the Onassis vessels was technically owned by a separate holding company established for that purpose alone.

Olympic presented acceptable credit references from a New York bank that would not divulge further information about the company's finances. Olympic had hired or was hiring an impressive array of consultants to design and locate the refinery and "make it blend into the landscape," to design the deepwater terminal, and to investigate the environmental consequences of both as required in the permitting process.

EFFECTS ON THE SHOALS LABORATORY

The televised announcement by Olympic on November 27 touched off a major reaction in the New Hampshire coastal area. Scores of legitimate questions, our own among them, surfaced immediately and demanded answering. The refinery issue started on the front page and stayed there. Until the crucial votes some three months later, some aspect of the issue made headlines on the front page of the *Portsmouth Herald* nine days out of ten, but Olympic was not prepared with answers.

I found out all I could at UNH and elsewhere in the seacoast area during an emergency trip from Ithaca the weekend after the announcement was made. Back in Ithaca, I immersed myself in publications dealing with effects of oil refineries, supertankers, and spills. The Cornell libraries and the Water Resources and Marine Sciences Center had nearly everything I needed to get a basic grasp of the subject. It was immediately obvious that a major terminal at the Shoals would present serious problems for the Laboratory. Problems could be classed under three major heads: possibility of a spill, results of routine oil leaks dissolved in the water, and effects of heavy, large vessels operating in our immediate vicinity. The latter included such things as exhaust into the air; heat discharge into the water; deck runoff; encumbrance of several square miles of water to our exclusion; prop wash damage to the bottom; damage to shorelines by the wakes of large tugs and launches; damage of blasting, filling, and dredging needed for laying pipes and building a terminal; danger of collision with laboratory boats; and danger of explosion or fire. We would also suffer aesthetic deterioration.

Administrative offices at Cornell were supportive, but had little experience or advice to offer in a matter of this kind. Concern was expressed that the university's tax-exempt status not be jeopardized by attempts to sway legislation (lobbying). The University Counsel determined that the IRS constraints against lobbying do not apply if an institution's life is threatened, and he agreed that the Olympic proposal constituted a genuine threat to the survival of the laboratory. Though I could legally attempt to influence legislation, I was to keep in mind that the function of the laboratory is education and research. I was not at liberty to advance arguments against the terminal on any other basis, such as the historical or aesthetic aspects. I could not speak for Cornell University without appropriate approval (a formal statement might require action by the trustees), and I was to make clear always that I was not speaking for the University of New Hampshire or the State University of New York.

No administrative office at Cornell volunteered to help fund a response from its own budget, and the Laboratory budget had absolutely no slack in it for such a contingency. I appealed to several of our major supporters whose rapid and generous contributions subsequently allowed me to do what I thought best without serious financial constraint. I still had to meet my own classes in Ithaca regularly, or find a guest lecturer for the times when I absolutely had to be away.

Since all else was confusion, the laboratory's best defense at first seemed to be intervention in the federal permit process, but it wasn't clear what that was going to be. Accordingly, letters setting forth our concern for the continued integrity of the Laboratory were sent to all federal regulatory agencies, all New England and New York senators, and the two federal representatives for the Shoals. The purpose was to establish a base from which future action might be taken in federal proceedings. The laboratory also approached Maine and Massachusetts officials for the same reason. The main weakness of this position was that Olympic would have spent several millions of dollars to improve its ideas and strengthen its case by the time it sought formal permits, and its position would have hardened correspondingly.

However, matters developed differently. Freed of lobbying inhibitions, I accepted invitations to participate in a first round of public meetings in seacoast New Hampshire, became aware of the surprisingly vigorous initial antirefinery reaction among many seacoast people, and concluded that it would be worth a try to stop the Olympic proposal before it reached the federal level. Subsequently, all efforts of the Shoals Lab went into obtaining, digesting, and presenting as much information as possible to the voters of the seacoast region about supertankers, terminals, oil, and their effects, even though firm details from Olympic were still lacking.

Many others shared my convictions. In the time between the November announcement and the March votes, a tremendous number of meetings were held, letters and editorials published, statements made, bills introduced, questions asked, positions advanced, and polls taken. Local organizations taking significant action included Save Our Shores (SOS), the Seacoast Antipollution League, the Committee on Regional Oil Planning, the New Hampshire Commercial Fishermen's Association, Save our Refinery, the Concerned Citizens of Rye, and the Star Island Corporation.

A PLETHORA OF EVENTS

Something important happened nearly every day between November 27 and March 6. Here is a skimming of how things developed, arranged more or less chronologically.

Save Our Shores, the first and ultimately the most important of the antirefinery groups in the end, was founded by Nancy Sandberg when the refinery was still just a rumor. The Sandbergs inhabited a 40-acre saltwater farm on Durham Point. Mrs. Sandberg made this issue her whole life during the crucial months. SOS grew rapidly, obtained excellent technical and legal advice, and became the focal point for the Durham opposition.

In early December the governor approved an outline for the UNH report on the impact of a refinery that he had requested, and university officials thought they had adequate assurance of their freedom to release the report to the public at the same time they submitted it to the governor. The UNH experts went to work on a major report due 90 days later. The university had other problems just then. It announced that because of the fuel shortage (caused by the OPEC oil embargo at that time), classes would end early for the fall semester and the university would be closed throughout January to save fuel oil. That same shortage was beginning to be felt in lines at gasoline filling stations. It intensified in succeeding weeks, and had a definite bearing on how a refinery might be received by the general public.

Later, just before the critical town meeting votes, William E. Simon, then head of the Federal Energy Administration, telegraphed the following message to Governor Thomson: "Congratulations on the progress you are making in New Hampshire toward the construction of a refinery in your state. This forward step and your progress with the proposed nuclear generating station will substantially help our country achieve energy independence by 1980 in accord with the president's goals. You may be assured that when your refinery becomes operational, the additional availability of heating oil and gasoline will be of substantial benefit to the citizens of your state and region." This telegram was reproduced prominently in the Olympic advertising campaign. A quick reading could leave the impression that if New Hampshire voters brought a refinery to the state, they would have more oil and gasoline in periods of acute shortage. Was this a fair (let alone accurate) way to state the case? Moreover, what was the propriety of a major federal agency lending its support to the activities of a single corporation such as Olympic, particularly when the entire corporate stock is privately held? Mr. Simon must have felt uncomfortable with the reaction to his telegram, for his office subsequently released a statement that the telegram did not refer to a particular refinery. How many refineries were then proposed for the state? How naive did he think those natives were?

Save Our Shores held a public meeting in Durham on December 4. More than seven hundred people attended; 663 signed a petition opposing a refinery. That was the first of several polls of the citizens of Durham. Those polls, uniformly expressing strong disapproval of a refinery for the town, were generally criticized by prorefinery interests as biased, unrepresentative, or dominated by students.

Olympic intensified its attempts to obtain options on the private Shoals islands (Star and Lunging) in New Hampshire's waters. Officers of the Star Island Corporation were invited to the governor's office in Concord, where Olympic representatives offered them $1 million for title to the 45-acre island (a much bigger sum then than it seems now). Olympic guaranteed that the corporation could continue to occupy and use its conference center there. The offer was refused. Subsequently the Star Island Corporation voted to "take such action as deemed necessary to oppose any use of the Isles of Shoals and adjacent waters which may in any way be detrimental to the conference center and the present largely undisturbed environment."

Lunging Island had been owned by the Robert Randall family for 48 years. A son was buried there and the family had deep attachment for this five-acre spot of granite and gravel. Unfortunately, the Town of Rye (in which it falls) had just reassessed all shore-front property. The Randall's taxes had gone from $74 to $1,043 in one year. They had consequently employed a lawyer to seek relief, particularly because they were taxed at full mainland rates, yet they received no useful town services. Their arguments for a lesser valuation brought tax abatement (to $643), but left a file in the town offices that they feared could be used against them in any action to

243

Lunging Island (Square Rock to right).

take the island by eminent domain. Given the choice (as they saw it) of losing the island by eminent domain or by sale to Olympic at a very high price, they chose to accept the Olympic option to purchase. But they expressed themselves as praying that Olympic would never exercise the option.

Possession of Lunging Island by Olympic was a severe psychological shock to other landowners at the Shoals. The Star Island Corporation amplified its public statement: "We cannot conceive of a set of circumstances, financial or other, which would induce us to alienate (Star Island). We believe we have the resources, human and financial, to maintain our position on Star Island, and will utilize those resources to the fullest extent to protect our interests." Miss Rosamond Thaxter (owner of Smuttynose Island) announced to the press in her indomitable way, "Only over my dead body will anyone unload tankers there!" Lobsterman Norman Foye (whose family owns Cedar Island) wrote, "Eventually there will be a terrific oil spill and then people living on the New England coast won't have to buy any oil; they'll be able to bail it off the coast. Put me and my sons down as being against any oil terminal anywhere near the Shoals." Lobstermen Ed Warrington and Rodney Sullivan, both landowners on Appledore Island, expressed similar sentiments and spoke against the proposal at public meetings. As director of the Shoals Lab, I was quoted in local and Boston papers as stating that "even a small oil spill in that area would be enough to put us out of business." Aristotle Onassis had earlier expressed his opinion that "you don't force with money, you seduce with it." If any of this reached Mr. Onassis's ears, he may have been surprised at the degree to which ruggedly individualistic New Englanders (and particularly Shoalers) were immune to fiscal seduction.

Publick Occurrences obtained and published a list of all options on Durham Point, naming names, purchase prices, and acreages. Now everyone could see who had settled for what. Two options were for approximately $1 million each. Some owners, comparing their figures with others, felt they had been "had." Many felt taken by the stories the realtors had told in obtaining the options. Evelyn Browne, a long-time resident of Durham Point and teacher at UNH, said that Olympic had obtained its option on her land by false representations and she would not honor it. No deed to Olympic would bear her signature. Her vigorous, embattled stance attracted much publicity adverse to Olympic and eventually it gave her back her option.

On December 10 Alden Winn, chairman of the Durham Board of Selectmen and professor of electrical engineering at UNH, released a letter from Governor Thomson that read as follows: "Neither the Olympic group nor this office has any desire to impose an oil refinery on a town that would be reluctant to accept the benefits that could flow from such an economic addition to a community. If in a proper, orderly and legal manner the Town of Durham should reject the proposed Olympic refinery, it would certainly be your town's loss and a great loss to the state, but this office has no intention of trying to force such a benefit on any community." He repeated that statement in public on at least two subsequent occasions.

The exact benefits of a refinery came immediately into contention. As far as taxes went, both Olympic and Durham Town Attorney Joseph Millimet said property taxes would be reduced very substantially (about 80 percent) if the refinery were built. Professor Samuel Reid, an economist at UNH, predicted on the other hand that immediate relief would be no greater than 29 percent. Subsequent estimates varied within those limits, but no one could state definitely what would happen because of uncertainty about how various refinery properties would be taxed under somewhat ambiguous state law. Are tanks part of the plumbing (therefore untaxed as machinery) or part of the real property? Can pipelines be taxed if privately owned? Can the oil itself be taxed? Only in later weeks did people become concerned about the longer-term effects as opposed to the immediate ones. What about need for additional roads, schools, fire protection, water, and other town services, and what might they mean in taxes in future decades? Even the exact life of a refinery was uncertain—perhaps about 40 years. What would happen if foreign crude oil suddenly could not be obtained?

The state legislature meets biennially in New Hampshire, but can be convened briefly in an "off" year if needed. It had been reconvened for a scheduled total of 15 days in January, February, and March 1974. A number of bills were suddenly introduced into the special session in an attempt to legislate answers in some of these ambiguous areas. Some felt that the state was as bad as Olympic in not having answers to the important questions.

Mr. Onassis announced that he would visit Durham on December 19. That day he and his entourage flew over Durham and the Shoals in a jet at twenty thousand feet, in a small plane at two thousand feet, and in a helicopter at a few hundred feet. They then landed at Manchester and hosted a major public-relations reception. Some five hundred people, including many from Durham, attended. Only those from state offices got near Mr. Onassis. The Durham selectmen were not able to talk with him and were miffed at the situation. Mr. Onassis promised cheaper oil for New Hampshire and favored status when supplies were short. He said the refinery would be "as clean as a clinic without smoke or smell," and that Olympic might fund a pollution research laboratory at the University of New Hampshire. The paradox of this proposal did not seem to occur to Olympic.

Money for public relations flowed yet more freely. Olympic opened an office at the local Ramada Inn and John "Tex" McCrary (of the then popular Tex and Jinx radio show) began operations from it just before Christmas. Serious funding had also gone to the Olympic consultants. The Durham selectmen were informed by Olympic that the consultants had received authorization sometime around December 10 to undertake all necessary land use and environmental impact studies. In all, it was said, Olympic expected to spend from $700,000 to $1 million on preliminaries before it sought permits.

On December 17, Dudley Dudley, state representative from Durham, presented Governor Thomson a petition against the refinery signed by four thousand local people. Five minutes after entering the governor's office she reemerged saying she had been "very badly used." The governor in turn said she was "provocative and belligerent."

As a result of the Dudley petition, five state legislators signed a letter authored by Representative George Gordon and directed to President Bonner of the University of New Hampshire asking for a poll of all university students, faculty, and employees. If a majority were found to be against a refinery, the legislators concluded that "we cannot in good conscience vote favorably toward any part of the capital budget which would

Students studying field marine biology must take a close view.

provide funding for the expansion of physical facilities at the college which would require one kilowatt of electricity or a single gallon of fuel oil for its operation." President Bonner demurred and the poll was not taken.

On December 21 the newspapers reported that a number of refinery-related bills had been approved by the Rules Committee of the state House of Representatives for presentation to the special session of the legislature. House Bill 34 (Roberts & Coutermarsh) authorized the creation of a single state committee with authority to override all other state agencies in approving and regulating any oil refineries to be built in the state. The bill also would impose a tax on all refined petroleum products moved out of the state, exempting those for use in New Hampshire. House Bill 18 (Dudley) would require a local referendum and majority vote to approve siting a refinery in towns and a two-thirds vote of the city council or a majority vote of the citizens in cities before construction of a refinery could be approved by the state.

Several other bills either had direct bearing on the refinery question or could serve as logical vehicles for amendments to the same effect. Principal among them was Senate Bill 17 (Foley), which related to the State Port Authority at Portsmouth. Many people saw the Port Authority as a possible way in which the state itself could develop a deepwater oil terminal, or a means by which the state's power of eminent domain might be brought to bear on the problem of land availability at the Shoals, thereby overriding existing town control in these matters.

Yet another bill, also introduced by Coutermarsh, sought to deal with any energy emergency by creating a nine-member state commission with power to override all state and local laws and regulations. Violation of the commission's rules or orders would be a felony. Horror stories began to appear in the press extrapolating situations from these premises, and even Governor Thomson initially disassociated himself from the bill. Representative Coutermarsh agreed that, among other things, the bill would give the state the power to override local rule in siting a refinery.

As the Olympic consultants began to go to work in earnest, the Durham town office was swamped with requests for information. The selectmen considered hiring their own experts and were very much concerned that they not give any appearance of favoring one side or the other in case partisanship could later be used against them in court, should it come to that.

A number of technical reports appeared. Professor Ted Loder of UNH presented the results of his drifter studies measuring how water moves in the vicinity of the Shoals. His chart of trajectories, widely republished in the press, looked like a mass of arrows shot from the vicinity of the Shoals, impinging densely on all the best beaches from southern Maine to Salisbury, Massachusetts, with several going as far as the Plum Island Wildlife Refuge and even to Cape Ann. The commissioner of the New Hampshire Department of Resources and Economic Development (DRED) released a study requested by the governor of the number of jobs and other economic benefits that might come from a refinery. When queried later about the surprisingly high figure of fifteen thousand jobs, he said that he had adapted his results from a study at the Massachusetts Institute of Technology of siting a refinery in the Boston area, and that most of the jobs actually related to petrochemical plants that would be attracted to the vicinity of a refinery. Would or should that happen in southern New Hampshire? Olympic claimed no interest in such parietal development. Arthur Martin, a naval architect by profession whose family had owned land on Appledore Island, began speaking out on the design of supertankers and their dangers, especially in treacherous waters like those at the Shoals. John Hallett, a retired naval commander, well-connected businessman, and member of the Kittery Planning Board, investigated how the major oil companies saw the Durham region for a refinery (negatively) and what the Town of Kittery and State of Maine might do to protect their interests against spills. Martin and Hallett

Students studying field marine biology must take a close view.

became the major guiding force behind the Committee on Regional Oil
Planning, a loosely organized group that set about publishing a series of
informational pamphlets opposing the refinery and the terminal.

In a number of public meetings attorney Charles Tucker, head of
the Southeastern New Hampshire Regional Planning Commission, reviewed
the major economic and sociological characteristics of the seacoast area and
made some predictions about what would change if a refinery came. Jobs
would increase; so would suicides. He observed that no matter what kind of
detailed information came forth, elected representatives would base their
votes more on the mood of the public than on informed recommendations in
technical reports. This prediction proved eminently correct.

Professor Fred Hochgraf, a UNH specialist in pipeline metals,
presented much information in public meetings about the benefits, dangers,
and costs in moving oil by pipeline. He pointed out particularly the difficulty
of protecting a pipeline from the shore to the Shoals, necessarily going
directly across the Portsmouth ship channel, against damage by anchor, and
recommended that the state adopt stringent pipeline construction codes (it
had none).

Most of the faculty at the University of New Hampshire whose expertise related to the refinery issue were deeply engaged in developing the preliminary report scheduled to appear in late February. They were torn in a number of directions. First, they did not wish to damage the university (the governor sits on the UNH Board of Trustees ex officio and has the authority to veto university budget bills). Second, most of them were residents of Durham and would have to vote on any zoning change or in a town referendum on the refinery issue. Third, and usually most important, each must maintain his professional integrity by calling the shots honestly. Several felt strongly enough about the issue to speak forth at public meetings and in the press in their areas of expertise: biology, oceanography, engineering, economics, and others. Little that came forth in that way was supportive of the refinery or of the terminal.

The Portsmouth City Council kept trying by letter and by meetings to get information out of Olympic. It was mostly unsuccessful because Olympic did not yet have the necessary answers from its consultants.

The Federal Environmental Protection Agency took an active interest in the situation. Eventually it released a position paper on refineries and deepwater ports in New England that contained recommendations strongly detrimental to Olympic's position. Some of its desiderata would appear to rule out a supertanker terminal at the Shoals: "Port facilities should be located some distance from the coast—between ten to 25 miles—and in areas assuring freedom from navigational hazards, protection of unique environmental values, and having the capacity to absorb or contain oil spills. . . .It is our opinion that refineries should not be situated in areas with unique and critical environmental assets such as along valuable and limited coastlines or in wetlands."

The deepwater-port situation was eventually complicated by three distinct proposals: First, Olympic proposed a privately owned and operated terminal at the Shoals that would serve only itself. Second, Commissioner Gilman of DRED proposed that the state own and operate a terminal at the Shoals that would serve as many as wished to use it. Third, Tuned Spheres, Inc., a Nashua corporation, proposed to construct a tuned-sphere terminal (a cross between a single-point mooring buoy and a giganitc spherical barge) twice as far out to sea as the Shoals, whose ownership and use were not determined. Olympic's proposal, however, was the only proposal with ready money behind it during the months in question.

At the request of groups in Rye, Portsmouth, and Kittery, James Garvin of Strawbery Banke pulled together the necessary information and completed forms nominating the Isles of Shoals for designation as a National Historic Site. Because that designation requires prior approval at the state

Students studying field marine biology must take a close view.

level, the application had to be submitted to Washington through the appropriate state department, respectively, in Maine and New Hampshire, each for the Shoals islands in its particular jurisdiction. The Maine islands (Appledore, Smuttynose, Cedar, and Duck) were designated a National Historic Site in early summer of 1974. The New Hampshire islands (Star, White, Seavey, and Lunging) were still undesignated in 1979 when I stepped down as director of the Lab.

Why the difference? Are the New Hampshire islands less historic than the Maine islands? No. The answer probably lies in a peculiarity of state government. In New Hampshire, perhaps for economy, the commissioner of the Department of Resources and Economic Development is also the head of the state department that forwards applications for historic registry status to Washington for federal approval.

PUBLIC MEETINGS

A questing and aroused public found numerous opportunities to hear both sides of the issue presented at public meetings convened by interested groups and by the seacoast towns themselves.

The informational meeting held by the Town of Rye on January 23, barely more than a month before the regular annual town meeting, brought out nearly one thousand people. I will describe what happened there in some detail as it was characteristic of such meetings.

It was said to be the biggest turnout since the first transatlantic cable came ashore at Rye. Many were turned away, and the evening was punctuated by announcements that automobiles were blocking traffic on the main street. The school stage held two tables and a lectern. A microphone was set up in the middle of the audience. At one table were those to speak for and against the refinery and terminal proposal. At the other were town officials and local representatives to the state legislature. They were to ask the first questions following the presentations. The Olympic representatives (Mr. Booras, supported by the following representatives of Olympic's consultants: Mr. Greene of Purvin & Gertz, Mr. Harlow of Harris Associates, and Mr. Moore of Kling Associates) were delayed by a prior television commitment. They arrived about halfway through the presentations of those speaking against the refinery. The latter consisted of Professor Hochgraf, Mr. Keppler of the Environmental Protection Agency's Boston office, and me.

I feel generous in characterizing Olympic's presentation as inept. After a few introductory words, Olympic's representatives ran a film for citizens of Rye that depicted the building and dedication of a deepwater terminal off Kuwait. The film was narrated by a person with a refined British accent; the sound track was of martial music; and the initial scenes showed burnoosed Arab dignitaries reviewing troops, making speeches, and pressing a button that started oil flowing through the pipeline to the offshore terminal. Then scenes showed how the pipeline had been built on shore, clad in heavy cement, and dragged into the water. The Kuwaiti shores are unpopulated barren sand. About a square mile of shore seemed to be taken up by churning tractors and other devastating machinery. One could see the citizens of Rye transferring that image onto their own shore at Concord Point. In what was, I supposed, calculated British understatement, the announcer said that the construction crews had to deal with an occasional recalcitrant rock. This was accompanied on screen by a dynamite blast close to shore sending a mass of water to the skies. One could see the citizens of Rye comparing that with the fact that there is little but rock between Concord Point and the Shoals.

Students studying field marine biology must take a close view.

When it came time for questions, town officials directed them entirely to the Olympic people, who did their best to answer. Unfortunately for them, information needed for answers was still sparse or unavailable. I learned from Mr. Harlow, for example, that his company did not yet have figures for wind and sea conditions at the Shoals, and had only recently hired a vessel to make soundings of the bottom from Concord Point to the Shoals. At this juncture, the dearth of such information was especially damaging, for town meetings were scarcely more than a month away. Mr. Tucker, chairman of the Rye Board of Adjustment, was particularly tenacious, like a terrier with a sock, in keeping the Olympic people to the point until he got a "we don't know the answer to that yet, but we are working on it" out of them repeatedly. Among significant questions was one from the town table pointing out that Olympic had earlier assured Durham that if it didn't want the refinery, it wouldn't have to have it. Would Olympic assure Rye that if it didn't want the pipeline, it wouldn't have to have it? After some hesitation, Mr. Booras replied that the question involved a major policy decision and major policy decisions were made in New York. Rye citizens do not take kindly to having decisions affecting them made in New York.

As is common at such occasions, questions from the floor somehow turned into statements. All comment was directed toward Olympic and most was obviously unsympathetic, though reasonably polite. As is also usual at such meetings, one or two town characters had their say. The townspeople knew what to expect when these people went to the microphone, but the Olympic people didn't. One individual, red-faced and emotional, waving his fist in the air, inferred a Communist conspiracy on the part of Olympic. His enlarged picture appeared prominently in the New York Times the next day. I heard subsequently that the Olympic group felt it had been badly used. Beginning about a week later Olympic representatives refused to attend any further public meetings until the time when they would be in charge of the show in their presentation scheduled for Durham in late February.

I think Olympic's trademark backfired, too. It consisted of an outline map of New Hampshire with a bull's-eye of concentric circles over the seacoast area.

At their own public meetings and in releases Olympic set forth occasional new pieces of information in December, January, and early February. The nature of the pipelines became reasonably clear. For instance, crude would be taken ashore through two 48-inch pipes. There would also be a 42-inch pipe for taking ballast water ashore and another of similar size for returning it, together with all refinery process water, to the offshore terminal. Thus all ballast from incoming empty product tankers and all process water from the refinery would in effect be shipped out as ballast for discharge somewhere in the oceans beyond American control. Product pipelines would include one or more for liquefied gas going to the truck terminal proposed at Interstate 95 in Portsmouth, and four, varying in diameter from 24 to 36 inches, for fuel oil and gasoline going out to the Shoals. Olympic also absolved the local real-estate firms of duplicity in misrepresenting the purpose of the options they sought in Durham by saying they had not been informed why the land they were asked to option was being sought or by whom. Mr. Greene, of Purvin & Gertz, admitted that when Olympic asked him to determine a site for a refinery in New Hampshire, he had done so by examining topographic maps of the area and by searching from a helicopter for a sparsely settled site. That's how he chose Durham Point.

I suppose to a Texan like Mr. Greene, southeastern New Hampshire looks, from the air, well-supplied with water. In Olympic's first releases the refinery was said to need six thousand gallons of fresh water per minute. When hydrologists pointed out that this amount was more than all the communities and cities in the area were using together, and it was absolutely all the region could be expected to be able to furnish from all

Students studying field marine biology must take a close view.

sources ever, Mr. Greene had to do some major recalculating. To use all the available water would obviously prevent all further housing and commercial development in the area. By stratagems such as proposing to employ waste water from neighboring communities, Mr. Greene worked the figure down to fifteen hundred gallons per minute of new water needed. This amount Olympic said was available from the Lamprey River. Others said that this estimate of needs was unrealistically low compared with current figures for modern refineries of the size proposed here and that the Lamprey River was an inadequate source even for the lesser amount during periods of drought. Would Olympic eventually request use of water from Lake Winnipesaukee? If so, thousands more New Hampshire voters and summer residents would become immediately and personally concerned about the issue.

A minor issue that kept reappearing in various guises was how well the refinery, with its three two-hundred-foot stacks, could be made to blend into the environment. Mr. Onassis said the stacks with their warning lights would be as pretty as a Christmas tree on the winter horizon. *Publick Occurrences's* cartoonist depicted them with Ionic, Doric, and Corinthian capitals.

From the beginning Olympic had issued statements concerning what permits it would seek and when. It would need a zoning change from Durham, a state permit or permits from a source not yet clearly defined in state law, and a number of federal permits. Little was said of the federal permits except to point out how many were required and to imply that they gave the public full protection against air and water pollution. The state situation was complicated by confusion as to whether a refinery could be considered a public utility or not. If so, it would come under the authority of a single state agency, the Site Evaluation Commission. If not, it would need permits from several agencies. The purpose of House Bill 34 (Roberts) was essentially to define a refinery as a public utility. The immediately critical action needed, however, was a zoning change in Durham. None of Durham was zoned for heavy industry. Without a zoning change the refinery could not locate at Durham Point unless the state found a way to override the town's zoning.

Zoning changes can be brought about only in an orderly fashion after legally mandated opportunity for public hearings. In order to place a major zoning change on the warrant for the annual town meeting, hearings had to be scheduled several weeks in advance. Despite repeated announcements that they intended to, Olympic's consultants were unable to acquire enough information or have sufficiently detailed plans ready in time to seek a zoning change or a permit from the state before the legislative sessions concluded. In the end no formal applications for either permits or a zoning change were ever made by Olympic at any level of government.

THE MONTH OF FEBRUARY

In late January, citizens of Durham took matters into their own hands in the absence of action from Olympic. They petitioned an article into the town warrant seeking a vote whether a zoning change should be allowed by the Zoning Board if later requested by Olympic. Citizens of Rye, observing that the town had overlooked Lunging Island in its zoning ordinance (though not in its tax office), petitioned an article into their warrant seeking to zone Lunging for single residential use.

Olympic announced that it would be ready to make a major public presentation in Durham on February 19 to convince the voters of the benefits and safeguards associated with the refinery. But it still was not able to get ready in time and had to postpone that meeting until February 27. It asked for four hours uninterrupted by questions from citizens either during or after the presentation. The Durham selectmen finally reached agreement with Olympic to split the meeting into two sessions, February 27 and March 3

256

(just three days before town meeting), and to allow questions from citizens at each presentation. Presentations were also scheduled by Olympic in Concord, Portsmouth, and Rye at about the same time.

Forbes Magazine stirred local waters with an article entitled "Is Croesus Losing His Touch?" calling into question Mr. Onassis's current financial condition and present profitability. It was widely quoted locally. Other flaps made headlines on nearly a daily basis as a decision drew daily nearer. News of every tanker grounding or spill that reached the attention of the editor of the *Portsmouth Herald* appeared on the front page. Should the selectmen of Durham visit a modern refinery at Olympic's expense, or would that be improper? What role had the possibility of drilling for offshore oil played in the governor's fight with Maine over relocating the state line? What indemnification would Olympic give the area fishermen against the damage of spills? Why did Olympic present the frugal Durham selectmen with folders bound in imitation leather but with few useful documents inside? How much money had Olympic already spent on public relations, and how much more was it prepared to spend? Was Olympic eyeing possible refinery sites in Rhode Island seriously, as reported in the press, or was that merely a ploy to pressure New Hampshire toward a rapid positive decision? Would Olympic be able to obtain the permissions necessary to take its pipelines across Pease Air Force Base, which stood on the path from Concord Point to Durham Point? What were the merits of placing a refinery adjacent to a major air defense base, which in turn was near a major naval yard? The questions were endless.

Why had not the major American oil companies already made a refinery proposal for the Durham-Shoals area if it were as suitable a location as Olympic claimed? Why had the Army Engineers' report failed to support this area as a terminal possibility? Could the state use the Port Authority to supersede local ordinances? What would prevent Olympic from operating the refinery at break-even, passing any profit back into the transportation of oil to the refinery in ships of Liberian registry beyond the reach of American taxation on profits? Where refineries had been built recently, what had been the actual effect on taxes? How noisy is a refinery? What would be the effect of a superport and refinery on the tourist industry in the seacoast area? Even without a spill? What is the life of a refinery, and what happens when one reaches the end of its useful life? Could modern refineries be really clean, or would the New Hampshire coast become another New Jersey Turnpike? Why had Governor Thomson been the only holdout when the New England governors attempted to deal with the oil problem on a regional basis? How could little New Hampshire (whose annual unrestricted state income then was $124 million and total bonded indebtedness $136 million) protect itself against the kind of relationships that often develop when a single industry dominates the state scene? Citizens had no shortage of questions, only of answers.

In any event the Shoals Laboratory's conviction that a supertanker terminal next to Appledore Island would severely hamper the objectives and operation of the laboratory and might put it right out of business was reinforced in the period leading to the town meetings. I reviewed the biological effects of oil in the environment in some detail. The major weapon used by the laboratory was its newsletter, in which I published our findings and conclusions much as you see them here. Copies were widely distributed in New Hampshire. One reader even gave a copy to Governor Thomson. He replied that it was "inadequately researched." I also gave many talks, both formal and informal, in the seacoast area. Because my salary was not paid by the State of New Hampshire as were the salaries of my colleagues at the University of New Hampshire, I was in a somewhat more comfortable position to do this than were they. My position was that better informed citizens would make better decisions when they voted. I still believe it is better to leave decisions of this magnitude to the voters than to politicians who are supposed to represent them.

THE FINAL THREE WEEKS

The two critical review reports, Olympic's and the University of New Hampshire's, were imminent. The UNH report was ready in draft by its 90-day deadline. Representatives of the governor's office were to review the draft, per agreement, for editorial style before the final printing was ordered. The review was detailed, careful, and time-consuming. Numerous changes were suggested in the original language. Many were simple changes in punctuation, or the substitution of one word for another. Some were requests for further explanation or substantiation of statements that were unclear or did not seem adequately supported to the reviewer. But in one major case, at least, there was substantial impasse. The governor's representative objected to the recommendations set forth in the section entitled "The Impact of a Crude Oil Refinery on the New Hampshire Environment," and lengthy conferences were held in an attempt to resolve the differences. The differences were never resolved. When it became apparent that the whole report would be seriously or permanently delayed in the governor's office otherwise, the authors of that section agreed to its appearance in the report without their recommendations. Even so, the UNH report did not come out in time to help the voters of Durham.

Olympic released a multivolume report on the impact of the proposed refinery about the same time as it held public presentations. The report represented a large amount of work on the part of Olympic's consultants. But it, too, did not help the voters much because it did not appear enough in advance of town meetings for adequate reporting, review, and digestion. Neither report was easy bedtime reading.

On February 15, sensing that the vote in Durham was going to go against the refinery despite Olympic's best efforts to sell it at the public meetings soon forthcoming, Governor Thomson expressed the opinion that state interests should be placed ahead of those of localities and suggested that whether Durham should have a refinery or not should be decided by statewide referendum. The press regarded this as reneging on his promise that if Durham didn't want the refinery, it needn't have it. But the governor remained firm in his new position. He advised that because it was too late to get a statewide referendum in advance of town meetings, each community should add the question to its own warrant under "new business." Many localities did so.

At about the same time, the Olympic team of lobbyists was completed. Those people registered themselves with the state legislature for the purpose of promoting votes favorable to Olympic's interests in the upcoming legislative sessions. The team consisted of Marshall W. Cobleigh, a former Speaker of the House; William H. Craig, former House Minority Leader and state Democratic Chairman; and David C. Hamblett, an influential lawyer and newspaper vice president of Nashua. The General Court began its session on February 19. It was to meet a total of 15 days between that date and April 4, and thus would be intermittently in session during the time of the town meetings.

A team of experts from several oil-handling states was invited to Concord to provide background for the legislators and officials of the state. They pointed out that, despite Olympic's continued representations to the contrary, the first amendment to the U.S. Constitution prevents any oil company from giving preferential treatment to a given state during a fuel shortage. They also pointed out that tourism was still the largest industry in seacoast New Jersey despite the presence of refineries on part of the shoreline.

After several argumentative meetings during which they heard from Olympic's Mr. Harlow, the New Hampshire Commercial Fishermen's Association voted 31 to 5 against the refinery and allocated $100 from its treasury to the Concerned Citizens of Rye to fight it. Although it had no direct bearing on the refinery question, Olympic's public image was not helped by an announcement of the New Hampshire Attorney General that Peter Booras was under investigation for alleged campaign financing irregularities when he ran for the U.S. Senate in 1972.

Finally came the first big day, February 25, the day the Olympic computer-sculpted model of the refinery was unveiled by the governor in the Executive Council chambers at the State House in Concord. This implicit stamp of executive approval was bitterly resented by some of the citizens of the state. The model was moved to Durham for the first of the two informational meetings there on February 27, and the presentation was accompanied by a lengthy brochure mailed to all voters of the town. Townspeople at the informational meeting were clearly inimical to the proposal, but order was maintained and Olympic had its say. Jobs, economic impact, cleanliness, aesthetic appearance of the refinery, pollution control, and details of the pipelines and terminals were set forth. The environmental impact was discussed in some detail.

We learned that despite its purchase options on nearly one-fourth the town at somewhat less than $2,000 per acre, Olympic would use only about 1,200 acres (less than half) of it for the refinery itself. Other land would be used for roads, housing, support services, and the like, and 600 acres would be developed as a public park. The refinery would receive and process light Arabian high-sulfur crude oil at the rate of four hundred thousand barrels a day, using only fifteen hundred gallons of freshwater per minute at minimum. When two thousand gallons per minute was not available from the Lamprey River, the plans included the option of using treated municipal effluent or stored water. The refinery would employ 950 workers at an average salary of $10,000 per year. The majority of those people would be obtained from the local work force, but some 15 percent would be skilled laborers brought in from somewhere else, according to Olympic. Unless distribution pipelines were constructed from the refinery to major points of use in southern New England, the truck terminal proposed for Interstate 95 at Portsmouth would have to handle four hundred trucks a day. The truck terminal and tanks would be on the final approach to the main runway at Pease Air Force Base. Much larger tank storage would be necessary at the refinery itself, just beyond the other end of the Pease runway. Here nearly 30 million barrels had to be accommodated. Sulfur, a major byproduct of refining, would be removed by rail or truck. Effluents, consisting of ballast water from arriving product-removal tankers and process water from the refinery, would be piped out to the tanker terminal to serve as ballast for the departing empty crude tankers.

The placement and characteristics of the terminal were also described in some detail for the first time. It would consist of two man-made sea islands: a double berth beyond the one hundred foot depth contour about six thousand feet to the southwest of Lunging Island to accommodate approximately 90 supertankers per year; and the other, also a double berth, in shallower water to the southwest of Appledore Island, to serve about 170 smaller tankers per year. With fixed terminals (as opposed to single-point-moorings), turning radius would be about two thousand feet. With the terminals not closer than five and one-half miles from shore, tankers would not come closer to the mainland than four and one-half miles. Two four-foot-diameter crude pipelines along the sea bottom, crossing on land through Rye and Portsmouth to Durham, would allow the relatively low-power pumps on the crude tankers to push the oil ashore, making unnecessary the installation of either pumps or tanks at the Shoals. This would not have been possible with a single-point-mooring system with its poorer throughput characteristics. However, two four-foot-diameter pipes give twice the capacity needed for moving the proposed amount of oil with high-pressure pumps. The refinery size could therefore be doubled (as Olympic had suggested earlier) using the existing pipelines if appropriate pumps were later installed at the Shoals. The terminal itself would require a work force of about 60 people and the installation of some complex electronic equipment for communications and navigation of supertankers into heavily populated, constricted, shoal waters.

Of the nine pipelines between Concord Point and the Shoals, four would carry refinery products to the small terminal off Appledore Island. They would consist of a 36-inch line for number six oil, a 30-inch line for number two oil, a 24-inch line for leaded gasoline, and a 24-inch line for unleaded gasoline. The product pipelines would be capable of handling on a routine basis 65 to 70 percent of the output of the refinery. Olympic promised that none of this would be exported beyond the United States.

Olympic's consultants estimated that the presence of a refinery at Durham Point would reduce the tax rate by 71 percent.

Thus, by the time of the first public meeting in Durham, Olympic was coming forth with the kind of detail long sought by the general public and the answers to some of the oft-repeated questions of municipal officials in the seacoast region. But Olympic made some serious mistakes, too, in its presentations, perhaps from the haste of preparation. Its highly touted computer-sculpted model showed access rights of way on land Olympic had been unable to option despite repeated attempts. Its model of the terminal at the Isles of Shoals showed a large radar installation on Star Island, prompting Mrs. Barbara Rutledge to observe (before television cameras) that "Star won't sell you an inch of land at any price at all." That became a segment in the nationally televised review of the Olympic proposal by *The Today Show*. That review was, intentionally or otherwise, a subtle summary of subsurface significance. The three clips advocating the refinery presented Governor Thomson with residual Georgia accent from his youth—sounding like a sort of reverse carpet-bagger; Mr. Greene, by accent a Texan; and Mr. Papanicolaou of recent roots in Greece. The three speaking against the refinery and terminal spoke with local accents, clearly defending their homeland from foreign invasion.

About the time Olympic was courting Durham voters, the *Boston Globe* featured a story that Mr. Onassis planned to go into partnership with King Faisal to obtain simultaneously the capital he needed to build the refinery and a guaranteed source of crude oil to run it. Olympic's new president, Mr. Gratsos, observed that the king and Mr. Onassis were long-time friends, but would neither confirm nor deny the report. The Durham people were forced to consider the possibility, accurate or not, of a large amount of Arab capital in their midst.

Just before Olympic's first Durham presentation, it filed papers to incorporate as a New Hampshire corporation. Officers were listed as: Mr. Gratsos, president; Mr. Papanicolaou, vice president and treasurer; Mr. Thomas R. Lincoln of Greenwich, Connecticut, secretary; and Mr. David C. Hamblett of Nashua (one of the paid lobbyists), clerk. None of those people were full-time employees of the new company. Mr. Papanicolaou announced that the company was fully owned by the Onassis family and that financial information would not be made public. The company had already spent $2 million on studies, plans, and promotion for the refinery and terminal.

Despite its earlier promise that no terminal would be built in Durham if the citizens didn't want one, Olympic admitted just before the town vote that it would indeed build the refinery over the objections of the town if the state gave it the right.

Beginning on March 4 citizens of New Hampshire were presented with a gigantic publicity campaign by Olympic to convince them through the public media that building a refinery at Durham with its terminal at the Isles of Shoals was in their best interest and to seek their support in the upcoming local and state votes. The campaign had two principal parts. On March 4 an eight-page advertisement was distributed as a supplement to every newspaper published in the state. For $10,000 Olympic spread 193,500 copies throughout the state. The supplement was cast in news format, containing no direct evidence that it was in fact paid advertising, and it was unsigned. However, it was so blatantly argumentative and prorefinery that only the most naive person would not have suspected its true nature, if not its immediate source. In addition, the citizens experienced nine hundred spot announcements over 30 radio stations at a cost to Olympic of $6,900. As with the newspaper supplements, the sponsorship of these announcements was not named.

In retrospect, Olympic's publicity campaign misfired in three respects. First, its heavyhandedness was widely resented by the people of the state. Their votes could not be bought in that way. Second, complaints were made that the unsigned supplement was illegal. The attorney general ruled (in due course, but not in time for the votes) that it was indeed an unsigned paid advertisement with a purpose of influencing votes and as such was illegal under state law. Third, in the newspaper supplement Olympic published the names, addresses, and telephone numbers of every one of the four hundred state representatives and 24 senators with a plea for citizens to express their opinions on the refinery to their legislators. Apparently many citizens did just that, but their opinions were not exactly what Olympic expected. This expression of opinion, facilitated by Olympic's press release, was probably an important factor in how the state legislators voted later that week on bills concerned with the refinery and home rule.

IT WAS ALL DECIDED IN JUST FOUR DAYS

The first municipality to express itself officially on the refinery question was the City of Portsmouth. For some months the city government had been attempting to inform itself about the refinery proposal and its consequences to the city. The question of official support for the refinery was brought before a vote of City Council on March 4. Support was voted down six to one.

On March 5 the Shoals Marine Laboratory announced that, although it had funds in hand for a new laboratory building, all construction on Appledore Island would cease until the refinery question was settled. Further investment of capital by Cornell University could not be justified if a refinery terminal was to be built at the Shoals. I admit now that I withheld the announcement of that decision (which was mine to make) until I thought it would have the greatest play in the newspapers and the greatest impact on voters, those of Durham especially.

Newmarket and Rye voted on March 5. In Newmarket, which lies adjacent to Durham and where large mills once utilized the Lamprey River for power, the vote was close, but favorable to siting a refinery *in Durham* (523 (57 percent) in favor; 401 (43 percent) opposed). Rye, on the other hand, was decidedly against Olympic's proposal. Several articles in the Rye warrant dealt with the issue. Perhaps the most significant was the article zoning Lunging Island (the one to which Olympic held option) for single residential use. On that question, 87 percent of the townspeople voted for the restrictive zoning.

The vote of the greatest significance was, of course, that of the townspeople of Durham. The critical vote came on March 6, the second day of the annual meeting. Of the population of 5,300, around 2,900 were registered voters. Voters have to be physically present at a town meeting to cast their votes. Durham voters cast 1,398 ballots, or approximately twice the number of ballots cast in the preceding year and far higher than that of a usual turnout for town meeting. Of these, 1,254 (90 percent) were against rezoning Durham for heavy industry; 144 (10 percent) voted for rezoning if Olympic requested it.

Expressing themselves then or by later votes, all other towns in seacoast New Hampshire which might house a refinery voted decidedly against it with two exceptions. Those were Rochester and Seabrook (plus previously mentioned Newmarket). Up to then, at least, Olympic had repeatedly stated that only Durham would be acceptable to it.

Most observers concluded that the refinery proposal had been soundly defeated at the local level in the seacoast area, especially in light of the Durham vote. Governor Thomson drew a different conclusion. He said, "It is amazing that after an all-out campaign effort, the SOS group has demonstrated its apparent lack of strength among Durham citizens. This is evident in that the total of 1,398 ballots cast on the refinery question represented a low of 48 percent of the total of 2,939 Durham citizens who are registered and qualified to vote. The vote is unimpressive when considered in the light that a silent majority of about 52 percent of Durham residents qualified to vote were reticent to take a position on the refinery question before all facts are available."

Would the state override Durham? That was now the crucial question. As described earlier, a number of bills concerned with the refinery question were before the legislature. The crucial vote came on March 7, the day after Durham's decision. Disposition of House Bill 34 (Roberts) became the key issue. The basic intent of that bill was to place a refinery in such relation to state permit machinery that the permit process would be carried out by a single state agency and would have to be accomplished in no more than a year from receipt of application. The bill also carried a provision for a five cent per barrel tax on refined oil leaving the state. Olympic's lobbyists objected vigorously to that provision, saying Olympic could not do business in New Hampshire under those terms. This tax provision was removed from the bill and sent back to committee for further study and later reintroduction should that be found appropriate.

An amendment (the Read amendment) to the Roberts Bill then became the focus of attention by the House of Representatives. It stated that "an application for a permit for the construction and operation of an oil refinery and associated terminals, pipelines, and other related facilities shall not be denied on the basis of any state law requiring compliance with a municipal ordinance or regulation. Issuance of a permit for such construction and operation shall authorize the applicant to proceed in accordance with its terms and conditions at locations approved by the committee, notwithstanding any municipal ordinances or regulations otherwise applicable thereto." The question was clearly "home rule or state rule." On roll call, the representatives defeated the Read amendment by a vote of 233 to 109. The Roberts Bill then went on to pass, and House Bill 18 (Dudley), calling for approval of a refinery by mandatory vote of local citizens or city government before the state could issue a construction permit, was also passed by voice vote.

On March 8, reading the situation differently from the way the governor saw it, Olympic conceded defeat and its principal officers returned to New York City. They expressed interest, still, in finding a way to build a refinery in the state, possibly in Newmarket, but under different terms. "We have no intention of going through another hassle or taking any more of the abuse we did in Durham," reported Mr. Papanicolaou.

In *Oil and Water* I concluded this story with a couple of pages of commentary on anticlimactic events and speculation on what Olympic might do next. Principal among the events was a ruling by the attorney general that Olympic's unsigned lobbying by newspaper and radio constituted "one of the more blatant violations" of the state's statutes on political activity. Also significant was the governor's pronouncement about the UNH refinery study that "if a few university officials have exceeded their commitment, they may have jeopardized the emergence of a cooperative effort between the university and the state. . . .I want to make clear that I asked for no conclusions and am prepared to accept no conclusions that imply that this state cannot handle a major industry." What escaped the governor was that whether the state could or not, the seacoast citizens wouldn't accept a refinery or a terminal, and the representatives of the citizens of the entire state had decided to uphold the right of a town's citizens to decide such issues.

What did Olympic do next? Passage of time showed that it did the realistic thing—nothing—but because Olympic would not announce its intentions, prudence required us to keep up our defenses for a while longer.

CONCLUSIONS

Exactly why Olympic Refineries did the things it did in New Hampshire may never become public. Danger lies, perhaps, in reading into actions more than the expressed purposes. Even if one grants considerable latitude for expressed and implied purposes of profitability and business advantage to a company previously engaged in transporting oil at a time when that function was being disrupted by world events, Olympic's proposal for a refinery at Durham Point and a deepwater terminal at the Shoals raised important questions of corporate purpose that were never adequately answered.

Why situate it in New Hampshire, for instance, especially when other oil companies had decided against locating a refinery there? The answer must be compatible with the following facts: Olympic's first move was to acquire land at Durham Point and the Shoals. That move occurred several months before Olympic had access to very much technical information about the region. Remember that Mr. Greene located the refinery at Durham Point by map and by helicopter—not by research and inspection—upon instruction to place a refinery in New Hampshire. The state was chosen before the locality, and the locality before the technical facts were known to support such a choice. The changes in Olympic's position on its need for fresh water and from using a single-point mooring (favored at first) to a fixed-berth terminal (favored in the end) were significant. Those major changes and others were forced by information, not difficult to obtain but which Olympic did not have when it decided to build the refinery at Durham.

What fact could be important enough to counterbalance lack of knowledge of the area and its physical and social characteristics? I believe the answer was political expediency, specifically the governor's support and the probable implication that, consequently, state approval of a refinery proposal could be readily attained. New Hampshire's coastal zone is limited and its protection was then less developed than in other New England states. Was that a factor? Perhaps the haste with which events took place can be explained by the observation that Governor Thomson was after whatever refinery he could get, as he himself had implied publicly. Attracting industry was a matter of first importance in his administration and he needed results; he had made overtures to several American oil companies. If Olympic didn't move fast perhaps another company would. No fault can be found in any of that, but in trying to justify ex post facto on technical grounds a proposal put forth hurriedly for political reasons, and being unable to do so by the time of town meetings, Olympic lost the initiative to the people of the towns. And Durham just didn't want the refinery.

Why a terminal at the Shoals? Why bring fragile supertankers within a few boat lengths of jagged granite rocks in exposed coastal waters? Alternatives have their own problems, but they exist. I think one factor, never stated, may have loomed very large in Olympic's motivation. To place a terminal in the lee of the Shoals is to place it within the three-mile territorial limit (which is drawn around the islands as well as along the mainland coast). In fact, close to the Shoals is the only location along the New Hampshire coast where the water is deep enough for the tankers to get within that limit. Neither federal nor local governments control the ocean bottom from tide line to the three-mile limit; that span is solely under the control of the state. At the time of the Olympic proposal, pipelines and terminals needed only state permits so far as use of the bottom was concerned (though the Army Engineers remain concerned for effects on free use of the waters above the bottom). Maybe this advantage seemed greater to Olympic than the obvious dangers of the Shoals rocks, the political and legal problems of proximity to Maine, or of partially blocking the entrance to Portsmouth Harbor. Initially Olympic was prepared to pay nearly $2 million for the private New Hampshire islands. After the votes, it said it really didn't need any of the islands to build the terminal, but it still wished to keep the terminal close to the Shoals. The real reason was not entirely a matter of "lee" as Olympic originally argued.

In the national press coverage, including that of *Time Magazine*, the defeat of the Olympic proposal was set forth as another victory of the environmentalists. *Not so*, say I. Those people who draw further conclusions from that bias will draw bad conclusions. People who are deeply concerned with protection of the environment were certainly involved in the antirefinery battle, but the conservation arguments were only one segment of the issue. For most voters, I think they were minor. Remember that the environmental consequences of the refinery or terminal were never closely focused for discussion because of the lack of timely information from Olympic. No federal permit was sought and no environmental impact statement was prepared as required in the permit review. Minds were made up before the Olympic public presentations, and few were changed at that time.

How did the people make up their minds? Emotionally. In such circumstances, negativity has a stronger force than acquiescence. Status quo is easier than change. The seacoast votes were votes *against,* not votes *for* anything, environmental or otherwise. They were votes against the arrogance of big business in thinking the votes could be bought. They were votes against public relations pressure and what it implied about the voters' intelligence. They were votes in fear of a corporation that had bought up nearly a quarter of a town in secret. They were votes against the power of a political body in Concord to rule over the people of Durham and the fear statewide of that power as it might be expressed otherwise and in other communities. They were votes of disbelief in corporate and governmental promises, of distrust of motives, and of dislike of change, whether forced by state government or big business, particularly big business with foreign roots. The votes begged the basic questions.

The basic questions remain. Does energy-hungry New England have a moral obligation to pay the environmental costs for a large refinery? If one is accepted, how should it be sited? Should the town-meeting mechanism, developed to govern small, isolated, homogeneous communities of the 1700s, be called upon to resolve regional issues of this sort? If it is unable to do so, what other mechanisms exist to deal with such an issue?

More questions would have arisen if Olympic had been able to seek permits as it expected. How should always complex and often foggy federal regulatory machinery function? Is it even capable of producing a clear "no" in a situation such as described above? Or will its answer always be a qualified "yes," with the actual force of the answer depending on the ability of the proposing parties to get what they want out of the qualifications by whatever means they can over whatever length of time it takes to do it, the whole process mostly out of public view? Should industry be able to invest several millions of dollars in a project before being subjected to some initial regulatory and planning control and public reaction to it? Or does the ability to spend large amounts of money up front tend to generate unwise management in which further massive sums are spent simply to protect the initial investment or the ego of management? The public ultimately pays the cost of unwise management either in increased taxes to regulate it better or through increased cost of product.

Above all, how can quiet wisdom be made to temper raw emotion in reaching decisions of this magnitude and import?

SEABROOK

The Shoals Lab would have liked to have had a say in the Seabrook Nuclear Power Station controversy that came hard on the heels of the refinery proposal. When the Seabrook people said in their early press releases that the generator would have no greater effect on local marine biology than a blue whale anchored offshore, I pointed out to Shoals Lab newsletter readers that the net effect of the heat coming out the Seabrook cooling tunnel would be equivalent in local waters of moving the Laboratory to a point south of Boston or the sun northward in the sky by about its diameter. That angered the Seabrook people sufficiently to provoke a letter attacking me personally (but not my conclusions) that their management sent to various public officials and to the presidents of the University of New Hampshire and Cornell (who ignored it so far as I ever found out). I spoke at one or two public meetings about the power plant, but no reasonable showing could be made that the power station would threaten the actual existence of our island laboratory, so my hands were essentially tied. Furthermore, I was exhausted from simultaneously battling the refinery proposal, managing construction on Appledore Island, and fulfilling my professional duties both at the Shoals and in Ithaca.

Sometimes I wonder how the Seabrook fiasco (financial, if nothing else) might have turned out if the seacoast area had not been already

Students viewing Seabrook and the rest of the horizon from the White Island lighthouse.

exhausted by the Olympic battle and the laboratory's hands had not been tied. In 1974, the Three Mile Island and Chernobyl accidents had not yet happened. Now we see similar possibilities, faint though they may be, literally on our Appledore Island horizon.

Chapter Twelve

BACK ON TRACK
1974

NOT ALL GLOOM AND DESPAIR

Although occasional disquieting statements by Governor Thomson and Olympic representatives issued during 1974 and 1975 caused the Shoals Lab to remain on alert, passage of time slowly demonstrated that there would be no refinery in the New Hampshire seacoast area and no supertanker terminal at the Shoals. We could get back to the business of constructing and operating the Lab. It was high time. Just a six-month hiatus to fight Olympic had severely damaged our circumstances. All plans for new construction had been put on hold and could not be reactivated in time for the 1974 construction season. Funding appeals had ceased. Who would contribute to an outfit that might have to go out of business soon if Onassis and the governor of New Hampshire had their way? Most people, deep in their souls, thought we would have to go out of business, money and politics being what they are.

Dominic Gratta would have to be content in 1974 with finishing some of the projects already begun. Little time had been available for setting up the regular teaching program; its existing momentum would have to carry it forward in 1974. There had been no annual spring fiancial showdown with the Cornell administration, which realized the seriousness of the Olympic situation and was satisfied that, with the slowdown of construction, we wouldn't be able to get very deeply in financial trouble that summer anyway. Instead, the senior administrators renewed their efforts to get Gratta Construction caught up on its billing.

A few heartening moments broke the heavy and relentless thrust of the oil crisis in the spring of 1974. The cod chowder dinner at Cornell was one. Our island chef had been instructed to keep extra food in the walk-in freezer at all times all summer in case we had a storm and couldn't get supplies out from the mainland for several days. He had access to some of the best cod in the world, which could be bought for around a half-dollar a pound right off the top of the hold when a trawler stopped at the Appledore Island dock. Repeatedly during the summer, selected large codfish were carried up the shore to Kiggins Commons and frozen immediately. There is none better.

When the alumni groups had departed at the close of the 1974 season, a lot of cod was still in the freezer. The close-up crew couldn't begin to make a dent in it.

Waste that cod? No way. Here's what we did. Rob Morris, who had cooked for the construction crew, had student connections with the dairy department at Cornell. Before Olympic surfaced, the Shoals staff in Ithaca had arranged with Rob's help to rent for one evening Cornell's Dairy Bar, which served breakfast and lunch, but was normally closed at night. For a reasonable price we had a three-hundred-seat dining hall in which to put on a "feed" for Shoals people and the general campus public.

The frozen cod was trucked to a freezer at Cornell. Everyone available, including some volunteer Shoals students, went to work. They planned an old-fashioned New England cod chowder dinner with all the fixings, and they invited Captain Carlo Sinagra, a Gloucester draggerman (who might have caught those particular cod) to come and lecture about the New England fishing business following the meal. Could they fill three hundred places in the dead of February?

Wendy Zomparelli printed tickets and put up posters. The three hundred seats were sold out almost instantly. Mr. Sinagra who, unlike most Gloucester fishermen, was comfortable lecturing before an audience because he taught commercial fishing in the Gloucester public schools, accepted the invitation. The only difficulty that arose in the total success of this effort happened when Carlo had a mild heart attack just before the event and couldn't come. In his place I gave an impromptu fishing lecture, drawing on what I had learned from listening to the visiting fishermen at the Shoals over the years.

The appointed evening brought together all the elements of the diverse Cornell community, from custodians to university senior administrators, who rarely mix informally like this. A great time was had by all. Three hundred Ithacans now knew what a New England fish chowder was all about. Not least, the distant Shoals Lab took on a greater reality at Cornell.

Another serendipitous event took place early that season at the Shoals. This one had consequences that persist to today.

Always on the search for people with resources who could perhaps be enticed into supporting the Appledore project, I used to scan the vessels at anchor in Gosport Harbor daily. When I saw a particularly large or distinguished one, I might hop into the Whaler and tootle out into the harbor with a view to starting a conversation with anyone aboard. One day the brand-new *Harvey Gamage* appeared in Gosport. She is a large wooden-hulled schooner, 95 feet long, now familiar in New England and Caribbean waters.

I had no trouble talking my way aboard; I found, to my great surprise, that my name was already recognized on that vessel.

Eben Whitcomb, the owner and builder of the *Harvey Gamage,* had a strong desire to put a vessel of that kind into academic service. He had heard of the Appledore project, and thought he might learn something from me about the academic side of the business. We went below to meet yet another person with similar interests. That was Corwith "Cory" Cramer, who had just founded the Sea Education Association and taken possession of the staysail schooner *Westward*, a little larger than the *Harvey Gamage,* and steel hulled. Cory wished to combine for students an academic marine education with open-ocean training under sail. Although we came from entirely different backgrounds, all three of us had strong opinions about what constituted a proper marine education, but less than perfect ideas of what was economically supportable. Each of us had risked large amounts of money on an unknown ability to make something work. We had an old-fashioned bull session lasting into the wee hours the next morning. It was greatly useful to me, and I think to the others, too.

Cory and I arranged on the spot to trade classes that summer. He would bring the *Westward* to the Shoals, his class would come ashore for a day's work at the Lab, and the Shoals students would board *Westward* for a day's work at sea. This took place without a hitch later in the summer with excellent educational results for both parties and was the beginning of the formal relationship between the Sea Education Association of Woods Hole and the Shoals Lab that persists to today. I had obtained something far better even than a cash contribution from those aboard that large vessel in Gosport Harbor.

The Olympic crisis, taking place mostly during the winter, was over before the 1974 Shoals season began. Most of the New Hampshire state legislators, like most New Hampshire natives, had never been out to the

The Sea Education Association's staysail schooner Westward *anchored off Appledore Island; UNH's research vessel* Jere Chase *in foreground. Below: Students aboard* Westward.

Aboard Westward; *"Haul away."*

Shoals and had only a hazy idea of what was under contention out there as legislative matters progressed. They couldn't go out to the Shoals in the winter months—the trip was too rough and chancy. Under the urging of representative Dudley Dudley, a small number of legislators arranged to go out in early spring aboard UNH's *Jere Chase.* They got as far as the mouth of the Piscataqua River before they were forced to turn back by rough seas. Later, when students had arrived on Appledore Island, I asked Dudley Dudley if she would like to try again. She found that more than one hundred people (legislators, their families, and friends) wanted to come out. Given that number, they would have to come on a special run of the ferry.

As was often the case in June, the *Viking* hit a wall of fog at the mouth of the river. In the wheelhouse I asked skipper Bob Whittaker (if memory serves) if he could pick up on radar the tanker then anchored just offshore waiting for the right tide to run upriver to the Sprague terminal. He could see it easily. Why not give the legislators a first-hand look at a tanker? Head for her. Bob did.

Running up on a tanker in the fog is a memorable experience. Just when the darkening horizon looming ahead begins to make people take notice, it materializes into a massive wall of plates and welds extending far overhead. We picked up the tanker at her bow, ran her full length to the stern, noticed from her name and port of call that she was the *Olympic Gulf* registered in Monrovia, and then ducked under her stern and ran forward along the starboard side before heading off to Appledore Island. With no particular comment from me, this made a major impression on the legislators, most of whom by then had no remaining sense of direction. They felt as if they had just had a monumental experience somewhere out in the middle of the Atlantic Ocean. After another half hour of dense fog and no landmarks, Star Island congealed into view dead ahead. We landed as usual and shuttled the legislators across to Appledore Island.

At the close of the day's events, the New Hampshire legislators gathered in the Kiggins Commons dining room. Here they heard some words on the work of the Laboratory, the value of the location for such work, and its effect on students' lives, some of which they had already plumbed for themselves in conversation. I then opened the gathering to questions, which were prompt in coming. After a time, one legislator at the back of the room, obviously impressed with what he had seen, asked, "How can we in the New Hampshire legislature help you out here?" I answered that if the New Hampshire legislature was in position to vote funds for a private New York institution operating in facilities leased from a Massachusetts religious corporation and located in the State of Maine, more power to it. I prophesied that it could never happen, political divisions being what they are, and except for funds spent through UNH it never did despite the legislators' obvious interest, good will, and best of intentions. I suggested that they could work hard to keep another Onassis off our backs, and they might see if they could hurry DRED Commissioner Gus Gilman along in approving the New Hampshire islands for inclusion in the National Registry of Historic Places, as Maine had already done for the island on which we stood.

OWED TO A GRAECIAN EARN
(Coined by Arthur Borror.)

A report prepared by Jay Freer for a meeting with Mr. Peterson in May, after the Olympic crisis had mostly passed, showed that attention was urgently needed to the matter of funding. That was no surprise. The teaching program of 1973, as always, had operated in the black, and a realistically balanced budget had been constructed for 1974. The problem was, as always, in the construction funding. To date, as near as could be figured, $470,000 had been spent or committed to complete the Grass Foundation Lab, to renovate the Coast Guard building, to bring Kiggins Commons to 80 percent

Adult-education programs are important at the Shoals Lab.

completion, to restore at least partially the old cottages (Hewitt and Laighton), and to create the island infrastructure (roads, docks, and utilities). Funds were in hand with which to build the Palmer-Kinne Laboratory; no debt was anticipated in that project. On the other hand, the sudden near-cessation of contributions coupled with the administration's recent success in getting some bills out of the Grattas, plus unexpected rampant inflation and a subtle increase in the quality (and cost) of new construction to enhance the Lab's ability to house adult-education programs comfortably (not envisioned in the original planning), all had conspired to put the Lab's construction account balances actually in the red for the first time. Of the $125,000 debt authorization, $85,000 was now in use at a cost of nine percent interest.

The 1973 teaching program had been able to pick up $10,000 (about half) of the island operating costs (the construction budget had covered the rest), allowing Jay to project that the Lab should be able to meet all operating costs from the teaching budget when the island was utilized to designed capacity. Absence of adequate dormitory space and beds prevented that now. Remaining payments on the SUNY contract, grants, and pledges would cover more than $100,000 of debt if fully realized as expected, so the Lab would not be in serious financial trouble if construction stopped at this point. On the other hand, the future operating budget would be in trouble if the beds needed for expansion to capacity were not soon provided through new construction.

Mr. Peterson easily saw all that. He also realized that funds had been coming in from donors up to the Olympic crisis about as fast as construction spending required, and he felt this could be expected to resume. Further analysis showed that total costs on Appledore Island (including the infrastructure) had worked out to only about $30 per square foot of functional space created. Compared with the home campus, educational space had been built at the Shoals at less cost, and that space had demonstrated a greater educational result per student per hour of use.

The only real problem appeared to be that the project had now reached the overall cap of $450,000 that the trustees had voted originally, and probably exceeded it by a bit, considering unbilled debts. Jay and I proposed that the trustees be asked to raise the cap to $850,000 to include construction of the Palmer-Kinne Lab and new dorms, the latter contingent on finding funds. Mr. Peterson agreed and I suppose the trustees did, too, though I think no one in the administration ever bothered to tell us so. They would have told us quickly enough if the trustees had not agreed!

Costs escalated significantly and unexpectedly in the summer of 1974 when the main (60-kilowatt) generator quit for good. Old Oscar had always suffered from excessive vibration, which was eventually diagnosed as owed to a sag in the main shaft occasioned by long years of standby idleness at the Manchester, New Hampshire Veterans Administration Hospital. We knew that choosing a 20-year-old machine was a gamble, but it had very low hours of use and seemed to run well when we checked it out. But a machine free of purchase cost becomes an investment when it has been installed on an offshore island, and represents further cost at an unknown time in the future when it has to go back to the mainland for repair.

Old Oscar's main bearing housing had finally cracked. The first effect was, unexpectedly, a reversal of phase. That made electric motors run backwards, a development that was immediately detected in the various island pumps and also in the kitchen when the machine that made bread crumbs out of slices of bread began hurling the slices back out and up to the ceiling. This situation didn't last long; the main bearing itself let loose and sprayed its small steel balls throughout the generator room, bringing to a cessation all power generation. The 15-kilowatt generator was pressed into service, but it could not handle the entire island load simultaneously. The engineers had to isolate the salt-water pump, the refrigeration compressors, and other major users of power and run them individually as needed by shutting all power to everything else for as long as necessary. Resulting power outages were usually announced but sometimes came as surprises. Never a dull moment.

The 60-kilowatt antique was replaced as soon as possible by a modern, well-used but thoroughly rebuilt standard commercial 30-kilowatt generator that proved adequate to meet the full electrical needs of the island even if the lights dimmed a bit when the salt-water pump came on. The new generator was much less temperamental than Old Oscar and it used significantly less diesel fuel, but it was a major unexpected expense.

Another unexpected event, this one without budgetary consequences, happened a few weeks before the island closed for the season. A small, bright yellow seaplane swooped low over Appledore Island, made another pass or two along the water near the dock, and then landed just offshore and taxied to our float. The unaccompanied pilot got out and introduced himself as Bob Bryam to all who been drawn to the excitement at the dock. Fortunately, I had heard of the Labrador Foundation and Reverend Mr. Bryam's work ministering to the populations of the tiny, isolated communities of fishing families that dot Labrador and other far northern shores. I knew also that he was half of the duo that had created the Burt & I Down East records when he was a student at Yale.

Just what attracted Bob Bryam to Appledore Island I don't know. Perhaps he thought we needed the professional attentions of a minister, just as had Massachusetts, whose Society for the Propagation of the Faith among Indians and Others had sent a minister to lawless Star Island centuries earlier. In any event we all had a pleasant visit. Bob asked on leaving if I would like to have him serve (at no cost) as the island chaplain. I said sure, if he recognized that we were ecclesiastically mixed, his attentions had to be nondenominational and ecumenical, and most particularly if he didn't mind the students asking him to do *Burt & I* routines when they found out who he really was, as they surely would.

Bob Bryam said those conditions were no problem. He came back once or twice in the next year or two, to everyone's delight, but eventually stopped dropping in (literally). Maybe he decided our civilization was in good shape and his attentions were needed elsewhere more than at the Shoals.

ALUMNI EAT RUSSIAN SHARK

Toward the end of the summer season, when the alumni short sessions were in progress, Rob Morris returned to Appledore Island bearing a very large frozen blue shark, courtesy of the Russian trawler *Belagorsk*. Rob had just spent some time aboard the *Belagorsk* as an exchange student from the National Marine Fishery Service's laboratory at Woods Hole. He cooked up the Russian shark for the alumni. One of them, Jean Cooper, wrote the following (abridged and slightly modified) for a class column in the *Cornell Alumni News*:

Peter and I had an unusual experience this September. We spent three days at the Isles of Shoals ten miles off the coast of New Hampshire. There are six islands, all tiny. If you miss the lighthouse on White Island, then your next stop is England. This was important for us because we arrived by sailboat.

The Shoals Marine Lab is on Appledore Island. In September after the kids have left, Jack Kingsbury conducts a program there for Cornell's Adult University in marine biology, ecology, and the like. Attendance is restricted to 44 people because of Appledore's limited housing facilities. Dormitory living is the first adventure. The Appledore "Hilton" and the Appledore "Statler" are leftovers from the past, drafty, leaky, and unpainted. Each room has a cot or two, a chair, and one bare light bulb. But they provoke instant comment and are the best conversational ice-breakers I've ever seen. We are kids again on our first camp out. The limited available funds have been devoted not to housing but to the construction of a science building and equipment, and a lecture and dining hall, and a better library.

You arrive from the mainland on a ferry that is met off the island by the Lab's own lobster boat. (The dock on Star Island had been closed for the season; visitors to Appledore Island were moved directly from the deck of the new ferry the *Viking Queen,* hove to off Appledore's shore, to the deck of the *Wrack*.) It took two trips to get everyone and their gear ashore. Since Peter and I had sailed up from Long Island, we missed this part and arrived just as the last sleeping bag was unloaded. We met for lunch about an hour later in the lecture-dining hall and here began our second adventure. Many of the foods served were products of the sea, cooked and used in fascinating ways. Lunch was flounder chowder, home-made honey bread, and salad. Dinner was an oven-fried shark steak from a blue shark caught and frozen during the summer. The next day we had a haddock newburg for lunch and boiled lobster for dinner. Before the lobster, we had mushroom caps stuffed with fish, haddock, and grilled cheese on toast, and steamed periwinkles gathered by the group that morning. If you closed your eyes as you dipped them in melted butter you'd swear they were escargots, only smaller. Sunday lunch was a bouillabaisse—hot, rich, and loaded with all the seafood, shellfish, and lobster we couldn't finish in the prior two days. It was

Above: It's important to find White Island.
Below: The new ferry, Viking Queen.

all great, but to me, the shark was the best, and I had two helpings.

Believe it or not, we were busy between meals. Bird banding went on at all hours. Nature walks began at six each morning. On Saturday, with Jack in the lead, we scrambled up and down the rocky coast of Appledore Island, learning about zonation, intertidal growth, seaweeds (we even ate some), and red tides. After lunch there was a talk on the island's gulls and a lecture and slide show on seaweeds. After dinner we had a lecture on commercial fishing and lobstering in the area followed by an eyewitness account of Olympic's foiled attempt last year to build a deepwater oil port at Appledore Island. Friday night we saw Jacques Cousteau's film on whales. Sunday we worked at the sea lab in the old library and climbed almost but not quite to the top of the radar tower. It was a sparkling day and the view was forever, but I chickened out at the last level when I realized there was no guard rail around the roof.

At our final gathering and lecture over lunch on Sunday, we were 44 friends who had arrived strangers two days before on this small rock island. More than one person remarked, "How am I ever going to explain this weekend to my friends at home? I slept in an abandoned barracks, gorged on seafood, sloshed in the rain and dark at night to get to the head, climbed rocks, chased birds, counted gulls, and talked a lot about seaweed. They'll never believe me!"

Later in the autumn of 1974 I was invited to debate with the Commissioner of New Hampshire's Department of Resources and Economic Development (DRED) on the still-hot topic of oil. We met on the stage of a large lecture hall at UNH before an audience of representatives from New England historical societies. Commissioner Gus Gilman was a logical choice for one side of this debate because, in addition to the responsibilities of office suggested by his title, he was, by a peculiarity of New Hampshire governance, also the head of the state committee that nominates places such as the New Hampshire islands at the Shoals for listing as National Historic Sites.

The debate was lively, to put it mildly. Nonetheless, both debaters came out of it with increased respect for each other as persons, if not for each other's position. Gus Gilman became a strong supporter of the Shoals Marine Laboratory.

In November the 1974 annual meeting was faced with some important decisions. Those assembled—including Cory Cramer of the Sea Education Association and Arthur Peterson, treasurer of Cornell—heard that the Shoals' teaching program had operated in the black yet again and had been able to pick up more of the island operating costs (though still not all). The student exchange with SEA's *Westward* had gone well. So had the Cornell and UNH alumni programs. Island systems and facilities had moved from largely jury-rigged to comfortably functional though still massively unfinished. The Palmer-Kinne Laboratory had been drawn and sited.

Decisions made by vote at the meeting were to join with the Sea Education Association in presenting *Sea Semester*, the shore component of which would be conducted on Appledore Island; to complete the Palmer-Kinne Laboratory; and to charge the full cost of operating the island to the teaching program in 1975 (none to construction) if possible. These decisions meant adding a second course (*Introduction to Nautical Science*) to our one existing course at the Shoals. In doing so we would have to be sure not to tread inadvertently on any toes in the College of Engineering. Offering elements of celestial navigation and piloting under a biological sciences course number might be difficult to get approved by the faculty of the Division of Biological Sciences, and a biological sciences course number might raise some eyebrows connected to engineering toes.

ON THINKING LIKE A LOBSTER

The fish chowder supper we sponsored at Cornell in the winter of 1973 had been so well received by the campus community that the pressure was on us to do it again. This time we chose to present Shoals lobsters, "finest-kind" as the fishermen say. Arthur and Helen Peterson came to the dinner. The lobsters, steamed with seaweed in the large milk-pasteurizer kettles were done to perfection and came apart easily, sometimes too easily. By the time they had been handled several times, a few had lost a claw. Mr. Peterson got such a one-armed lobster as he went down the line. As was his nature he accepted it as a fact of chance and said nothing. But I noted for future attention that Cornell's treasurer had not received his money's worth.

Having had suddenly to substitute for a fisherman the year before, I chose this year to prepare a presentation in which I pretended to be a Maine-coast lobsterman. Preparation consisted of listening once again to tapes of lectures Mr. Norman Foye had given to the classes at Appledore Island. The evening presentation was well received. I learned later that some in the audience who didn't recognize me thought I actually was a lobsterman.

Norm Foye (as he was known to everyone) was the dean of lobster fishermen at the Shoals, senior in age and experience to the half dozen others who fished there. He also was a true Maine-coaster of many generations' descent. The Foye family owned Cedar Island. In the winter, the Foyes—Norm, Mary, and the boys—lived in a small mainland cottage on the

Norm Foye often jigged for cod on Sundays when lobstering was illegal (unless it was foggy enough). Above he demonstrates "Here's how it's done." Below: "Now you try."

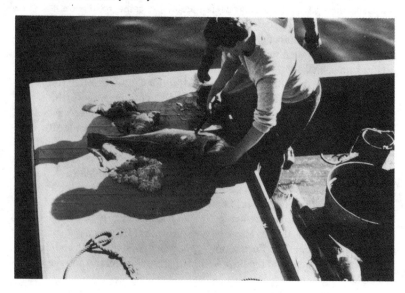

What's left after proper filleting.

riverfront behind the Congregational Church in Kittery. The family moved to Cedar Island each summer for the fishing season. One of the boys, George, was working into the business at that time.

Norm Foye never considered himself a lecturer, but he liked to talk about lobsters and lobstering, which he did both with proper Down East accent and wit. "Dean" Foye, with little formal education nevertheless knew more about lobsters and lobstering than did all the students or professors on the island. After the class had heard about lobsters as invertebrates from Professor Anderson, and then eaten them, Norm Foye would go to the front of the dining hall in Kiggins Commons, lean against a lobster trap on the lecture table, and begin.

"Well, I don't know just what Dr. Kingsbury wanted me to talk about. There ain't much to lobstering—really. You have to have a good trap—this one, I don't know. The head here's too loose. Whoever knitted that just got it too loose. This one wouldn't hold em. No, it just wouldn't. A good trap, it'll hold every one that goes in. See, they go in here, into the kitchen. And they get a free meal. That's where the bait is. We give 'em a good free meal, every one that goes in, shots (shorts) and all. We figger we've

Professor Anderson preparing the class for Norm Foye's lecture.

fed every keeper plenty of free meals before he gets big enough to keep. Then they crawl up through this other head, here, into the parlor—we call it the parlor. Once they get in there, they don't get out. Just no way. They just don't do it! If the pot's made right, not like this one—this must be one of Sullie's. Of course if the pot gets turned over or broken up in a storm, then they'll get out. Sooner or later, they get out if we don't haul 'em first. Worms get the wood and it breaks up. A lost pot and all, it just breaks up after a while. That's how it works. That's about all there is to it."

Of course that is not all there is to it. Lobstering may seem simple to one who does it all the time, but so far as the students' curiosity is concerned, Norm had hardly scratched the surface. The questions would begin. (The following is excerpted from an actual lecture):

Student (S): "What wood is best for making traps?"

Norm Foye (F): "Oak. Oak. It's tough and worms—teredos—well, they do a good job on it, but if you use spruce or pine, it'll only last six months and it's all gone. Oak pots will last three years if you dry 'em every six months. But if you start with one hundred pots, in three years if you had ten left, you'd be darn lucky. Storms, worms, boats, they all get 'em; anything like that."

A derelict pot of the kind that washed up on Appledore Island occasionally.

S: "Does a trap that has algae and stuff like that on it catch more lobsters than one that doesn't?"

F: "No, no, it don't fish as good. You take a brand new trap right out and set it, they won't catch anything. Even with good lobstering. But if you let 'em brown—brownin' up we call it—they'll fish like the devil. But if they get all that algae over 'em, you've got to take them aground and scrape 'em off. Lobsters don't care for all that—we call it slop—on 'em. No offense to Dr. Kingsbury. But you've got to dry 'em out about every three or four months, especially in the warm seasons. Those they set out in the spring—right now they're getting horrible, shoal water, you know, and all that. Lobsters will go into a clean pot a lot better than one of those we've just been talking about—all moss. No good."

S: "How do you make the buoys? Turn them out on a lathe or have them made for you?"

F: "They're made. Most all are now Styrofoam. 'Course you can't use Styrofoam out here—the siggles (seagulls) gobble it all up. You have to use wood because they'll just eat a Styrofoam buoy right up. Two nights and it's all gone."

S: "What do you use for bait?"

F: "Well, herrin' we think is the best bait."

S: "You just put the herring in the parlor?"

F: "No, right here in the kitchen end; it's on a cleat. Some pots have a bait hook and you put it in there."

S: "Then what would make them go through into the parlor?"

F: "Gee, I dunno; I never asked one; but that's where they go. We don't know how many go out of a trap. I've never seen pictures of it. Down on the bottom I've watched a lobster walk right by one. It's common to see the lobsters crawling by and never even stop. You see 'em—we haul 'em a lot of times—one would be sitting on the side head there. They seem to be going in, most of 'em, going in head first, the ones we catch at it. Once he gets in there—I don't know why he goes in the back. But you'll catch an awful lot, long's they're crawling."

S: "Is it true they like rotten herring?"

F: "No. No. I know people say it, but it's not really true. They like oily bait, but really rotten, I'd say no. You won't get anything. No, they won't touch it."

Kingsbury (K): "How rotten does it have to be before they won't eat it?"

F: "Well, what we call 'sweet.' I don't know how you'd explain it. But a bait with no salt on it, like if you got herrin' and it was going to pieces and you put it in as bait, you wouldn't get no lobsters. But if you got it salted, with the oil coming out, you'd get 'em. But right rotten, so's there's maggots, you don't get nothing. You wouldn't use it."

S: "Do you have to have a license to go lobstering?"

F: "Yes, you're supposed to. (Laughter) Well, it don't cost anything. Used to be a dollar; now they've upped it to ten dollars. But you've got to be a resident of the state and things like that."

S: "How does the state boundary war affect fishermen?"

F: "Not a bit! Just New Hampshire trying to gobble up a few thousand acres of our fishing grounds, that's all. I don't think they'll make out. I don't see any reason why they should. Well, it never should've got out of hand. They pinched one guy; then the governor got into it and blew it all up. It's more or less simmered down now, but the line has always been there. There's been fishermen get over it a little bit but nobody cared one way or another. The governor really got it cannon-ballin' where it shouldn't even of happened. If somebody got over the line, all they've got to say, 'Hey, get your gear back.' That's what we always do. We never, *never* had any trouble, but when you get the bigwigs and the politicians in it, they really get it goin'. I don't know how it's all going to end up."

K: "How much power does a lobster have in its claw?"

F: "Quite a lot!"

"Keepers" are pegged and transferred to a crate called a "car" moored in the water.

S: "Ever get pinched by one?"

F: "You get more than pinched. They've got tremendous power in that crusher claw. It's just like a guy took a pair of visegrips and come right down on you. And they don't let go! The other cutter claw ain't too bad, but that crusher claw can really make your eyeballs pop. Really. They can really do it, and the pressure keeps coming down and down. It'll turn your whole knuckle all black."

S: "Well, what can you do if one clamps on your finger?"

F: "Grin and bear it! If you don't jump or something, they'll let go and drop off after a while. But if you ever move, then you've got to stomp him or something. Very, very seldom do we get bit, say once a year. They're not that hard to handle. Well, I suppose they are if *you* reach in like we do, in a whole bunch of them with those snappers and all the claws going. But we don't panic. We've got gloves on."

S: "Isn't there a special way of plugging them?"

F: "Oh yes. Just grab 'em with one hand and put the plugs in with the other. (Laughter) Well, what I mean is, see, you hold the claws in both hands. . . .If you had a live one here, I'd show you. There's a little trick to it.

If you was trying it, he'd probably reach around and grab you with the other one. All we got to do is catch 'em. We don't have no trouble pluggin' 'em."

S: "Do you ever try to recover buoys and traps that have washed up?"

F: "Yeah. In fact, I got to get Dr. Kingsbury for this one. I think it's $50 for taking a trap off the beach. (Laughter) Yeah. That's what it is."

K: "I didn't have anything to do with that one!"

F: "Tell it to the judge." (Laughter, applause)

S: "Has anyone caught that fellow who was taking pots that didn't belong to him off Duck Island?"

F: "Down to Duck Island? No, he was helping himself. No, he had too much power. We'd like to catch him."

S: "What would you do to him if you caught him?"

F: "Heh, heh, heh. As a rule, they don't come back a second time! But all in all, we're not bothered too much by that. But if they're caught, as a rule they *don't* come back. That's all I can say on that one." (Laughter)

K: "You never enlist the legal authorities?"

F: "No. No. Never bother them. No, we do it ourselves." (Laughter, applause)

S: "Can you give us some idea of how much a lobsterman makes?"

F: "Well, I dunno. I *have* made good money, what we consider good. But now, I dunno. I can make as much or better than the average machinist or quarterman—a lot better'n he can. That's the only way to answer that. I've never had a problem making a living fishing. But I might have been a hard fisherman. We went in hard weather and worked hard—long hours—but I always made what I considered was a good living. I don't mean somebody else starting out could. There'd be no money as far as a novice starting out—just no money in it. He just couldn't break in. Be no way. You'd go bankrupt. We're half lobster and half fish anyway. That's how we make out."

K: "What would a full supply of pots cost you?"

F: "Jeez. Well, they'll cost you $15 apiece and if a guy is going to be big, he's got to have four hundred to six hundred of them. Then you've got to have half again as many on land for the storms. We've got a wharf full in there (Kittery) now. We used to have a tremendous amount of gear, but, like I say, I've slowed down. But if a guy's startin' in, if he's got six hundred overboard, he's got to have another four hundred on the wharf ready to go, because he's going to lose... It's quite a poker game. Quite a game."

S: "How does one cope... Now don't take offense, but I've heard all lobstermen are drunk because it's so cold out there."

F: "No, I wouldn't take no offense. But I'll tell yuh, in the winter if you was ever out there drunk—you might do it a few times, but you'd never come home. You'd never come home. Some gustin' rough out there in the winter. Unbelievable. No, far's the cold, you're dressed for it and you work and it doesn't bother you. Our hands—we're in to it every day and it don't bother. Probably if you went out there and stuck your hand in it and the air blew on it, why, most all the greenhorns we take out, they never go a second time. Not in the winter."

S: "What do you do to supplement your income when lobsters aren't running?"

F: "We've never had no problem. We've always made enough on the ocean. I've never worked for anybody in my life. I've never had no problem making a living."

S: "But you don't have any retirement contract. . ."

F: "No. No. I would never look forward to retirement. I would like to work as long as I could and then, plunk, and that'd be the end of it."

One year, toward the end of a question-and-answer period like the preceding one, a student, obviously wanting to try the lobstering business out himself, asked, "In the end, Mr. Foye, what does it take to make a successful lobsterman?" Norm contemplated this for just about ten seconds, and responded, "You've got to think like a lobster." To my mind, there is more wisdom in those seven words than in many entire college lectures. Think about it.

HOODS VERSUS CORNELL

Something happened in the summer of 1974 that had significance at the time, and even more dramatic effects in 1975. It had to do with Hoods's billing practices versus Cornell's check writing.

Chef Stu Feigenbaum could go shopping ashore only once a week. Obtaining milk and milk products capable of lasting a full week without either running out or going bad was a major challenge. Stu bought directly and in person from the Hoods Milk Company branch in Portsmouth. He asked that Hoods send the bill to our Portsmouth Post Office address so it could go out to Appledore Island for initialling and then we would send it on to Ithaca for payment. This Hoods agreed to.

After a month or so, Stu was surprised to learn on seeking his weekly milk in Portsmouth that Hoods had not yet been paid anything by Cornell. Stu responded that the Hoods bills had been passing through Appledore and going to Ithaca promptly. Even so, the process took time. Hoods understood; the milk flow continued unabated.

After two months, Hoods was still not getting paid. It had received nothing at all, and our account was getting quite large. Stu checked with me, and as soon as I could get ashore to a telephone I checked with Jay Freer. He said he had been passing the bills, properly approved for payment, to Cornell's check-writing department right after he got them. He would investigate, but he reminded me that Cornell wrote checks only once a week, and any check might be as much as two weeks late just in the normal processing.

After two and a half months, Stu reported that Hoods still had not been paid and he was having to get down on his knees to get his orders filled. I called Ithaca again. Jay said the bills *were* being paid.

After three months, as we were about to discharge the last alumni group, Stu was refused further milk. Hoods had received absolutely no payment all summer. Fortunately, alumni use less milk than the college-age crowd. Shortly thereafter we found out what had happened.

Cornell's checks are often difficult to decipher. The attached stub usually bears a few cryptic letters to identify what the check is for. Cornell had been sending the checks to Hoods's main office in Boston, which originated the bills for the Portsmouth branch. The Boston office had no idea that "Cornell University" meant "Shoals Marine Lab" and could find no account against which to credit the checks. The checks piled up uncashed in Boston for a while. Toward the end of the summer, noting that the checks came from Ithaca, New York, Hoods-Boston sent them on to Saratoga, the headquarters of Hoods for upstate New York. Hoods-Saratoga had no idea what they were for, either, and had no hope of finding out because the Portsmouth account they were to credit was handled in Boston. Finally, after some more arrived, Hoods-Saratoga called Cornell, which traced the pile of uncashed checks to Jay Freer, and then everything became plain.

At the close of the season, back in Ithaca, I represented to Mr. Peterson that this was no way to do business. On the island we absolutely depended on the good will of all our suppliers. At best, when everything worked right, Cornell's reimbursement was slow. Some of the Portsmouth area suppliers, we found, would not even sell to the University of New Hampshire because the State of New Hampshire was even slower in paying than was Cornell. We needed to be able to pay our local bills on time, and in person if possible, to get out from under this bureaucratic cloud. Mr. Peterson said he would look into it.

Chapter Thirteen

A TANK, A TELEPHONE, AND A DOLPHIN
1975

A TRAVEL ADVANCE

In the spring of 1975 Jay Freer and I learned the nature of Cornell's plan to enable the Shoals Lab to make local payments in New Hampshire. The university wrote me a personal check for $7,000, debited to a Shoals account in Ithaca, which it identified as a travel advance. I was to keep a record of how I spent the money just as I would have done on a prepaid trip. When the money was exhausted and fully accounted for, the university would issue another check.

A check for $7,000, payable simply to John Kingsbury, represented a vast sum of money to me at the time; actually it was equal to a full quarter of my annual salary. I ran to a Portsmouth bank with that check as if it were a hot potato, and I deposited it there to create a checking account in the name of the Shoals Marine Laboratory. I was then able to write checks to Hoods and other suppliers on the spot, as needed. That was a considerable help.

I worried, though, how the IRS might view things when they got my annual personal return. All supporting bills and receipts for how the money was spent had to go to the university to justify the expenditures. I kept the cancelled checks from the Portsmouth bank as my only personal proof of how Cornell's money had been spent. This led, in due course, to a major confrontation with the university auditor (in person, in my office, with Jay Freer as witness). He demanded the cancelled checks. I refused to relinquish them, saying his proof of what Cornell had done with the $7,000 was my signature endorsing the back of the university's check. He said that any checks on any account in the Shoals Lab name had to remain in the possession of an officer of the university (meaning him). I pointed out that, as defined in university documents, faculty members are officers of the university. If it helped, I would keep the checks in my campus office, but the Shoals Lab checks would remain with me. I would need them in case of a personal IRS audit, and I doubted my ability to get them back if I ever let them go.

The final blow from this arrangement hit when the time came to pay the regular faculty honoraria. I found I was supposed to write myself an honorarium check from money that was already mine according to university accounts. I refused. To make matters worse, Cornell then began dunning me personally for a two-month-overdue loan of $7,000. It had not managed to identify the Shoals Lab receipts with the money paid me as a travel advance despite Jay's best effort. In addition to IRS vulnerability, my personal credit standing was now also in danger. In the end, it took a vigorous letter from me and a five-page memo from Jay to get this situation straightened out in Cornell's accounting labyrinth.

This awkward situation, difficult for all, arose from trustee legislation at Cornell requiring in effect that all university checking accounts be approved in advance by the trustees. Mr. Peterson had not wanted to bother the trustees with a picky request for a small, seasonal account in Portsmouth, New Hampshire.

In the end, though, that is what he had to do. Mr. Peterson recommended that, for 1976, the trustees approve such an account, he and I the designated signatories. They approved. Now Jay could move funds from our Ithaca accounts directly into the new Portsmouth account, or even deposit tuition payments and other income directly into it if he chose. Again we had won by force of circumstance rather than design an ability not normally given by the university to a junior professor or, in fact, to anyone. Now the auditor could have all the cancelled checks he wished.

While all this was working its way through administrative offices in the winter of 1975, another problem surfaced with the administration: the naming of buildings on Appledore Island. When I had started raising construction money from donors, I thought I had obtained permission in the right Cornell offices to name buildings according to the donor's wishes. Following those wishes, I had begun casually identifying buildings in conversations, on the island maps, and in the newsletter by their donors' names. A strongly worded letter arrived from someone in the Development Office telling me that I had no such right; only the trustees could name Cornell buildings. I was to inform the Development Office immediately of *all* buildings on Appledore Island that were being named after their donors. I responded promptly, fully, and accurately with a list of four buildings on the island: Kiggins Commons; the Palmer-Kinne Laboratory; the Grass Foundation Laboratory; and Gift-from-the-Sea, our outhouse.

Needless to say, the trustees saw only three of those names.

CHARLIE WERLY'S TANK

Charlie Werly came to visit Appledore Island one day in the summer of 1975 with his wife, Jane. He was one of the very first people to put money behind the Shoals idea back in 1966, when he was a trustee. He remains a faithful and committed friend of the Laboratory to the present day. On that particular summer day in 1975 we were offloading 55-gallon barrels of diesel oil from the *Wrack* to go to the Grass Foundation building to power the island generator. Charlie looked at the *Wrack's* slipping-drum winch, the delicate handling of rope loops around its power head, and the possibility of dropped barrels. Visions of split thumbs and worse passed through his head. He said, "That's not a very good way to do that. You need a storage tank on land filled directly from the water."

"I know that, Charlie, but we can't afford it. They cost real money."

"You find one and I'll pay for it."

With the help of Cornell alumnus Eli Manchester, a superb fifteen-thousand-gallon tank was soon located at the Naugahyde plant in Naugatuck, Connecticut. The factory had been built during World War II, when natural rubber was in critically short supply, to become the first major national producer of synthetic rubber. The process used large quantities of mild acid. A special tank used for acid storage was for sale as the factory was now being dismantled. Mr. Manchester went to check it out. He observed that the tank was built about twice as heavily as is standard for oil storage tanks. It had been kept in immaculate condition; absolutely no rust. Also, in his informed opinion the price was right. I went to Connecticut for a look, and agreed.

We bought it. Arrangements were made to have it shipped on a flatbed truck to Kittery. Simultaneously discussion began as to how to get the tank out to Appledore Island. The tank weighed six tons or a little more so far as we could determine. Why not simply plug its ports, roll it into the

*Above: The Werly tank arriving at Appledore Island. (Where is the barge?)
Below: Off the barge and onto shore.*

water, hitch a line to it, and drag it out? Some said it probably would not be a stable shape for towing and might yaw about, sweeping back and forth across the harbor. Then why not raft it alongside the *Wrack?* It might overtop her, or chafe violently against her, or overwhelm the *Wrack's* ability to steer, or all three. The most conservative thing to do would be to put it on the barge. We knew from practice that the barge acted predictably under tow even when heavily loaded. Even if the barge were submerged by the weight of the tank, the tow would probably be safer than without the barge, provided the whole business didn't overturn. Here's what we did.

Several weeks later, an extra-wide truck showed up at Frisbee's with the tank aboard. Ron Harelstad was there with the barge. The driver tried but eventually gave up attempting to get the tank onto the barge there. He couldn't get down to the dock properly with so large a rig. Ron redirected him to the State Port Authority dock at Portsmouth, and went upriver with the barge. With the help of the people and crane at the Port Authority dock, the tank was unloaded from the truck and placed on the barge and thoroughly dogged down. The day was nearly over by the time the tow was ready and the tide was right to start out to Appledore Island.

As it happened, purely by chance, Charlie Werly had come out to Appledore Island for a second seasonal visit that same day. He had expected to see the tank in place on the island. Instead, nothing had yet happened on the island, and nothing happened there all day. Finally, late in the day, I took Charlie back to shore in the lab's Aquasport. As we approached Whaleback Light, we saw what looked like a submarine coming down from the Portsmouth Navy Yard. The Aquasport closed rapidly with it and the *Wrack's* silhouette soon materialized in front of a gigantic circular shape riding high astern. We had met the tank! But the barge was nowhere to be seen. It was almost completely under water. Charlie was impressed; so was I.

The tank arrived safely at Appledore Island after a very slow tow. On the next high tide it was floated into the swimming pool. Dominic gave much thought about how to get it ashore and where to put it. In the end, he constructed a temporary railway with some rails salvaged from the old Coast Guard marine railway in Babb's Cove. With that in place there was finally a use for those telephone poles obtained from military surplus years earlier. They were just right as rollers under the tank.

With the backhoe scurrying about, the tank was oriented toward shore, its front-end jacked up, a telephone pole roller placed underneath, and the tank dragged forward inch by inch. Another roller was placed beneath the front of the tank before the first one reached the midpoint of the tank. Slowly and haltingly the tank climbed the beach; additional rollers were added as necessary. When a roller came out from under the back end of the

Dominic positioning the next telephone pole roller.

tank it was taken to the front and used again. The tank moved onto a second section of rails. The first rails were removed from behind and shifted into place ahead. Through this process of leap-frogging rails and poles the tank moved slowly across the road to the location where it now lies. There Dominic had used a little judicious dynamite to help the backhoe dig a hole for the tank deep enough to get it at least half buried, and it came to rest in a bed of sand in that hole. All of this took nearly a week of major effort.

Fifteen-thousand gallons of diesel oil would run Appledore Island for two years. The cost of fifteen-thousand gallons of diesel oil was a major expense. Getting it delivered was another. Here's how we solved the delivery problem for the first filling of the Werly Tank.

The generators at the White Island Light require that the Coast Guard make occasional deliveries of diesel oil to that island. The *Hornbeam,* their large buoy-tender out of Woods Hole, was equipped with tanks, pumps, and hoses to make such deliveries. Perhaps we could get the *Hornbeam* to stop at Appledore Island if we paid for the oil. I put the paperwork into motion. After several exchanges it became clear that the *Hornbeam* would

The Hornbeam *positioned for oil delivery at Appledore Island.*

be willing to pick up enough Number 2 fuel oil at the Sprague terminal in Portsmouth to meet the needs of both Appledore and White Islands. The crew would pump us full on the way to White Island and the Coast Guard would charge us only for the gallons of oil it took to do that. We were told in detail what to do to get ready and what hoses and connections we had to have to join our tank to the *Hornbeam*. I was doubly pleased by all this; not only did we avoid the considerable costs of hiring a commercial tanker from Portland (the nearest available), but also, if some oil were spilled on this first attempt to get it ashore, we would be operating under the direct supervision of the Coast Guard, which was the policing authority.

It was a great day when the *Hornbeam* appeared. Radio contact was made. They picked up our mooring. We took their hose ashore with the Whaler and connected it to ours. Oil began flowing into the Werly tank. It flowed for four hours. The whole transfer, 13,705 gallons, was made without one drop of spillage on land or water. Sprague Oil Company charged the Coast Guard 31.45 cents a gallon under a low-cost government contract. When we finally got the bill, the fuel cost us very much less that what we would have paid for it from a truck on the Kittery dock.

This situation proved too good to last. Although the Coast Guard was happy to do this favor for us (we often hunted for lost boats in Gosport Harbor at Coast Guard request), a commercial tanker company had complained to the Coast Guard that it was illegal under federal regulation for the government to provide a service in competition with private business. The tanker company was ready to provide that service to Appledore Island, and had the right to compete for it free of governmental undercutting. We never found out who complained, nor how they learned of the Coast Guard delivery to Appledore, but we suspect the company used for its corporate benefit information gained from listening to the marine radio frequencies on which we conversed with the *Hornbeam*, which is illegal.

ON IGNORING CORNELL'S TRUSTEES, AND OTHER EVENTS

Let's return to the matter of names one more time. The Werly tank got me into trouble again. It's not a building, I reasoned, and should not be subject to the requirement of trustee approval of building names. Charlie was obviously proud of what we had done together, he and the Shoals people, in finding and installing that tank. I asked him if we could call it the Werly Tank on the island map. He was delighted with that idea. People in Cornell's Development Office weren't so delighted, however, when they saw the name on the island map. I was charged with being disrespectful to a donor.

The next time Charlie Werly came to Appledore Island he went through the lunch line as usual with the students and the rest of us. It was standard practice in those days (and still is, I think) to introduce all strangers who happened to be with us at mealtimes. As lunch concluded I rose to introduce Charlie Werly, and mentioned that among many other nice things he had done for the lab, he was personally responsible for the Werly Tank. I then gave Charlie the floor. He stood up, looked around the room, and said with deep emotion and obvious pride, "There are many college buildings named after donors. There are even entire campuses named after donors. But I doubt if anyone else has a fuel tank named after him on any other campus in this country." He sat down to loud and prolonged applause. Charlie Werly is a true island person.

Earlier, a great deal of thought had been given to the best names for Kiggins Commons and the Palmer-Kinne Lab. Specifics had been discussed at length with the respective donors. When the time had come to tell Jim and Martha that I needed to bring a formal name to the trustees of the university for approval, immediately Jim said, "Call it the Martha Kinne Palmer Lab." Martha said simultaneously, "Name it the James B. Palmer

Construction of the Palmer-Kinne Laboratory. Above: First wall erected;
Below: Front wall and beams in place.

Palmer-Kinne Laboratory: Exterior and interior completed.

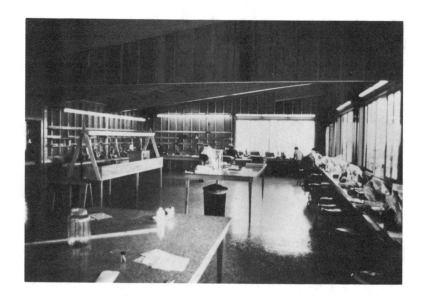

Above: Jim and Martha Palmer.
Below: President (of Cornell) Dale Corson with ever-present camera.

Laboratory." After some gyrations we settled on "The Palmer-Kinne Laboratory," recognizing in that name not only both of them but also those several others in Jim's Palmer line whose lives had been influenced by Cornell, and Martha's Cornell relatives of the Kinne name. It was an appropriate name, too, for the several Palmer children and grandchildren who had garnered Cornell degrees through the years (much to the delight and pride of their forebears). So far as I know (though I have never checked), the Cornell trustees approved that name.

It was not so easy in the matter of Kiggins Commons. Willard Kiggins said, as soon as he heard it, that the formal "Willard A. and Kathryn Kiggins, Jr. Commons" was too awkward. He opined that "Kiggins Commons" had a lot more going for it. "Let's call it that." Heartily in agreement I submitted that name. In due course notification came back that the trustees had approved calling the new building "The Willard A. Kiggins, Jr. Commons." Someone in the layers of decision had helpfully changed what I had requested apparently thinking an ordinary professor would not have been careful to be accurate or respectful enough. I wrote Willard about this miscarriage of his wishes and suggested that we ignore the trustees. He responded that ignoring the Cornell trustees was exactly the right thing to do.

Apart from successful top-notch courses on Appledore Island, which by now were taken for granted by all, the high points of the summer of 1975 were several. Paramount was Dominic's building of the Palmer-Kinne Lab, which was up and operational by midsummer.

The Palmer-Kinne Lab is grand both in appearance and in function. It has become one of the main foci of island life. As the Palmers wished, it is similar in outline and profile to the Brookfield Building on Star Island. This low profile was a major plus as it turned out.

Way back in 1966 when I first examined it, I wondered what real use could be made of that gigantic, indestructible radar tower perched on a high point of Appledore Island. The best use crystallized in our minds when the time came to design a salt-water system for sea tables and toilets. The fourth level up in the radar tower, the last to which a stairway came, would be ideal for a salt-water storage tank. Pressure generated from that elevation would be ample to serve the entire island.

Dominic erected a retaining wall inside the fourth level, separating off the stairwell, and installed a supply pipeline across the rocks and down into the ocean just outside where the dock is. He built a small housing above high tide for a very large pump. Although we had the usual start-up problems with intake fouling and breaks, this general design has worked well. In the first year or two, though, it gave Dominic some special grief. He had decided that the bottom level of the radar tower was a convenient place to store carpenter tools and equipment, always a problem on the island.

The pump on the shore was controlled by a float-switch in the radar tower. When the tank was full, the float-switch was supposed to shut off the pump. Sometimes it stuck open. Then the tank level soon spilled over the retaining wall, raining seawater down the stairways and onto Dominic's tools below until someone noticed and shut off the pump. Before Palmer-Kinne was built, the radar tower was well isolated and it could be hours before someone did notice an overflow. Dominic tinkered unsuccessfully with the float-switch. After a few more floods, he got a new one. The new one also stuck open occasionally.

Dominic's opinion of float-switch engineers, already low, got lower with each flooding of his tools. Finally, he gave up looking for a float-switch that *always* worked. Instead he drilled a hole just below flood level through the outside wall of the radar tower facing Kiggins Commons. Now when the float-switch stuck, that fact was immediately proclaimed visibly by a widening streak of water down the outside concrete of the radar tower for all to see. A fast run to the pump switch in the tower could still save the tools from another wetting.

When it came time to site the Palmer-Kinne Lab, there was really only one choice. Sea tables need running seawater as nearly the same temperature as that of the ocean as possible. Long stretches of slowly flowing distribution pipes out in the summer sun defeat that objective. The solution is to keep supply lines for sea tables as short as possible. Obviously, the Palmer-Kinne Lab, housing the most heavily used sea tables on the island, should be built immediately adjacent to the radar tower. And so it was.

The low profile of this new building next to the radar tower not only reduced somewhat the sore-thumb effect of the latter, but also was almost invisible from Star Island, a condition of our lease, even though the building is on a high point of the island with a great view.

In the break between courses we had a bang-up dedication of the Palmer-Kinne Laboratory. The timing coincided with the 50th wedding anniversary of Jim and Martha Palmer. The Palmer family, especially David and Nancy, took the dedication as an opportunity to celebrate doubly. Largely through their efforts, all but one of the 30-plus children and grandchildren, many Cornellians among them, made it to Appledore Island on the appointed day. So did Nellie and Dale Corson, then president of Cornell; Mr. and Mrs. Eugene Mills, then president of the University of New Hampshire; Rik Clark, of Cornell's Northeast Regional Office; and many other special guests. Stu Feigenbaum and his kitchen staff outdid themselves.

The simple ceremonies of the dedication suited well both the island spirit and a gathering there of great warmth and happiness that will be long remembered by all who were present.

Dale Corson attended a gull nest on Appledore Island for some time to obtain the picture above of a just-hatched gull chick. Below: Same, dried out and fluffed up.

Dale and Nellie Corson stayed on the island two days and nights on that occasion. Dale used this as an opportunity to check things out closely. Who knows what he might have heard in Ithaca about the doings on Appledore Island? In his quiet but perspicacious way he quizzed students, watched the kitchen crew in operation, participated in operating the *Wrack's* new radar (his professional interest), and fathomed Dominic insofar as that is possible. He even challenged me on the contents of a book I had recently published (*The Rocky Shore*). Why had I termed the showy part of a particular plant the flower when as a Cornell botanist I knew full well that the showy part of that plant was really a bract? This demonstrates that one should never write down to an audience, especially if Cornell's physicist president is to be included in it. Dale went away well pleased with what he saw and heard.

With the Palmer-Kinne Lab completed, Dominic had time to get to some long-neglected matters, especially at Kiggins Commons. When he heard that the historic Jordan Marsh building in Boston was being taken down, he managed to obtain a truly massive timber from the salvage. It was soon incorporated as the bumper in a new loading platform at the rear of Kiggins Commons. A spiral staircase was installed inside, and also a fireproof ceiling in the kitchen. Polished Ogunquit green granite counters were laid in the washrooms.

All summer we had been climbing a ladder to reach the front door of Kiggins Commons. In spare moments Dominic had been building, in his mind, a stone stairway for that entrance. He had spotted various rocks all around the island that "felt right" for the purpose. Gradually he accumulated the actual rocks at the site and then went to work freehand on a flight of doorway stairs that represent Dominic at his finest. It is truly a work of monumental art.

Toward the end of the summer Willard and Kathryn Kiggins paid us a visit to see how things were going. They walked across the island, climbed Dominic's stairs, noted John Bender's sculpted wood sign identifying Kiggins Commons, and went inside. They turned simultaneously though separately to enter the dining room from either end of the serving corridor. Like most visitors, they were struck by the beauty of that room with its spectacular floor, arches, and view—until each looked up to see six bare three-hundred-watt bulbs in naked porcelain fittings in the ceiling. Simultaneously but independently each of them decided something would have to be done about that. Fortunately, they decided on the same something. Willard and Kathryn told me they knew exactly what to do about obtaining suitable light fixtures for that room. Could I send them some pictures of the room, particularly its vaulted ceiling, as soon as possible? That I did.

306

Here's what they did. They showed the pictures to Sam Ogden, a neighbor of theirs in Londonderry, Vermont, who is a distinguished artist in metal sculpture. Willard and Kathryn asked him to create appropriate fixtures. Later that season Sam Ogden personally delivered to Appledore Island six original light fixtures in which he had captured in an inverse way the sweep and curves of the Kiggins Commons dining room. He installed them himself as a final Kiggins touch to that magnificent building.

A REAL TELEPHONE OUT THERE?

In the summer of 1975 two seemingly simple events culminated two years of hard paperpushing. As the reader may have gathered, the radio links from the Island to the mainland left much to be desired. Dominic Gratta was regularly frustrated getting building materials. Stu Feigenbaum had massive misunderstandings with his food suppliers in Portsmouth. The island office was often inhibited or thoroughly thwarted when it came to communicating to and from Ithaca or even just Durham.

Wouldn't it be great if we had a regular telephone on Appledore Island? Given the insurmountable difficulties of radio, especially CB, the desire to have a real telephone ran very high at times. The cost of submarine communications cable was way out of sight. Could we get suitable cable from surplus? None had appeared on the lists or in the state warehouses. Even if by some miracle we got the cable, where would we go ashore with it? If we got it ashore, would the telephone company be willing to hitch us up to its system? All in all, a true telephone seemed an unattainable dream.

Then I learned by chance of Huc Hauser at Simplex Wire and Cable, up the Piscataqua River, who might be able to help. It turned out that the navy was then retrieving cable that had been laid during World War II on the floor of the Atlantic Ocean, which it was delivering to Simplex for evaluation and reconditioning. We had seen the navy cable-layer with its unmistakable bow going in and out of the river from time to time. Each trip brought many miles of cable to the Simplex dock. We needed only eight.

That was a temptation too great to resist. I started looking into it—and found a large iceberg dead ahead. To lay a communications cable, not only do you have to have the cable, you must also have permission from the U.S. Army Engineers to put it in marine waters anywhere, the additional approval of appropriate state agencies and affected towns to put such cable within the three-mile territorial limit and across the near-shore bottom and intertidal zone, and the approval of all landowners contiguous to the properties involved. All these permissions are necessary in addition to the approval of the telephone company for hitching into its system. In those days when telephones were not available for public purchase, you also had to find a source for them, but that was the least of our worries.

How we did achieve a real telephone on Appledore Island is a very long story. The pile of permit paper and correspondence was a full foot high by the time it eventually happened. Two college presidents, four senators, two states, three seacoast towns (Kittery, New Castle, and Rye), the U.S. Navy, the U.S. Army, the U.S. Coast Guard, Simplex Wire and Cable, and Western Electric all were in the picture before the cable was laid. Here are the high points.

Huc Hauser from Simplex encouraged us that the navy would probably be willing to support our nonprofit marine educational efforts with a gift of cable if we convinced them of the need and worthiness of our request. He suggested letters to the navy from the presidents of Cornell and the University of New Hampshire with copies to the senators representing those states. I proposed the text for such a letter to the two college presidents and both sent letters. One of the senators who received copies immediately took a personal interest and assigned someone in his office to keep after the navy until a decision had been made. So far, so good.

At the same time, I wrote the Army Engineers in Waltham, Massachusetts, asking what we needed in the way of a permit to lay the cable. I pointed out to them that Appledore Island had served as a center for cable communications during World War II, so designated cable paths from the island to the mainland were already on the marine charts.

We really had only two choices of where to land our cable: the Coast Guard base at Portsmouth (actually in the Town of New Castle) or Rosamond Thaxter's exposed shore-front property at Champernowne Farm in Kittery Point. The cable paths on the official marine charts went to New Castle. I tried that first.

This brought the Coast Guard First District Office in Boston into the picture, but we approached it through the Portsmouth Coast Guard base. We found, to our surprise, that the Portsmouth Coast Guard base not only housed the usual search and rescue people, but also had a contingent of specialists who were responsible for all communications to lighthouses and offshore installations from Rhode Island to the Canadian border. They knew all about telephones and cables, and they were happy to be of help to us. They saw no reason why our cable couldn't come ashore at their base and tie into the telephone company on the same terminal that served their cable out to White Island.

The Boston office saw it somewhat differently. The people there were worried about the legal aspects and also about the possibility that our cable might foul their White Island cable if laid near it. But basically they wished to cooperate. It was, of course, to their advantage to have reliable communications with offshore islands, and we had been of considerable service to them over the years looking for missing boats in Gosport Harbor and the like, many times saving them a trip out.

The Coast Guard cable from White Island to Portsmouth had an extra pair of lines in it. In the end, Boston offered us the use of that pair in preference to our laying a cable all the way to the mainland next to theirs. We jumped at the offer. It meant we would need to scrounge and lay only about a mile of cable instead of the eight miles originally envisaged, and there was already a direct cable path on the charts between Appledore and White Islands.

In the meantime, I had received a massive document from the Army Engineers with directions and forms for an application. I studied it carefully. Among other things it required a scale drawing of the exact path of the cable, including a profile representation of depths and passage across the intertidal zone. Of course, they expected drawings from a professional engineer. That we did not have. Instead, Cynthia Hyde, the student working as our assistant chef that summer, who had taken a course or two in drawing, volunteered to make them. She did so with pen and india ink on onion skin paper through which she traced the marine chart lines, adding to them as necessary.

There was a single electric typewriter on the island, in the island office, which worked when the generator did. After several attempts it finally produced an application form properly filled out and readable. The directions said to submit the form in quadruplicate (or some such number). Being unable to do that easily, I sent off the one-and-only application form with Cynthia's original drawings.

The matter of how to get some actual telephones needed attention. In such circumstances I commonly asked Cornell's Development Office to see if there were any Cornell contacts in useful places. It responded on this occasion that the executive vice president of Western Electric was a Cornell graduate. I wrote him about our telephone problem. He wrote back that he would see what he could do if I would send a complete description and specifications for the system of phones we wanted on Appledore Island.

One of the communications technicians at the Portsmouth Coast Guard base (Russ Belleville) was happy to do some moonlighting. The Coast Guard used Western Electric equipment exclusively and he knew exactly what to order. He came out to Appledore Island, discussed what we needed, and wrote a detailed proposal. After a few weeks I had it in hand and sent it off to Phil Hogin, Western Electric's executive vice president. Within a very few days Western Electric had approved a grant from its philanthropic foundation in the amount necessary to cover its internal costs, and it shipped the equipment to the Coast Guard base at Portsmouth. The next time I saw

Russ Belleville he exclaimed, "Who do you know? It takes us at least six months to get an order like that delivered."

With the push from college and senatorial offices, the navy readily agreed to give us the cable we needed. Then it started trying to figure how to do so legally. The navy had assumed that we had some kind of federal funding that would have made a transfer possible. We had none. After considerable communication by telephone, some involving Simplex Wire and Cable Company, I received indirect word to call off the senator's office. The glare of senatorial attention made progress very difficult for the navy in the absence of a clear-cut way to transfer ownership of government cable. The navy shied at taking visible action to transfer the cable to us while they were being quizzed weekly about it at the senatorial level.

Thus it was that the two college presidents sent letters to their respective senators thanking the senators most warmly for their interest in the cable matter and informing them that the navy had been most helpful on our behalf (without actually saying we had the cable). At that point, of course, we didn't.

The Army Engineers surprised us with a prompt response to our application. They sent it right back saying I hadn't provided the required copies. I returned it to them immediately, without copies, but with a letter pointing out that the person reading my letter probably was sitting within 30 feet of a photocopy machine, that I didn't have access to one within ten miles of ocean, and that under these circumstances it would be kind of them to make the copies they needed themselves. They might even send an extra one back to me, too, because I had none at all. And I had no telephone to tell them so, which was the purpose of our application in the first place.

That was the end of that foolishness. Our application started through the labyrinthine U.S. Army Engineers administrative review procedures and we heard nothing more for some time.

The application had to be supplemented by a show of approval from abutting landowners. That meant checking with our few fishermen neighbors on Appledore Island, none of whom objected; actually a telephone on the island would have benefitted them almost as much as us in an emergency. There were no abutters on White Island. I wondered how long it would take the Army Engineers to realize that if there were no abutters, I didn't have to get their approval. Instead, the Army Engineers eventually involved all the abutters of the Coast Guard Base in New Castle in the permit application, and I had to make an appearance at the New Castle Town Offices.

The Engineers eventually made the preliminary finding that if we laid the cable on the natural ocean floor without modifying the bottom, it would present no environmental damage, and if we laid it in the existing charted cable path, it would pose no navigational difficulties. They distributed these findings to all local radio stations, to newspapers, to post offices for posting, by mail to all abutters, and to the town offices of the towns involved, and to the departments responsible for environmental protection in Maine and New Hampshire. All people and agencies opposed to the Army Engineers issuing the requested permit were invited to object by mail or in person.

The only response that crossed my desk was a letter from the Maine Department of Environmental Conservation (DEC) stating that it agreed with the engineer's findings in general, but was concerned about how we were going to protect the cable as it crossed over our shoreline and through the intertidal zone. Sensing a potential problem here, I responded to them very carefully that we planned to lay the cable across the rocky shore between the rocks. At most we might move a few rocks over it by hand (no powered equipment) if absolutely necessary. To appreciate what is involved, the reader needs to visualize oceanic communications cable: it is about as thick as a human wrist; its exposed surface consists of a tightly wound layer of heavy stainless steel wire enclosing a thick, dense rubber core inside; and the pair of copper conductors seem almost negligible at the center of all this protective covering. Oceanic communications cable is not delicate.

Eventually the Maine DEC responded that if we planned to move any rocks over the cable, even by hand, we would need a wetlands permit. By then I was fed up with permits. I wrote back that we would not move any rocks over the cable by hand or in any other way. If necessary, we would instead thread the cable under and between the rocks without disturbing them even slightly.

That should have ended that ridiculousness, but some months later, after the cable had been laid and no rocks moved, I received a somewhat intense letter from the Maine DEC complaining that when its inspectors had gone to Kittery to check on what we had done, they couldn't get out to the island. I responded that the inspectors were welcome on Appledore Island any time they wanted to come, but it wasn't incumbent on us to send a boat in for them. The state would have to find a way to get them out if they were going to come. They never came.

Earlier, as if by magic, two large reels of oceanic communications cable appeared on the deck of our barge after we had positioned it alongside the NOAA R/V *Ferrell* at the Simplex Cable Company's dock on a particular date as someone had suggested would happen if the barge was there then. I suppose the navy inventories still show this particular cable as being on the floor of the Atlantic Ocean—which, of course, is exactly where it still is.

The Appledore cable-layer in action.

Finally, the permit from the Army Engineers came! It was a disappointingly small piece of ordinary paper with a few short typewritten insertions—nothing like the grand embossed and red-sealed document you might expect for all the work involved. We could now lay the cable. The telephone system was being installed in the buildings on the island by Russ Belleville. The cable itself was out at the Shoals, ready to go. All the pieces were now assembled, *and no significant bills had been involved.*

Laying the cable (in the summer of 1976) proved the easiest part of the whole operation. Our cable-laying crew just unreeled it slowly over the side of the barge with the Whaler providing the forward motion.

But our problems were not over. The telephone company balked at providing service to a terminal at a federal base located in the Portsmouth exchange (New Hampshire area code) to serve a telephone not of its ownership that was located at a private address in a different town, a different state, and a different area code. It claimed a signal could not travel ten miles without amplification. Our Coast Guard technician claimed it could, though perhaps attenuated a bit.

Above: Joining the intra-building cable to the marine cable.
Below: The first telephone call!

I asked Phil Hogin, the executive vice president at Western Electric if he would intervene with the New Hampshire telephone company on our behalf. He did and it connected us despite the irregularities and misgivings.

It was truly a great day when that Western Electric telephone first called to the mainland from the Shoals Lab office on Appledore Island, and a very pleasant sound when it rang with the first incoming call. You can barely imagine the "high" we all felt on the island that golden day. Now Dominic and Rachel could do their business in private, and so could the rest of us without having to go ashore.

But, sad to say, it didn't last. Two winters later, seacoast New England experienced what was called the "storm of the century." Not only was our cable to White Island broken in more than one place, but the Coast Guard's own cable from White Island to the mainland was severed. It took the Coast Guard two years to get its cable repaired. In the meantime, the Portsmouth base relied on radio communications with White Island, and we went back to radio, also. Transistors and miniaturization were making radio links more reliable, more convenient, and less expensive. Frequency modulation (FM) had replaced the old AM marine telephone frequencies, resulting in much clearer transmissions. More channels were suddenly available and synthesized sets made crystals unnecessary. Splicing a broken underwater cable is not child's play, as we found when Russ Belleville had to splice ours after one break the first winter (1976-77). Just locating the break and lifting the cable was a challenge.

Reluctantly, we decided not to try for a cable connection again. Now, after several generations of intermediate solutions to the communications problem, Appledore Island is served by a microwave telephone system that is almost equivalent (when it is working right) to having a regular dial telephone. No mobile or marine operator is involved, and the frequencies are not quite as open to public listening as in either the mobile or marine services.

WELL BOTTOMS AND OTHER THINGS

Returning to the important events of 1975, the presentation of a *Sea Semester* jointly with the Sea Education Association ranked high. A *Sea Semester* consists of two parts: a land-based introduction to marine and nautical sciences at Woods Hole, followed by an equal time at sea studying aboard and handling a large schooner. We proposed to offer the land component at Appledore Island instead of at Woods Hole and the students

314

The Westward *as seen from the deck of her sister ship, the* Corwith Cramer, *1989. Both vessels are owned and operated by the Sea Education Association of Woods Hole, with which the Shoals Marine Lab is a formal associate.*

would board the R/V *Westward* directly from Appledore for the second half of the program. In preparation, the Shoals Lab obtained faculty approval to present a new two-week course on Appledore, *Introduction to Nautical Science,* for three credits. This course would be offered in the open slot of three weeks between the first and second offerings of the regular *Introduction to Marine Science* course. *Seagoing Apprenticeship,* presented during seven weeks aboard *Westward,* was approved for eight credits at Cornell. The full *Sea Semester* consisted of all three courses for a total of 16 credits, equalling to a full semester on campus. These courses were staffed by a combination of faculty members from the Shoals Lab and SEA.

The joint *Sea Semester* was absolutely top-notch academically and in terms of student reception. It was something we should have kept doing. The only problem was a matter that Cory Cramer of SEA and I might have anticipated: in no way can two office staffs be kept gainfully employed simultaneously on the income from one set of students. SEA and the Shoals

Lab both lost money on the venture, seriously enough that we were forced to decide we could not do it again.

A special benefit that resulted by chance from the joint presentation of a *Sea Semester* was that it brought Professor George Lyon from Cornell's engineering college to help teach *Introduction to Nautical Science*. He used his instruments, his skills, and his spare time on Appledore Island to answer the nagging question of whether our main well might go brackish (as had the small shore-side well) if we used it too hard, too long. George was able to determine that the bottom of the main well, in the northern interior of the island, is just about at the same level as the high tide line on the shores of Appledore. Thus there is little chance heavy pumping will ever make it go detectably brackish.

As the Shoals Lab came closer and closer to operating at design capacity, interest intensified about whether operating income would cover the island's full operating expense as we had prophesied at the beginning. All available figures were reviewed with great diligence. Decisions made at the annual meeting took on a higher significance. Those assembled in the fall of 1975 heard that the operating budget had ended the summer in the black (barely) despite losses associated with *Sea Semester*, and the budget had assumed the full operating costs of the island (not including depreciation) for the first time. With a tuition and fees income of around $100,000 in 1975, we had instructed about three hundred students and alumni in our island facilities; presented or provided space for four courses totalling 20 credits, which appeared in various combinations on the transcripts of six colleges or universities; paid summer salaries or honoraria to about 50 faculty and graduate assistants; employed an island staff of seven and a year-round office staff of one and one-half; published a book and a checklist; mailed over a thousand copies of six issues of the Lab's newsletter; maintained and operated five powered boats, three diesel generators, two water systems, one sewer system, about one and one-half miles of "roads," and a radio communications net; maintained and operated one backhoe, one dump truck, one carryall, one farm tractor, one jeep, and one stepvan; occupied and maintained seven buildings and one large tent, including three laboratories with 90 student stations and ten research stations; spent money in the Lab's name through two state accounts and five endowed accounts at Cornell, one account at the University of New Hampshire, and a checking account in Portsmouth; and again raised about $150,000 from donors. Not bad for half a dozen seasons' hard work on Appledore Island.

Among the significant votes taken at the annual meeting was one that would bring the Shoals Lab to a major milestone in 1976. Those

Hetty Baiz enjoying a fringe benefit of her job as Shoals Lab factotum. Hetty was followed in that function in due course by Rita Hogan.

attending voted to increase from 40 to 58 the capacity of *Introduction to Marine Science* the second time it would be offered that summer. This would be easily possible if Dominic could get the first new dormitory up in time, and if not we could put up a second military tent which we had been holding in reserve in case something happened to the first one. If successful, this would bring island operations essentially to full capacity for the last month of the summer.

At the 1975 annual meeting attendees had also to deal with the problem of what to do about the three-week midsummer period between the two offerings of *Introduction to Marine Science*, after the departure of the *Sea Semester* courses. With the idea of providing some advanced studies that might attract graduates of the *Introduction to Marine Science* courses back to the island, six new courses were proposed. Varying in length from one to three weeks, they were *Anatomy of the Gull, Field Phycology, Invertebrate Embryology, Underwater Research, Research in Biology,* and *Poetry and Poetics.* The last was an existing course offered by Cornell's Department of English that could be moved to the Shoals, an experiment championed by Hetty Baiz, who had replaced Wendy Zomparelli as Shoals office factotum, and welcomed by the English department. The first five were new courses that required faculty approval both at Cornell and UNH. The reputation of the Shoals Lab had now grown in Ithaca and Durham to the point where there was little faculty resistance to any new courses we might propose—a marked change from the skepticism and negativity the first course had brought forth in 1966.

Adult education programs offered the potential of utilizing the Appledore facilities fully, generating perhaps a little higher level of income than realizable from student tuition, and introducing potential donors to the Shoals. Those attending the annual meeting voted to increase the number of adult education programs offered in September to the alumni of both universities, and to accept SEA's offer to make the *Westward* available for adult practicums at sea at the same time.

Presentations at the 1975 annual meeting were not all positive. Donald Squires had left the directorship of the SUNY Marine Sciences Research Center at Stony Brook to take on the directorship of the SUNY-Cornell Sea Grant Institute of New York. He was replaced by Jerry Schubel, who immediately ran into typical New York State/SUNY budgetary problems. Jerry thought the program at the Shoals was great, but he noted that its function was undergraduate education. Why should the Marine Sciences Research Institute, whose charter envisaged neither undergraduates nor teaching, be spending off the top of its particularly tight budget to pursue these functions? We were informed that, reluctantly, Jerry was severing the MSRC connections with the Shoals Lab, and we would not receive the sixth through tenth payments under the agreement Don Squires had arranged. This removed $75,000 of pledged payments toward construction needs, but would make little actual difference in the coming year because Cornell's administration was now much more relaxed about Shoals affairs. The Shoals Lab was now open and running essentially on income, had demonstrated repeatedly its ability to raise capital as needed, and to survive a confrontation of Olympic magnitude. The SUNY contract was no longer the matter of life and death it had been at the beginning: $15,000 a year was now only about five percent of the lab's annual cash flow.

A DOLPHIN IN THE FREEZER

There had to be a third annual takeover of the Dairy Bar in 1975; the Ithaca public demanded it. A second lobster feed was organized and presented. This time a dolphin was involved.

Lobsters and dolphin on route from Appledore Island to Ithaca.

About half way through the summer a dead Atlantic white-sided dolphin had washed up on the shores of Appledore Island. The gulls were just beginning to get at its exposed eye when I saw it. To preserve it, I got some help and wrestled it into the jeep, took it up to the kitchen, and prevailed on a somewhat unhappy chef to let me put it in the walk-in freezer.

Later that morning a letter went to the federal officials in Gloucester, Massachusetts, whose responsibilities included enforcing the terms of the Marine Mammals Protection Act. These required that all dead or distressed animals be reported and left strictly alone until a properly constituted authority took them in charge. The letter described what we had found and done and asked permission to transport the frozen dolphin to the Veterinary College at Cornell for a proper professional necropsy following the Smithsonian protocol for marine mammals.

There was no reply from Gloucester. When the time came to think about closing the island and turning off the refrigeration, that dolphin, solid as a board, was still standing on its tail in the freezer. I wrote to Gloucester again, pointing out that something would have to be decided soon. The answer was classic federal bureaucratese. I paraphrase: "It is illegal to

The season closed with adult education programs. Larry Kelts from Merrimack College instructed this one.

possess dead marine mammals, frozen or otherwise. It is illegal to move such specimens, especially across state boundaries. No official notice will be taken of a missing dolphin on Appledore Island or the arrival of a frozen dolphin in Ithaca unless forced. In the future please be sure no more marine mammals wash up on your shores."

The frozen dolphin was just as effective as a large block of ice in keeping the lobsters cold enroute from the Shoals to Cornell. It was later the object of a full public dissection, which lasted almost all day, performed by Howard Evans, J.B. Heiser and other experts.

At dinner, Arthur and Helen Peterson appeared again in the lobster line. This time Mr. Peterson got a lobster with both claws intact. After all of the three hundred diners had gone through the line and were seated, I sought their attention. "The treasurer of Cornell was short-changed last year," I announced, "by getting a lobster with only one claw. As the treasurer well knows, the Shoals Lab always honors its debts and obligations in full." With that brief statement I presented to Pete Peterson the missing lobster claw. That little byplay was much enjoyed by all present, and Pete lost some of the anonymity he generally tried to preserve on campus.

Andersons Ledge, entirely underwater at high tide, is the outermost of the low tide lands at the Isles of Shoals, marked by a solid steel pole about a foot thick at the base. Landing a class on it safely is tricky. Here is the phycology (seaweed) class on Andersons Ledge in 1979.

Chapter Fourteen

GROWING PAINS
1976

CHANGES

As applications came in during the spring of 1976, it became obvious that, although both sessions of *Introduction to Marine Science* would fill comfortably, the new midseason short courses were not drawing well. In the end only two of them (*Anatomy of the Gull* and *Underwater Research*) had enough enrollment to be offered. An informal, noncredit diving course was organized to meet the needs of inadequately qualified applicants for admission to *Underwater Research*.

Willard Kiggins and the Doherty Foundation provided funds sufficient to ensure that the first dormitory would be built. As usual I drew a floor plan and Dominic worked out the construction. He went to work on it as soon as the season allowed. Funds were also in hand, mostly from contributions of the Rosamond Thaxter Foundation and members of the Laighton family, to allow simultaneously a major rebuilding of Laighton House, urgently needed to make the old cottage structurally sound and fully useful.

A lot of thought went into the dormitories. Features I was able to incorporate in the plans included windows that function as fire escapes from each room, rooms sized small enough to discourage heavy partying and

Dormitory 1.

equipped with desks and lights for easy studying, fixed beds with storage underneath to facilitate cleaning and housekeeping and located away from windows (so as to stay dry in a sudden storm), doors that are not directly opposite (to give a bit more privacy and quietness in each room), and a roofed porch (to keep arriving and departing luggage dry). The floor and walls of the central hall were to be fully waterproofed and the walls supplied with hooks on which foul-weather gear could be hung to drip and the rooms thereby kept dry.

The dormitory floors were finished with waterproof spread polyurethane, as are all new floors and some renovated ones at the lab. We owe these classy and almost indestructable floors to Bert Hamm and his crews. The first floor Bert did was the clear polyurethane one in Kiggins.

Bert was so pleased with the opportunity to work on Appledore Island, and we with his work (including the very low cost), that he has been coming back repeatedly. In fact, he more or less requires the Shoals Lab to have a floor needing resurfacing each year so he can keep coming out.

To help keep costs down, Bert saves up the chips he uses for coloring the polyurethane layer that are left over from each of his jobs

Bert Hamm.

ashore, and brings them with him. When the time comes to chose a color for a chip floor he throws down a handful of this and a handful of that, until the mixture satisfies Dominic or whoever is in charge. Each chip polyurethane floor on Appledore Island is a one-of-a-kind work from Bert Hamm's hand.

Two of the early mainstays of the island staff were conspicuous by their absence in 1977. Chef Stu Feigenbaum, having graduated from the Cornell hotel school, had to take a real job. He went to New York City and soon became manager of the Playboy Club there. Sam Hayward, equally competent became the second head chef. Island engineer and *Wrack* skipper Ron Harelstad succumbed to the strong lure of exotic adventure. Over the course of more than a year, his colleagues Russ Nilson and Ric Martini had sailed Russ's ketch *Serenity* from Appledore Island to the Galapagos Islands and then across to Tahiti. There they had discovered William Robinson in retirement and his brigantine *Varua* moldering at the dock. Mr. Robinson gave *Varua* to Russ and Ric if they would agree to rebuild her. Ron went to make it a threesome. Their subsequent adventures with the two vessels in South Pacific, Australian, and Alaskan waters invites a book of its own, which perhaps Ric Martini will add to his list of publications some day if the others don't beat him to it.

324

Chef Sam Hayward receives a standing ovation for his efforts on a special occasion in 1978 (identified by the wine bottles on the table).

The alumni programs at the end of the summers shaped up well during those years. To make them more readily available, the distinction between the alumni of Cornell and the University of New Hampshire was dropped. Alumni bred by either university would henceforth be invited to participate in any program. The University of New Hampshire helpfully took over the printing of the alumni program flyer. The *Westward* was scheduled for four-day alumni practicums at sea in September; they could be combined with an island program and were well received.

The Barnacles, the alumni of Professor Jackson's Zoological Laboratory on Appledore Island during the 1930s, came back for their first formal reunion under the letter-writing stimulation of Olive Brock. Some 40 Barnacles showed up, a remarkable achievement. Those people already on the island were treated to some fascinating reminiscences of their times. Even more stimulating was to watch each Barnacle's reaction in comparing the actual Appledore of 1976 with memories of it that had gelled some 30 or 40 years earlier.

Celia's Garden: Site cleared, smoothed, and rototilled; cottage foundations in background.

CELIA'S CEREUS

From time to time several of the Barnacles have brought back to Appledore items that were earlier identified with the island. The most unusual, perhaps, were five rooted cuttings from a night-blooming cereus plant that had belonged to Celia Thaxter herself more than a full century earlier. These were delivered to Appledore Island by Olive Brock. Here's how she got them.

Celia's mother, Eliza Laighton (wife of Thomas Laighton, who built the original Appledore House Hotel) possessed a night-blooming cereus plant (*Hylocereus undatus*) in her Appledore Island cottage. Just when and how she got it is unknown. This plant is a scraggly, spineless cactus well suited to the summer rigors of the Shoals. It thrives on benign neglect and may reward its owner, usually after several years, by blooming once, at night. Heralded by a large bud that keeps well its secret of just which night is going to be *the* night, the blossom lasts only one night, wilting by dawn. Days of suspense are followed by a brief but truly spectacular and highly fragrant display, well worth the years of waiting and the nights of staying up to catch it in bloom.

Above: Garden fence built, beds lined out, and planting begun. Student Gary Boden was heavily involved in this work. Below: East end of the garden as it appeared in July, 1979.

In 1851, Eliza's daughter, Celia, married her former tutor, Levi Thaxter, and went with him to live in Watertown, Massachusetts, near the senior Thaxters. Among Celia's mainland friends was Elizabeth Hoxie, daughter of the Curzon family of Newburyport, Massachusetts. The Curzons owned a large mill on the Artichoke River, and the adjoining miller's house was vacant. Celia and Levi, on Appledore Island in the summers, began spending winters at Curzon's Mill in 1854. Probably on one of those fall moves to the mainland Celia took a cutting from her mother's plant (or perhaps the whole plant itself) ashore as a gift to the Hoxies. Later Elizabeth Hoxie's daughter gave it to a neighbor in Newburyport. That neighbor in turn gave it to Olive Brock, who as a graduate in 1937 of Professor Jackson's Marine Zoological Laboratory, recognized its historical significance. Olive brought it back to Appledore Island in the summer of 1976.

This event stirred my interest in Celia Thaxter's famous garden on Appledore Island, memorialized for all time in her book *An Island Garden,* which was illustrated by the noted American artist Childe Hassam and published first in 1893, the year before Celia's death. The detail and a plan in the book would allow exact recreation of the garden in its original spot, if we so desired. Audrey O'Connor of Cornell Plantations, I soon learned, would be happy to obtain seeds and cuttings and to start the necessary seedlings if asked, and members of the Rye Beach-Little Boar's Head Garden Club showed signs of wanting to make such a project financially possible. Having Celia's garden as the main feature of a public picnic area on the north end of the island would give our casual visitors something to see, and might keep them from wandering into the labs and classrooms as much as they did. All the pieces seemed in place except a picnic table. Eddie and Myrtle Donohue of Star Island announced they would provide a picnic table with benches.

In the autumn of 1976, with a donation of $1,000 from the Rye Beach-Little Boar's Head Garden Club in a Shoals account, I located the foundations of Celia's Cottage in the underbrush then rampant, traced out where the porch had been, and measured off the boundaries of the garden as given in Celia's book. Then I fired up the backhoe, trundled over, and using its toothed bucket as a grubhoe scratched out the wild sumac and the wild cherry thicket that was there. The next spring (1977) a rototiller was imported, a fence built, and the first plants installed. The detailed story of how the garden was brought back into being is told in the introduction to the Bullbrier Press edition of Celia Thaxter's *An Island Garden.*

Essentially all bakery products served at the Shoals Lab are made in the Kiggins Commons kitchen; Curtis Tanner punching down dough at left.

PURLOINED CHOP SUEY

The Shoals Lab kitchen in Kiggins Commons worked out well. Dominic sited it to get the best island breeze through its windows. My plan for large walk-in refrigeration and freezer rooms made life easier for the chefs, and the eclectic assortment of kitchen equipment scrounged from all sorts of sources seemed to meet the needs well if the meals that came from that kitchen under a succession of chefs were evidence. The sole piece of major new equipment was the gas-fired tilt-brazier which could cook almost any variety of eggs or pancakes as fast as the island population could eat them.

Many of the smaller items with which the kitchen was equipped at its start came from Cornell. There a fine tradition of gracious living had yielded to modern fast-food even in the residential housing, and separate kitchens were forced out of business by the efficiencies of mass production. Crockery, utensils, pots, pans, meat slicers, toasters, and much more came to Appledore Island from such places as the Clara Dickson and Risley dining halls and the Martha Van Rensselaer cafeteria as they were closed or changed over to scramble-line eating or to vending machines. For some

329

reason the flatware from these sources was mostly bent, battered, stingy, and vastly prejudiced against spoons.

I don't remember what brought Henry and Nancy Bartels to Appledore the first time—probably one of the adult education programs. Hank, who was the president of International Silver, took one look at our "silverware" and quietly disapproved. He asked me if I would like to augment it with a better product. Of course I would, and we needed spoons particularly, I said. Hank said he would see what kind of chop suey he could scrape together when he got back to Connecticut. Seeing the expression on my face, he hastened to let me know that "chop suey" was just a designation for the rejects in their production line. Most rejections came from small imperfections in stamping the client's name on the flatware. The utensils themselves were fine.

That explains why, if you dine in the Kiggins Commons on Appledore even today, you may find yourself holding silver that appears to have been purloined from Bell Laboratories, American Airlines, or some of America's finest hotels and hospitals.

ON PIGS, AND MASKING-TAPED UNH TRUSTEES

Dominic Gratta conceived that the garbage disposal problem on Appledore Island, increasing with the human population, could be advantageously solved by recruiting a couple of pigs. Meeting no serious objection, Dominic bought a couple of weanlings and delivered them to the island at the beginning of the 1976 season. He constructed a shelter and a fenced enclosure for them in the waist of the island, out of sight of casual view. The pigs worked out fine. They loved lobster shells and burgeoned on the garbage that came down the hill in buckets for their benefit. By the end of the summer those pigs were pushing two hundred pounds.

The pigs worked out so well in 1976 that Dominic brought two more out for the 1977 season, the first pair having met the usual porcine fate in the fall of 1976. The only problem was that the pigpen fence was not quite pig-proof at first, and the pigs loved both freedom and human company.

The members of the Rye Beach-Little Boar's Head Garden Club decided to visit the brand new reproduction of Celia's garden along about the middle of the summer. A score or so of garden club ladies appeared at the Appledore dock on the appointed day and we started walking over to the garden, growing resplendent within a new board fence carefully built (from pictures) to be just like the one Celia had, with two swinging gates. The pigs, now half grown, naturally chose that time to get loose. They immediately

Above: Appledore Island garbage disposal system.
Below: Louise Kingsbury feeding the system.

headed joyously toward the ladies to make friends. The ladies, not quite ready to reciprocate, instead charged off to the garden and retreated within the new garden fence until the pigs had been corralled.

As in 1975, the three-day break between classes was used in 1976 for a dedication; actually two of them simultaneously. The Grass and Kiggins families and friends joined us to dedicate the Grass Foundation Laboratory and Kiggins Commons. The dedication of Kiggins Commons had been delayed for two years because the building, though unfinished, was entirely functional and Dominic always had more urgent matters under attack. Eventually he got it done.

Dale and Nellie Corson came out for the dedications, along with many other local and distant dignitaries. This was the occasion that brought Helen Peterson and Arthur Peterson, Cornell's treasurer, out to Appledore Island for the first time. Having announced his retirement, Pete felt at liberty now to "endanger his judgment." Chef Sam Hayward and the kitchen staff mounted an 11-course dinner for the event, complete with wines and a menu entirely in French. (I once told James Barker Smith, owner of the Wentworth-by-the-Sea resort, in a moment of braggadocio, that I would match my kitchen against his any time.) The warmth of the Grass and Kiggins dedications matched that of the dedication of the Palmer-Kinne Lab a year earlier, though few who had attended the latter would have agreed that its equal would ever be possible.

The trustees of the University of New Hampshire decided to hold a summer meeting at the Shoals Lab in 1976 to see for themselves what we were all about. We were delighted and arranged to provide proper hospitality. One of the particular benefits of such a gathering would be a chance to encourage useful conversation between university trustees and some real students, neither of whom have much chance for direct interaction.

It worked out by chance that the trustees would come out on the same run of the ferry that had already been scheduled to bring the class back from its mainland salt-marsh expedition.

How would 45 muddy students get along with the UNH trustees? More particularly, how would we get the two groups talking together? Here's what we did.

The marsh we used for class trips was the one behind what was then the elegant Wentworth-by-the-Sea (no longer in business). Students and faculty inevitably got muddy chasing specimens on the mud flats. Some effected total coverage by accidental upsets in the slippery environment. James Barker Smith nobly allowed us to troop back from the marsh along the parked Cadillacs and Lincolns of his guests and down to a building at the

Dr. Borror leads the troops into the Wentworth saltmarsh.

head of his dock. That building contained showers, ample hot water, and towels. Most of the islanders who were generally allowed only one freshwater shower a week on Appledore, forewarned of this opportunity, took full advantage of the showers. They were a good deal less muddy when the ferry received them than they were as discharged from the saltmarsh, but were still clad in muddy clothes.

The students were accompanied by buckets of three-foot-long marine worms, sea slugs, and other prizes from the mud flats not necessarily endearing to the trustees.

All the islanders—students, faculty, assistants, island staff, and construction people—were expected to wear name tags at all times while they were on Appledore Island. No name tag at mealtimes meant no meal. We used the simple means of a roll of masking tape and a magic marker pen to label everyone. The students were asked to be sure they had a name label showing on the return trip from the mudflats.

With some trepidation the Shoals staff also managed to get masking-tape labels on each member of the trustees' party as they waited on the dock in Portsmouth. They were all very good sports about it.

Instructions to both parties were to talk with as many masking-tape-labeled strangers as they could. The masking tape worked extremely well to break the ice. Conversations between legislators and students were already numerous as we left the dock. The trustees' visit was a tremendous success in all respects but one. The trustees discovered afterwards that UNH trustees' meetings could not legally be held in Maine.

BARLOW'S BLOWERS AND SEELEY'S BEES

While the Kiggins kitchen was without a ceiling, no one noticed that there were no exhaust hoods over the cooking surfaces. Once the ceiling was finished, the lack of hoods began attracting attention. Stainless steel hoods and venting is expensive.

While standing in line for lunch, one of the UNH trustees said, "Shouldn't you have a hood over your stove?"

I said, "We'll have one as soon as we can afford one."

He said, "Well, let me tell you about a village school near where I live that burned recently. It was brand new, but fortunately fully insured. We've just rebuilt the school with the insurance money. A lot of the original equipment wasn't much damaged in the fire. It was removed and stored in a local farmer's chicken house. I wouldn't be surprised if you could find some good hoods and ducts there and we could probably arrange for them to be given to you."

"What did you find?" For Joseph Geraci, happiness is a three-foot worm.

Dominic visited the chicken house the next weekend. He found a lot of good stuff there, including an ample supply of top-class stainless steel hoods. They were soon installed in the Kiggins kitchen.

But there were no exhaust fans for the hoods. Therefore, in installing the hoods Dominic didn't go beyond placing them against the ceiling. He never made holes in the ceiling or the roof for the hood ducts to exhaust through. The stainless steel hoods looked great, but were functionally useless.

The Kiggins kitchen is very well cross ventilated, and the chefs never used much fat in cooking. The absence of functional hoods caused no actual problem. It might even have been a blessing because many institutional fires start in accumulations of fat in hoods and ducts.

At about this time, for some forgotten reason, I had to visit the Kittery Code Compliance Officer's office in the new town office building out on Route 1. The days of the informal offices on Main Street in town and the relaxed paper-pushing as described in the first chapter of this book were long gone by then. State law had caught Kittery up with modern times.

While the Kittery compliance officer was filling out some form or other, another official wandered through. The compliance officer asked him if he had been out to Appledore to inspect the kitchen.

He replied, "Appledore? That's out at the islands, isn't it?"

"Yes."

"Aren't the Isles of Shoals in New Hampshire?"

"Appledore's in Maine. In fact, it's in Kittery, and you'd better get out there when you can and have a look at the kitchen of the Shoals Marine Laboratory."

On the first of his continuing annual visits, the Kittery kitchen inspector never noticed that the hoods went nowhere. Basically, he liked our kitchen and our way of doing business.

Some time later, after I ceased being director, the kitchen inspector chanced to look more closely at the hoods and noticed their stasis. The lab would have to install roof vents and blowers at once. Fortunately, this difficulty was overheard by Barlow Ware of the Cornell Development Office, who happened to be on Appledore Island at the time. Knowing that there was absolutely no money in the budget to meet this emergency, Barlow offered to pay for the expensive new blowers himself, personally.

Barlow's blowers were bought and installed and Barlow's Blowers have now joined the Werly Tank in common language at the Lab. This time no one from the Cornell Development Office objected.

Tom Seeley, a graduate student at Harvard, came out to Appledore Island in 1975 and 1976 to work on his Ph.D. thesis problem. He needed a

The Sullivan house on Appledore Island (shuttered for the winter).

place to do some experiments concerning how bees choose a new home and communicate the decision within the swarm when the colony moves. This required a terrain for setting up his constructed experimental housing cavities where no competing natural choices such as hollow trees were present. Appledore Island seemed ideal.

When he arrived on the island with his bees, Tom was dressed and shorn, or more accurately unshorn, according to the mores of graduate students at that time. After considerable work, everything was ready for the big experiment and Tom released the bees. He watched and interpreted the dance of the scouts as they returned from exploring the island. Soon he came to me and announced that he thought the bees were heading off for one of the fisherman's cottages on the south shore of Appledore Island, specifically Rodney Sullivan's. He proposed to go over and see.

The Sullivan family valued its privacy, and Rodney kept a loaded shotgun behind his front door at all times. Students were instructed to keep well away from all private fishermen's property along Gosport Harbor. It was easy to picture disaster of several kinds if graduate student Seeley approached lobsterman Sullivan from the rear when bees were attacking his house, especially if Rodney found out that the bees were Tom's. What to do?

Here's what the lab director and the graduate student did. I told Tom that any approach had to be made from the front, meaning the water, where Rodney could see who was coming before we landed. I also told Tom he was to be very careful and do his best to get on the right side of Mr. Sullivan from the beginning. With great foreboding I got in the Whaler and we started out around the corner of the island into Gosport Harbor.

Rodney, who could be charming when he wanted to, heard the Whaler approaching and came out on his porch. He welcomed us loudly (most fishermen have good shouting voices) and told us to come on ashore. As Tom and I climbed up over the rocks of his side yard, Rodney started telling us exictedly about a great swarm of bees that had just come down his chimney and were buzzing about loudly in the horizontal stovepipe to his stove. He didn't know what to do about this emergency! Tom offered to help. He told Rodney he happened to know how to get the bees out of his stovepipe and take them away, and he would be happy to put some hardware cloth over the chimney for him if he wanted to keep bees out in the future. Rodney was delighted. We actually had a very pleasant visit, with the graduate student lecturing the fisherman on the habits of bees.

THE *WRACK* IS BOARDED

Regular *Wrack* runs had long since become a smooth routine disturbed only by the occasional barge trip or the more frequent use of the vessel for instruction. How a bottom-fishing net works is easy to talk about, but difficult for students to visualize when all they ever saw was a great pile of netting on the deck of a fishing boat tied up at our dock, with the two massive otter doors hanging near the stern. To remedy this the *Wrack* took classes to sea with a small demonstration bottom trawl just like the commercial ones in all respects but size. An hour's dragging using the fish-finder depth sounder usually resulted in a moderate catch of typical bottom-dwelling animals. Sometimes, just like the larger boats, we had bad luck and caught almost nothing. Sometimes we got a several large cod, a good catch of flat fish, or specimens of unusual species. Sometimes, like the commercial fishermen, we hung the net up on some bottom obstruction such as jettisoned military hardware. Whatever happened, the class learned from it. Also deployed from the *Wrack* as class demonstrations were gill nets, long lines, and other gear. Truth to tell, the Shoals Lab management favored exercises like these because they helped keep the food bill down. The kitchen took everything edible caught by the *Wrack* that did not end up as a specimens for study in the lab. It was comforting to realize that if mainland supply lines were severed and the commercial fishermen stopped coming by, the lab itself could supply the protein needs of the Appledore population indefinitely. Even more penetrating was the thought that this hunting method of nurturing a human population is about as close to primitive as can still be found in the world.

Good-weather trips by the *Wrack* between the mainland and the islands were routine; most of them simply boring. But you never knew what might happen. Perhaps you would meet a submarine coming downriver, or a LPG (liquified petroleum gas) tanker coming in. The tankers are treated like potential bombs by the Coast Guard and traffic is excluded from the river as they pass. The most exciting break in routine in my experience as skipper on hundreds of trips was neither of these.

The *Wrack* usually operated supply runs with a crew of two. I don't remember who was with me on this occasion, probably Ron, or which year it happened. The event itself is emblazoned on my permanent memory.

We were exiting the Piscataqua River on a sunny, lazy midsummer day. The mouth of the harbor contained the usual clustering of sailboats and power boats. A local lobsterman was flitting from buoy to buoy hauling pots. A typical sport-fishing power boat with a fellow in a particularly loud sportshirt at the wheel and fishing poles stuck at the transom corners was loafing along parallel to us as we passed Whaleback Light. Everything was boringly normal.

Suddenly the sport fisherman lept to full speed and headed directly at us. Simultaneously six uniformed officials, each fully armed with pistol and automatic rifle materialized on deck. In seconds they were alongside, demanding to board. The uniforms were not familiar, but certainly these were neither Kittery police nor Maine state police, nor military, nor Coast Guard officers. The circumstances were not propitious for asking to see identifications or warrants, or even to consider in a detached way the legalities of boarding within the three-mile territorial limit. They had grappled us and begun to board even before these thoughts had finished crossing my mind. The boarders started searching the *Wrack*. Soon they found our registration papers tacked to the the below-decks side of the main bulkhead.

"This vessel is owned by Cornell University?"

"Yes."

"You are working for the university?"

"Yes."

"Well, I guess that's all right then."

They departed as quickly as they had come.

Back on Appledore a lengthy discussion took place as to just what had happened. In the end the general conclusion was that these were Treasury agents looking for drugs, a new development on our coast.

Chapter Fifteen

CHANGE IS IN THE WIND
1977-1979

STAR ISLAND IS SINKING

The workings of the federal government are sometimes wondrous to behold. I thought I had had a pretty good exposure to the range of possibilities in the decade during which the Shoals Lab was conceived and largely built. Even so, an event that began in 1976 and ended in 1978 expanded my conception of the workings of federal agencies considerably.

The all-important yearly transect study of marine organisms from above high tide to as far down the rocks as the students can get at low tide depends on an exact knowledge of tidal levels. Fortunately, Star Island had served as one of the earliest observational reference points in federal studies to determine tidal characteristics on the East Coast. In conducting these studies, official reference points are identified permanently with bench marks set in the rocks. A bench mark consists of a heavy brass plate bearing the name of the agency emplanting it, the date, and a stamped identification number. The elevation of each bench mark is determined with an accuracy of a hundredth of a foot or so, and that figure could be obtained by querying the U.S. Coast & Geodetic Survey (now National Geodetic Survey). The exact elevation of one such bench mark, near the extreme high-tide line,

Benchmark 9751E on Appledore Island.

had been carried to the fifteen transect sites we chose on Star Island by a Cornell engineering student with transit, who closed the island with an accuracy of less than a half-inch deviation. In 1967 my brother and I, with hammer, star drill, and a pot of melted lead, placed a monel metal pin as a reference point at that elevation for each of the transect locations around Star Island (except the end of the dock and the swimming beach).

I give this detail to point out that the actual elevation of the government marker becomes the critical reference point for a tremendous amount of data collected by each class each year.

When classes moved from Star Island to Appledore Island, there were no government bench marks on the island. We did the best we could to carry the Star Island reference elevation across Gosport Harbor accurately, but it's not as easy as you might think. We really had no idea at first how accurate the new transect reference points were that we placed on Appledore Island that summer.

To get the right government agency to come to Appledore Island and put in an accurate bench mark just for us would be a major, if not impossible request, and I had not yet made the effort. That was the way the matter stood at the close of the summer season of 1976.

Students use secondary benchmarks as transect starting points.

Imagine our surprise on returning to Appledore Island in the early spring of 1977 to find some brand new bench marks on the shore rocks. It seems that, in connection with a tidal survey of the Piscataqua River, the National Ocean Survey had chosen Appledore Island as one of its references. In fact, that's what the R/V *Ferrell* had been working on when the telephone cable passed over her decks to our barge at the Simplex dock.

The Appledore bench marks carried the message, "For information write Director, National Ocean Survey, Washington, D.C." Eagerly, I did just that and mailed the letter from Portsmouth in May of 1977. Nothing happened. Busy with the summer's rush, I forgot about it. Nearly a full year later, in April 1978 to be exact, my letter came back unopened, marked "Insufficient Address." What the postal service had been doing with it for a year is hard to imagine, but I marvelled that after passing into the federal maze in Washington it came back intact or at all.

Knowing the elevations of the new bench marks was important to us. There were two choices: obtain and plow through thousands of pages of federal directories (which I could do on the Cornell campus), or let someone do it for me. Whom better to ask than Senator Daniel Patrick Moynihan of New York, himself a former professor? I sent my returned letter still unopened, to the senator at his Washington address on April 19, 1978, with the request that he bring the weight of his office to bear on getting the letter delivered to the right place. On June 2, 1978, a nice letter came from an aide to the senator, postmarked Oneonta, New York, saying that they had delivered my letter to the right address, which was really in Virginia, not Washington.

On July 18, 1978, the first actual response to the letter of May 1977 arrived at the Portsmouth post office. The return address was neither Washington nor Virginia, but Rockville, Maryland.

In the original letter I had identified one of the Appledore bench marks as "7951D-1976." The letter from Rockville politely informed me that there was no such bench mark on Appledore Island. They had a record of bench mark "9751D-1976" instead. Nothing was said about the other bench mark (9751E) for which I had also requested an elevation.

It turned out that the year's delay hadn't mattered because the National Ocean Survey had not yet done the computer analysis necessary to figure out what the actual elevations were. It would do this as soon as it could and would inform me.

Instead of what I had asked for, my federal correspondent included in his letter a sheet of elevations from 1968 for the bench marks on Star. The Star Island bench mark we had been using was listed on the datum sheet of 1950 as having an elevation of 12.51 feet above mean low water. According to the 1968 figures, it was really at an elevation of 12.18 feet. Had Star Island sunk nearly half a foot in 18 years? If so, here was geology in action! Or was there a misprint somewhere along the line? I asked the Rockville authority for an explanation and also pointed out that the Appledore bench mark really was 7951D and not 9751D, and I included a photograph of it as proof.

A response came from Rockville at the end of September, 1978. It turns out that Star Island was not really sinking at the rate of two feet per century. Instead, the government revises the ground rules (no pun) for determining elevations every 25 years or so. In doing this most recently, the National Ocean Survey had abandoned all data collected before 1941. That accounted for the change in figures for Star Island.

A few months later another letter came from Rockville. The governmental computer had functioned and the elevation for the Appledore bench mark in question was now known. Here's how the government put it (I quote exactly and carefully): "Bench Mark D (1976) is a standard disk, stamped '7951D 1976,' (miss stamped) set in a rock outcrop, 66 feet east of western shoreline 38 feet southwest of southwest corner of Grass Foundation Laboratory and 16 feet east of centerline of a dirt road running

Descendants of Thomas B. and Eliza Laighton who had contributed generously to the rebuilding of Laighton House were invited to its rededication in 1978.

around the western shoreline. Elevation: 22.92 feet above mean low water (14.26 feet above mean high water)."

Ignoring the possible sexist implication about the stamping, I thanked Rockville warmly. To have produced that small piece of information in any other way would probably have cost thousands, if not tens of thousands of dollars. A letter of thanks also went to Senator Moynihan.

In the meantime other letters had been circulating as a result of the senatorial intervention. I had been receiving copies of an exchange between the postmaster for the District of Columbia and the rear admiral in charge of the National Ocean Survey, giving the latter's correct forwarding address and pointing out that mail generated by the four hundred thousand bench marks in American rocks should be delivered (naturally enough) to Rockville. The admiral implied that neither rain, snow, nor movement of federal agencies over centuries of time should delay the mailman.

Another consequence of all this is that Senator Moynihan has sent me his newsletter regularly ever since.

CHANGE

The pace of construction on Appledore Island began slowing in 1977 and 1978. A new dorm, the second and third, was built each of those years and Dominic finished up a lot of loose ends including the exterior rebuilding of Laighton House, but the job he began in 1972 was now nearly over. His construction crew, which had dominated the island in the early years, had now become the smallest fraction of the island's human population as the teaching program reached capacity. The island staff took over building maintenance and repair. An epoch in the history of Appledore Island ended when Dominic Gratta departed the island for good.

Was my usefulness nearly finished too? The intensity of the building years had certainly taken a toll. Perhaps I needed a change. Perhaps the Shoals Lab needed a change from me.

My nascent thoughts on these matters, somewhat tumbled, found their way into the Lab's newsletter of November 1977.

No one, I said, knows better than the Shoals Lab's first director that the development and operation of the Shoals Lab was the result of the dedicated efforts of many individuals at all levels, from the inspired kitchen staff to the unconquerable engineering and boat-operating departments, from the indomitable Gratta family to indefatigably skeptical university administrations, from the office computer without compassion to the Shoals Lab's staff with infinite compassion, from the local fishermen who helped to

Contemplation.

the distant politicians who legislated, from the casual visitor whose eyes provided a fresh vision of the island to the seasoned residents whose dedicated tenure provided deeper perception, from the necessary help of the less-than-$25 donor to the necessary help of the more-than-$100,000 donor, from the enthusiastic teaching assistants to the wise professors, and especially from the entering student with expectations to the departing student with accomplishments immediate and distant. The director was merely the person at the center who manipulated the stage for all this ferment, focused the action, and expedited the means. The actual doing was by all those others.

I decided it was time for a change in directors.

It was time, I said, because the current director found the faces in photographs from the early days of the lab looking surprisingly youthful and inferred the reciprocal. The generation gap widens to no one's advantage.

It was time because the growth of the Shoals Lab begged significant review by the parent universities, which the director had been unable to obtain, and a resignation would force that review.

You can't trust anyone over thirty.

It was time because institutional health periodically requires new ideas, new perspectives, new thrust, free of preconditions, idiosyncrasies of personality, twists of history, or outdated restraints.

It was truly time, I said, for new enthusiasms, new visions, and new abilities to find expression at the center of the Appledore stage.

With these considered words made public in the Lab's newsletter, the first director of the Shoals Lab became a lame duck.

Finding a new director for the Shoals Lab was a slow process. Standard academic procedure requires a painstaking nationwide search. Because I had functioned without a job description, one had to be written. The anomalous relationship of the Shoals Lab to its parent universities had to be regularized in some measure and the new director protected from some of the unusual personal risks that had fallen on the first director by circumstance. A salary line had to be created for the position because my professorial salary would not be available. I did not plan to quit my regular duties at Cornell.

Following normal university procedures, the retiring director had little role in choosing the next incumbent or in ancilliary actions and decisions, and I will not attempt to summarize them here. The process was long and difficult, fraught with disappointments. After two years the national search brought to the top the name of one of the Shoals Lab's own graduates, John B. Heiser, universally known as "JB" The job was offered; he accepted. Although JB didn't take over formally until the summer of 1979, my active directorship ended in the winter of 1977. I leave it to JB, whose tenure in the directorship is now approaching my own in duration, to write the next volume of the history of the Shoals Lab. As those who have experienced the subsequent work of the Lab know, JB, too, will have a success story to tell.

EPILOGUE

I once toyed with the idea of titling this book *Here's How We'll Do It Despite Cornell University and the University of New Hampshire.* Deep in my soul I knew I couldn't. Senior administrators at both institutions have possessed the imagination, trust, dedication to a worthy academic goal, goodwill, and vision without which the unprecedented delegations of authority or anomalies of operation that the Shoals Lab necessitated would not have happened. The rise of the Shoals Lab from university parents such as these testifies *au fond* that both universities are blessed with some top administrators capable of bending rules when the rules need bending and finding new ways to do a worthy something when the something is not otherwise possible. This is a clear mark of collegiate excellence. Let's hope Cornell and UNH stay that way, and that governments let them.

Appledore Island is a magic place. Even the casual day visitor senses it. A didactic dissection of that magic, were it possible, would probably kill it. Looked at closely, it might vanish.

We can perhaps sneak up on island magic with words such as adventure, self-reliance, total immersion, community, roots, equality, camaraderie, enhanced vision, shared goals and hardships, peaceful contemplation, intense bullsessions, penetrating insight, and one-on-one learning. Learning is enhanced on islands by the close linking there of cause and effect. Islands make more easily visible the insight that cooperation works and the contrary does not. Islands are the epitome of "one for all and all for one." In more senses than one islands offer no place to hide.

Appledore Island displays the natural world as it is, sometimes raw, sometimes exquisite, always absorbing. The two-way street that constitutes the fundamental relationship of the human species with the natural environment is writ clearly on islands and cannot be ignored, as it seemingly is in the glass and steel canyons of urban campuses. The rocks of Appledore

348

Island serve a far more profound function than merely as a means of getting from one laboratory building to another. Islands are magic. It behooves us to keep them so. The trick of the future for many academic institutions will be to learn how best to maintain steady-state excellence in the absence of expansion. Inevitably this will be much more difficult than hiding deficiencies in the warm panacea of growth, or measuring success solely in increasing numbers. Perhaps the Shoals Marine Laboratory, constrained to circumscribed performance by the dimensions of a small island, will be at the forefront of academic steady-state excellence as we enter the twentieth century. If so, tiny Appledore Island will not only continue to exercise a disproportionate importance in the lives of students, but also, by example, perhaps it can foster a national improvement in quality of educational institutions generally.

An unattainable goal? That's what they said about the construction of the Shoals Lab in the first place, and now you know how we did that.

Photo Credits

J.M. Anderson 22t, 34bl, 43, 49t, 58t, 70t, 76t, 113, 118, 138b, 173, 174, 213, 226, 345; G. Boden 325; L. Bush 60,74; D. Corson 304t&b; J. Cutler 195t; J.R. Factor 30t, 205, 301t&b; R. Fink 330t; R. Harelstad 26b, 136t&b, 166b, 176b, 179, 193, 214t&b, 215t, 221b, 323; J.B. Heiser 318; S. Hitchner 252; P. Hodgdon 25b; A. Hulbert 336; H. Jackson 246; T. Keohler 328; T. Loder 28t, 243; P. Logemann 326b; D.J. Lord 285; P. McGill 312t; R. Meadows 178t, 231, 326t; A.H. Moore 221; G. Nace 30b, 334b; P. Randell 24b, 94, 98, 116, 147t, 189, 311, 316, 324; L.E. Rasmussen 32; B. Rivest 196 t&b; N. Rogers 346; M. Shepard 319; P. Sze 16t, 18b, 44, 147b, 167t, 299t; D. Wehle 287, 332b; C. Willand 268; V. Wirsig 38, 254.

Investigation.

The *NOAA Fisheries Research Vessel* Delaware II *arrives at Appledore Island for a class demonstration of commercial fishing gear and techniques. Below: Each square has a north, south, east, and west, and when you fix a tear, each must be knitted just right. Captain James Madruga.*

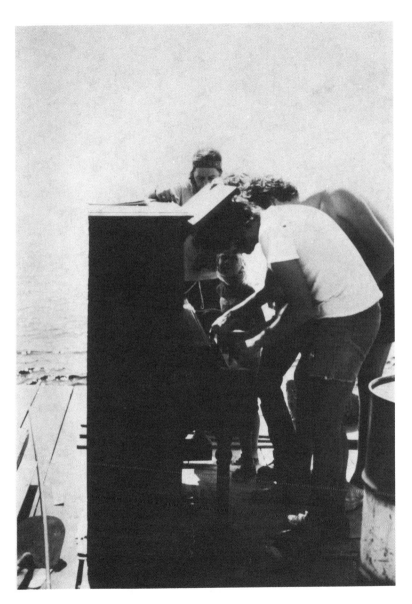

Culture arrived at Appledore Island by barge.

352

The Isles of Shoals is a place that gives perspective to the human soul.

INDEX

354